G000144295

Office Manager Escapes Clutches Of Desk

"At last I'm free, thanks to No[kia] Mobile Connectivity solution and it feels great" exclaims M[ary] Langer, office manager.

"I thought I was imprisoned at my desk forev[er] hope of any release – but at last I'm free. No[w] visit more suppliers, get better deals and whenever and however I want. Am I happy [...]

Secure, Reliable, Freedom and Flexibility

happy..." Mary enthused first taste of freedom.

Workers everywhere fro[m] to Account Managers a[re] rejoicing at the thought breakthrough in their wor[k]

"Mobile Connectivity fr[om] means I can make bett[er] my waiting time at the airport" said [...] Baker, "which gives me more family ti[me] get home".

Even sales manager John Patten was ov[er] he realised his field sales team could visit [...] customers, now that they were able [to] access company data while on the road [...] check emails from home, at the offi[ce] they're travelling" he said. "And best of [all] IT manager says it's no sweat as he [can] manage everything, give the right leve[l] the right people and still keep c[...] information secure".

Introducing a new era of secure, corporate business freedom and flexibility – Nokia Mobile Connectivity solutions.

Employees throughout an enterprise want to be more mobile and productive – and this can now be realised thanks to Nokia Mobile Connectivity solutions. CIO's and IT managers can provide the mobility and security of anytime, anywhere access to users while empowering everyone from the CEO to field salesforce teams with the information needed to do their work where and when they choose. Nokia Mobilae Connectivity solutions include a range of IPSec and SSL-based client and gateway products that provide secure, appropriate

access to corporate email and applications. Enterprises will discover new levels of efficiency from their workforce while giving them greater freedom to manage their business and personal lives. All solutions are easy to deploy and manage, are based on award winning technology and backed by Global Support and Services.

So if you want greater working freedom that's IT approved, go ahead and escape. Visit www.nokia.com/mobileaccess/emea or call 0161 601 8908

NOKIA
CONNECTING PEOPLE

Testimonials are fictionalised and do not depict actual Nokia customers. Copyright ©2003 Nokia. All rights reserved. Nokia and Nokia Connecting People are registered trademarks of

the
SECURE ONLINE BUSINESS HANDBOOK

We go a long way to give you
better business telecommunications.

(20,750 miles to be exact.)

We've gone to the lengths of investing nine billion pounds to develop a fibre optic
network that stretches over 20,000 miles. As a result, we can provide some of the
most technically advanced and resilient connections that are available. As well as
being highly efficient, the communication solutions we offer are flexible, so they fit the
needs of your business better. For more details, call us now on 0800 052 9000 and
switch to ntl's business division. We're better by miles.

www.business.ntl.com

Smarter communications at work

the
SECURE ONLINE BUSINESS BUSINESS HANDBOOK second edition

e-commerce, IT functionality & business continuity

RECOMMENDED BY
INSTITUTE OF DIRECTORS

KOGAN
PAGE

London and Sterling, VA

This book has been endorsed by the Institute of Directors.

The endorsement is given to selected Kogan Page books which the IoD recognizes as being of specific interest to its members and providing them with up-to-date, informative and practical resources for creating business success. Kogan Page books endorsed by the IoD represent the most authoritative guidance available on a wide range of subjects including management, finance, marketing, training and HR.

The views expressed in this book are those of the author and are not necessarily the same as those of the Institute of Directors.

Publisher's note
Every possible effort has been made to ensure that the information contained in this book is accurate at the time of going to press, and the publishers and authors cannot accept responsibility for any errors or omissions, however caused. No responsibility for loss or damage occasioned to any person acting, or refraining from action, as a result of the material in this publication can be accepted by the editor, the publisher or any of the authors.

First published in Great Britain and the United States in 2003 by Kogan Page Limited
Second edition 2004

Apart from any fair dealing for the purposes of research or private study, or criticism or review, as permitted under the Copyright, Designs and Patents Act 1988, this publication may only be reproduced, stored or transmitted, in any form or by any means, with the prior permission in writing of the publishers, or in the case of reprographic reproduction in accordance with the terms and licences issued by the CLA. Enquiries concerning reproduction outside these terms should be sent to the publishers at the undermentioned addresses:

120 Pentonville Road
London N1 9JN
United Kingdom
www.kogan-page.co.uk

22883 Quicksilver Drive
Sterling VA 20166–2012
USA

© Kogan Page and individual contributors, 2003, 2004

ISBN 0 7494 4221 2

British Library Cataloguing-in-Publication Data

A CIP record for this book is available from the British Library.

Library of Congress Cataloging-in-Publication Data

The secure online business handbook : e-Commerce, IT functionality, and business
continuity / consultant editor, Jonathan Reuvid.
    p. cm.
   Includes index.
   ISBN 0-7494-4221-2
   1. Computer security–Handbooks, manuals, etc. 2. Business–Data processing–Handbooks,
manuals etc. I Reuvid, Jonathan.
QA76.9.A25S3755 2004
005.8–dc22

Typeset by Saxon Graphics Ltd, Derby
Printed and bound in Great Britain by Scotprint

Global Experience

BSI Management Systems is one of the few truly global suppliers in both assessment and training for a wide range of products and services. BSI clients benefit from world-wide, multi-sector, multi personnel experience, covering all sectors of your business. You can join our world. Contact us now and we'll show you how.

- INFORMATION SECURITY
- QUALITY MANAGEMENT
- ENVIRONMENTAL MANAGEMENT
- OCCUPATIONAL HEALTH & SAFETY
- MANAGEMENT SYSTEMS TRAINING

shape the future

Group Headquarters BSI 389 Chiswick High Road London W4 4AL United Kingdom
Tel: +44 (0)20 8996 7720 Fax: +44(0)20 8996 7540 Email: client.services@bsi-global.com

www.bsi-global.com/emea

Management
Systems

Make the CD itself an experience.

maCrovision™

Protecting 200 million CDs worldwide

Macrovision boosts CD value to new heights, providing a robust, intuitive consumer experience while enabling media security. Now you can protect CD content against unauthorised ripping, copying and file trading - at the same time you deliver optimised playability within Windows Media® DRM environments (such as PCs and portable devices) and enhanced content. It ís a total win/win - giving consumers the flexibility and portability they demand and copyright owners the protection they deserve.

maCrovision™

www.macrovision.com

Macrovision UK Ltd. Malvern House, 14/18 Bell Street, Maidenhead, Berkshire. SL6 1BR
Tel: +44 (0) 870 871 1111   Fax: +44 (0) 870 871 1161
iodmusic@macrovision.com

Contents

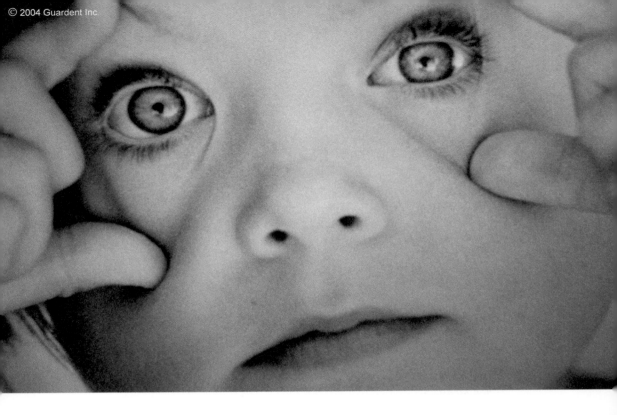

© 2004 Guardent Inc.

Straining to maintain focus 24x7 on information security?

Large enterprises spend millions of dollars every year to secure their information systems. With Guardent's managed security services, you can get that same enterprise protection at a fraction of the cost.

Want to learn more? Call +44.(0)1582.621211 and start sleeping like a baby.

24x7 Managed Security Services
World-class Security Consulting

To learn more about managed security services please donwload Gartner's MSSP Magic Quadrant report at: http://www.gartner.com/reprints/guardent/118599.html

Part 5: Contingency planning

Do more with NetScreen

When it comes to integrating critical security and VPN functions into a single appliance nobody does it better than NetScreen.

We give you everything you need including stateful inspection firewall, remote access or site to site VPN, traffic management, and attack detection and blocking, which means you can unfold from some of the most advanced security and VPN technology available today. Indeed more and more users are moving to NetScreen, helping us to grow by 76% over the last year*. Get tooled up.

NetScreen-25

NetScreen-50

NetScreen-204

NetScreen-208

NETSCREEN EMEA
Victoria House, London Square, Cross Lanes, Guildford, Surrey GU1 1UJ, United Kingdom
Phone: +44-8700-75-00-00
www.netscreen.com

NETSCREEN®

* Revenue growth measured for the quarter ended 30 June 2003 compared with the quarter ended 30 June 2002.

Copyright © 2004 NetScreen Technologies, Inc. All rights reserved. NetScreen, and the NetScreen logo are trademarks of NetScreen Technologies, Inc. All other trademarks are owned by their respective owners. For privacy policy please visit www.netscreen.com/privacy.jsp

Leatherman® and Pulse® are trademarks of Leatherman Tool Group, Inc.

pro|seq

*So **secure** you can **relax***

Internet **insecurity**.

Just one rogue packet – that's all it takes.

– Will you be watching your network when it hits?

Proseq services ensurex 24 x 7 x 365 vigilance and handling!

Proseq AS
Web: www.proseq.net

Norway	UK
Nygta 4	1 Liverpool Street
P.O. box 618	London
N-4809 Arendal	EC2M 7QD
	United Kingdom

Phone: +47 37 70 98 00   +44 20 7956 2033
Fax: +47 37 70 98 01   +44 20 7956 2001

Foreword

Hackers, viruses, fraud, denial of service and most recently blackmail against threat of electronic attack, are becoming genuine problems for organizations of all sizes: at a time when companies are expected to be continuously accessible to customers, suppliers and partners. Downtime in the modern world not only causes commercial loss but creates a crisis of confidence in the reliability and security of an organization. Sadly, this is widely recognized by those who wish to attack an organization's operation, either with criminal intent or for sheer malevolent satisfaction.

It is often not until an attack has happened or a system has crashed that the full implications for the business become clear. This book is designed to give directors a proper appreciation of the potential risks, explaining where their companies may be vulnerable. It draws on the expertise of specialists in the area, as well as lawyers, bankers, insurers and business consultants, to examine ways of developing an appropriate security policy.

As the book explains, there is no simple answer. Effective information security depends on taking a multi-layered approach, combining technical, organizational and legal counter-measures.

Nor, unfortunately, can directors rest there. A continuous process of checking and testing of security needs to be instituted. Slight changes in the configuration of a system can unwittingly create holes through which attacks on data and networks can be launched.

Looking at the worst situation where there is a major breach of security, the book reviews the back-up measures that could be put in place and discusses how a crisis can be managed to minimize its impact.

It's unfortunate and frustrating that all the advantages of modern technology have to be accompanied by such consideration. But they have to be faced and dealt with fully. Over the coming years, there is likely to be more than one catastrophic corporate failure brought about by an attack on 'information security'. The intention of this book is that it shouldn't be one of its readers.

George Cox
Director General
Institute of Directors

Think your business is secure?

Don't get caught out.

Having a secure IT system is critical to the success of any business. Our IT group has the knowledge and expertise necessary to provide you with straightforward but innovative legal advice. We can give you the assurance you need to feel confident that your IT security is watertight.

Simmons & Simmons

For further information, please contact:

David Barrett
T +44 (0)20 7825 4032
E david.barrett@simmons-simmons.com

Peter Brudenall
T +44 (0)20 7825 4346
E peter.brudenall@simmons-simmons.com

www.simmons-simmons.com
www.elexica.com

GET THE MOST OUT OF YOUR TRAINING BUDGET WITH MIS ON-SITE TRAINING

Keeping your staff up to date and at peak performance is one of the most crucial parts of running a successful team and profitable organisation. Its benefits are ten-fold, in investing in your staffs professional growth you are saying 'we think you are worth it' at the same time ensuring a consistent knowledge level throughout your whole team.

One of the most effective and cost efficient ways of training your team on the same subject is by having the training On-Site. MIS Training can bring any audit and information security courses to your organisation.

You choose the dates, course, and location. We provide the training. Perhaps you have installed a new system, recruited new staff members or have a specific audit approaching. You are probably keen to secure your network, take preventative measures to counteract fraud and to assess for risks.

For organisations with 5 or more people who require training on the same topic.

MIS can tailor training courses to meet your exact educational needs and budget, saving you up to 50% on normal training fees.

Our Instructors are expert at tailoring programmes to meet your specific learning goals, and we can also customise a new programme just for your organisation. Your staff don't spend valuable time (and budget) travelling, and they get the training they need without leaving the office.

On-site training can be just for your own staff, guaranteeing privacy for confidential issues and consultation for individual problems. Alternatively, you may choose to team with peer departments, either inside or outside your organisation.

All MIS Instructors are hands-on audit and security practitioners eager to share with you their knowledge and experience and serve as

your personal consultant. The training can be given in which ever form is most conducive to your departments learning, e.g. interactive, case-driven classroom courses or intensive hands-on workshops, or a combination of both.

MIS can deliver to your organisation:
- Any seminar in our catalogue or on our Web site off the shelf or tailored to your needs
- Any topic custom-designed for your organisation
- Dates to suit your team
- Hands-on or workshop style training
- Instructors with real-life experience and practical knowledge
- Flexible pricing structure to suit your budget

Some of the benefits of On-site training:
- **Save money** over public seminar fees in addition to savings on travel and accommodation costs.
- **Save time on travel** as the instructor will travel to you. Furthermore, the training can be held at the most convenient time for you.
- **Ensure the relevance** of the seminar for your organisation and industry. You may wish to tailor the structure and methodology of your seminar or customise the seminar to meet the expertise levels of your attending employees.
- **Assure confidentiality.** With only your own people present, sensitive or proprietary issues can be addressed and used as examples during the seminar.
- **Bring the best in the business** to your business. Instructors are hands-on, expert practitioners who are your subject matter consultants while they are at your location.
- **After class follow up.** Should you have any questions over the following months of training, our expert instructors are available by email to assist you and provide maximum value for your organisation.
- **Gain CPE points** and certificates for the number of training hours

Feedback from recent On-Site clients
OLD MUTUAL PLC
'We ran a 5 day IT Audit School based around 2 courses; IT Auditing and Controls and How to Audit Automated Business Applications. The aim was to introduce our non IT Auditors to IT Audit and the audit of computerised business applications.

'We chose MIS Training because they are leaders in the field of IT Audit training, their willingness to tailor courses to our requirements and the cost benefits after meeting critical mass thresholds for numbers on the course. The Instructor chosen for us was a very good presenter, with a strong

background in ISACA and a current IT audit practitioner. He was informative and drew from his experience as appropriate. MIS Training provided excellent support facilitating the course and presentation materials throughout the pre-course period. The course was well received by all participants and they all enjoyed the training and found the course materials most useful. We found that MIS are second to none in the provision of onsite training in Internal Audit, IT Audit and related matters because of the quality of product, excellent Instructors, outstanding support and the quality of documentation provided.'
Jonathan Birke
Deputy Chief Internal Auditor
UK, Europe and US Life Old Mutual PLC

JT INTERNATIONAL, AMSTERDAM
'We ran a 5 day tailored version of SAP R/3 Concepts and Audit Risks to prepare my team for a SAP R/3 post implementation audit. We chose On Site training with MIS Training because of the relevance of the course and the standard of the Instructor. The Instructor chosen had a good teaching style and encouraged participation. The On-Site Training was very easy to organise and I am planning to organise further training for next year.'
Marino Mata
Director IT Audit
JT International

Founded in 1978, MIS Training is the international leader in Audit, IT Audit and Information Security Training, with offices in the USA, UK and Asia. MIS' expertise draws on experience gained in training more than 100,000 delegates across five continents. MIS presents seminars and conferences in the areas of Internal and IT Audit; Information Security; Networks; E-commerce applications; Operating Platforms; and Enterprise Applications.

Full details of all training and conference events by MIS Training can be found at **www.mistieurope.com** or by calling **+44 (0) 207 7779 8292**

Examples of on-site training courses:
- SAP R/3 Concepts and Audit Risks and SAP R/3 Audit Information System
- IT Audit School
- Incident Response and Digital Forensic Investigations
- Security and Audit of Oracle Financials and More
- Securing and Auditing PeopleSoft Applications
- General Controls in a Web Based Operating Environment
- Audit and Security of Applications Development
- Creating Information Security Awareness
- Securing & Auditing Windows 2000 Server
- Intrusion & Detection Systems: Monitoring Your Network
- How To Audit SAP R/3 Basis
- Designing An Effective Information Security Architecture
- Sarbanes-Oxley-A Road Map To Compliance
- Power IT Auditing
- Uncovering Fraud In Core Business Functions
- Sarbanes-Oxley for IT Auditors
- Securing and Auditing SAP R/3 Revenue and Procurement Cycle
- Auditing Your Information Security Programme
- Securing & Auditing Oracle Databases
- Security & Audit of TCP/IP Networks
- How to Conduct a Fraud Investigation
- Writing Better Audit Reports in Less Time with Less Effort
- Security & Audit of UNIX
- Securing & Auditing your Website
- Using SQL Tools to Perform Data Analysis

Previous on-site training clients
- Old Mutual Plc
- Bahrain Petroleum
- Bank For International Settlements
- Barclays Bank
- Bank Muscat
- UNESCO
- Bank of Greece
- Saudi French Bank
- Department For Work and Pensions
- Daimler Chrysler
- Credit Suisse First Boston
- Hellenic American Union
- National Audit Office
- Ernst and Young
- JT International
- Nordea
- Citigroup
- ISACA Chapter Switzerland
- Statoil
- Sara Lee Corp
- ABN Amro
- ISACA Chapter Denmark
- Abu Dhabi National Oil Company
- Kuwait Petroleum
- ISACA Chapter Finland
- KPMG
- Office of the Deputy Prime Minister
- Alliance & Leicester
- Reuters
- Deloitte and Touche

Modular and flexible Risk-Management

International eBusiness needs Risk-Management on-demand, says Thomas D. Frueh, Wire Card's Head of Risk-Management. By employing the localized or industry-specific procedures and databases that have been tailored to national or international markets, a risk management process is then developed and adapted to the customer's business model.

The Wire Card AG Corporate Trust Center is an intelligent risk-management instrument for mail-order and electronic commerce companies as well as for banks and other companies. It boasts a number of national and international solutions including blacklists (hotlists), scoring, credit ratings, address verification or country exclusion procedures.

Flexible modification to your company's needs

The Corporate Trust Center uses multidimensional business profiles to model the special needs of customers. With business profiles you can precisely adapt the risk-management tools being used to customer needs such as localized or business-specific processes and data verification methods.

Wire Card CTC provides the following risk-management modules:
- Duplication Check
- Address verification/Address Check
- Scoring based on mosaik data/negative data
- Credit Rating (such as detailed information)
- IP Check (eg for country related Hotlists)
- Call-back Functionality

Payment-specific modules:
- Account Number and Bank Code Check
- Salary Check
- BIN Check (e.g. for country related Hotlists, crossover Checks with Address or IP-Address)
- CVC2/CVV2 Checking Procedures (including the Handling of recurrent Billing)
- AVS (Address Verification Services)
- LUHN Check
- Account Verification

According to Gartner Group fraud rates in MoTo/eCommerce businesses are 12 times higher than in the offline world

These modules are supplemented by sophisticated algorithms such as velocity monitoring, neuronal networks and limit checks, designed to detect fraud in advance and ultimately reduce its rate of incidence.

To create the optimum solution for the business and risk models of each customer, the CTC links its own risk modules and methods to the services of external national and international partners in the risk management sector. Wire Card AG based in Munich/Germany, cooperates with other leading companies such as German Schufa and international providers such as Experian, CyberSource or Fairlsaac.

By employing the localized or industry-specific procedures and databases that have been tailored to national or international markets, a risk management process is then developed and adapted to the customer's business model. The ability to vary the design of the risk-management process and the large number of risk-management modules and methods makes the CTC the ideal risk-management platform for all B2B/B2C companies, particularly for those involved in financial services, the mail-order business, and electronic commerce.

We enable our customers to fully outsource their payment and risk processes by acting as an extended Service Provider. We operate and host our software platforms centrally and thereby help our customers to reduce costs dramatically and increase operation efficiency.

Wire Card AG is a leading technology provider and service provider for electronic payment processing and integrated risk-management.
For further information please contact: Wire Card AG – Global Payment Solutions, Lilienthalstrasse 5, D-85399 Hallbergmoos/Munich. Tel. +49 (0) 811-5546 400 Fax +49 (0) 811-5546 499

info@wirecard.com   www.wirecard.com

Secure Online Business

Professional Services

Riskmanagement

Payment Solutions

WIRE CARD

GLOBAL PAYMENT SOLUTIONS

Wire Card solutions are developed to fulfill the highest security standards in online business. Corporate Trust Center and Card Corporate Clearing Center - go global with secure riskmanagement and online payment. **www.wirecard.com**

1

Information at risk

ARE YOU LOOKING FOR INFORMATION ON BEST PRACTICE IN BUSINESS CONTINUITY MANAGEMENT?

ARE YOU LOOKING TO INTRODUCE BUSINESS CONTINUITY MANAGEMENT INTO YOUR ORGANISATION?

ARE YOU LOOKING FOR A FULL TIME PROFESSIONAL CAREER IN BUSINESS CONTINUITY MANAGEMENT?

IF THE ANSWER IS YES TO ANY OF THESE QUESTIONS YOU SHOULD BE A MEMBER OF

THE

The Business Continuity Institute

THE WORLDWIDE INSTITUTE FOR BUSINESS CONTINUITY PRACTITIONERS

For Details Contact:

THE BUSINESS CONTINUITY INSTITUTE
PO BOX 4474, WORCESTER, WR6 5YA
UNITED KINGDOM
Telephone: +44 (0)870 603 8783
Facsimile: +44 (0)870 603 8761
Email: enquiries@thebci.org

THE BCI – LEADNG IN THE DEVELOPMENT OF BUSINESS CONTINUITY STANDARDS

The business case for IT security

Security is more than just about keeping the bad guys out it is also about iden-tifying and letting the good guys in, writes Andrew Steggles, Marketing Director, EMEA Nokia Enterprise Solutions.

For many years security was synonymous with having a solid firewall in place. Protecting the perimeter and thereby keeping the bad guys out was the main goal of network architects. However, recent surveys suggest that more than 70 per cent of all security breaches result from within the firewall, that is, from the people you trust – your employees, partners or consultants.

New viruses continue to employ blend threat techniques, exploiting multiple weak-nesses and attacking through multiple methods (for example, e-mail, file transfers and Web browsers) forcing organizations to purchase additional layers of anti-virus and content security products to deploy across the enterprise. Instant messaging has entered the corporate world and has brought with it another layer of security concerns. Instant messaging applications can provide attack points for hackers seeking to gain entry into corporate systems by presenting tunnels through firewalls.

Hacking toolkits and manuals can be found all over the Internet. Today, it is possible for a 10-year-old to break into a multinational bank and steal or alter the most sensitive kinds of information: balance statements, credit card information, access rights and so on.

Understanding threats

When organizations first begin to assess network security, the tendency is to focus almost exclusively on external-facing assets to defend against unauthorized attacks. However, to establish an effective security policy, organizations must examine both external facing, publicly accessible resources, and internal facing, private networks. Recent findings by the FBI and the Computer Security Institute indicate that internal attacks account for the majority of security breaches that organizations experience. This finding suggests that internal network security needs to be a higher priority for security and network administrators. Internal core network security is a requirement for all networks.

The threats to the security infrastructure of any network include packet sniffing, DNS spoofing (or domain name server spoofing: this is where a machine assumes the identity of a company's or service provider's Web address to an IP address look-up server), IP (Internet provider) address spoofing (where an unscrupulous person forges the address of the sending device to make it appear as if it has come from a different machine) and the proliferation of fake routing information. Spoofing occurs when an attacker sends network packets that falsely appear to be from a trusted host on the network. In general terms, these threats can be categorized as interception and impersonation.

Interception

The first type of attack involves interception of communication between two systems, such as a client and a server. In this scenario, an attacker exists somewhere on the network between communicating entities. The attacker observes the information passed between the client and server. The attacker might intercept and keep the information (reconnaissance), or might alter the information and send it on to the intended recipient (man-in-the-middle attack).

A man-in-the-middle, or bucket brigade, attack is one in which the attacker intercepts messages in an exchange and then retransmits them, substituting his or her own data for the requested one, such that the two original parties still appear to be communicating with each other directly. The attacker uses a program that, to the client appears to be the server, and to the server appears to be the client. The attack may be used simply to gain access to the messages, or enable the attacker to modify the messages before retransmitting them.

Impersonation

The second type of attack is impersonation of a particular host, either a client or a server. Using this strategy, an attacker pretends to be the intended recipient of a message. If the strategy works, the client remains unaware of the deception and continues to communicate with the impostor as if its traffic had successfully reached the destination.

Anticipating threats

Both of these attack techniques allow network information to be intercepted, potentially for hostile reasons. The results can be disastrous, whether that goal is achieved by listening for all packets (through a packet sniffer) on a network or by utilizing a compromised name server to redirect a certain network required to a maliciously duplicated, or compromised, host.

Over the last few years, falls in hardware prices have made it attractive and convenient for corporations and home users to go wireless, in particular using the 802.11 standard. But in the rush towards liberation from the tethers of computer cable, individuals and companies are opening the doors to a whole new type of computer intrusion. Without special software or hardware other than ordinary consumer wireless cards, hackers have found a new pastime: cruising around metropolitan areas with their laptops listening for the beacons of wireless networks and then accessing unprotected WLANs. War driving resembles the war dialling of the 1990s, with automated programs calling hundreds of phone numbers in search of poorly protected computer dial-ups.

Likewise, many hotels and airport lounges are providing free-of charge wireless LANs. Business travellers may automatically set up a WLAN and do not consider the security risks as they typically access the Internet, use instant messaging, or connect to corporate accounts. The public wireless connection exposes users to direct peer-to-peer hacking from anyone else connected to the over-the-air airport lounge network. Again, downloading files and instant messaging are common ways that hackers use to install spyware and hacking tools over the Internet. In the end, even safe VPN tunnels to corporate resources might be at risk since they are open to any intruder 'already on the PC'.

Protecting your corporate assets

The negative effects on a business of having insufficient security systems in place, or falling victim to security breaches and denial of service attacks, are well recorded and have made numerous media headlines. These headlines are increasing awareness of the importance of security amongst all businesses.

IT infrastructure security is clearly no longer just a concern for the IT department, but commands the attention of senior management as the face of security changes from an 'insurance policy', to a crucial business foundation. Not only is a watertight security solution mandatory, but also having the correct security systems in place can also positively impact an organization's business.

Until recently, security in the networked environment was about keeping the 'bad guys' out. Yet as organizations extend connectivity via extranets and the Internet, it is no longer enough to just lock out the 'bad guys'. A company has to allow a myriad of additional and valid users (such as suppliers, customers and employees) to access its data seamlessly – to let the 'good guys' in. In fact, by allowing trusted users to access its data, it is streamlining its business functions and creating economies of scale, which will ultimately justify the initial cost of implementing security technologies.

The number of valid users is rapidly increasing. IDC forecasts an explosion in the number of individuals accessing the Internet and corporate Intranets over the next four years. This means that corporate infrastructures will be exposed to an unprecedented number of users, all trying to access relevant corporate resource and information that they may need to conduct business.

In the global economy, many companies are based in disparate locations and have an increasing number of mobile workers, all of whom need to communicate and share information in real time. Availability and speed of access to information on the Internet, combined with the projected growth of Internet usage, pose an important consideration for companies: there is a need to optimize access to information while maintaining levels of security so that the business is not endangered. A business needs to assess the risk involved in opening its networks, whilst maintaining a secure environment – this is often a headache for IT professionals.

However, once a security policy and infrastructure are in place, a company can expect increased productivity within the business process, through the creation of trust, ensured privacy of data and maintenance of integrity.

Security as a business enabler

An overall view of security, taking into consideration the risks and benefits of using the Internet, will highlight the long-term benefits of a security infrastructure and policy. Here is a set of core elements that serve as a foundation to e-business:

■ **Trust**: by having a security policy (and necessary security systems to back this up) in place, customers and suppliers can trust your company and be encouraged to transact with you online.
■ **Privacy**: by assuring customers and suppliers that their data is secure, you are again promoting trust and encouraging more access and interactivity.
■ **Integrity**: by ensuring that your e-business systems are secure, you minimize the risk of attack and the loss of trust and brand equity of your company.

Security cannot be considered in isolation from a company's business goals. Technology is ultimately a tool to enable business, and security technology is no exception. Steps to consider when implementing security technology include:

■ Ensure that security is a board issue – it requires this level of governance.
■ Begin with your business objectives when planning a security policy.
■ Consider where your business will be in three years before implementing technology you will outgrow.
■ Choose a security partner that understands your business and has the technology solutions and reputable customer service.
■ Implement strong physical security.
■ Make sure you revisit and update your security policy and technology as your business grows.
■ Make sure that all users (staff and supply chain) are educated and trained.

To conclude, security is not an insurance policy. It is both a necessity for e-business and a positive element of infrastructure. This has been driven by the need for companies to nurture 'trusted relationships' with customers, partners, suppliers and channels. In many cases, a company's most valuable asset is its corporate data. The ability to use security technologies to enable greater access to corporate data increases the trust in these relationships. Ultimately, trusted relationships can yield significant benefits, such as higher transaction rates, lower cost per transaction and increasingly personalized services.

Nokia Enterprise Solutions focuses on mobile business devices and providing IP network perimeter security (firewalls and VPN), secure content management (anti-virus scanning and SPAM filtering), and mobile connectivity (remote access VPN and content) solutions designed to help companies to mobilize their workforces and increase productivity while ensuring the security and reliability of their networks.

For further information contact Nokia Enterprise Solutions on +44 161 601 8908, e-mail ipsecurity.emea@nokia.com. Full details of all Nokia Enterprise products can be found at: www.nokia.com/ipsecurity/emea

Recent attack trends

Online fraud has doubled in the last two years with a cybercrime being committed every 20 seconds. The Fraud Advisory Panel's Cybercrime Working Group reports on where companies are vulnerable.

Introduction

The Federation of Small Businesses has reported that Internet fraud costs the British economy £28 million a year, compared with £3.8 million in 2000.[1] The National Consumers League reported in January 2003 there had been an average loss of US $484 per person due to Internet fraud in the first six months of 2002. According to the Gartner Group, international losses from online fraud reached US $1.64 billion in 2002, that is to say they have doubled in the last two years, and with e-sales totalling approximately £91 million in 2002 it is not surprising that cybercrimes are being committed every 20 seconds.

The PriceWaterhouseCoopers Global Economic Crime Survey 2003 published in July interviewed more than 3,600 companies in 50 countries. Significant economic crimes were reported by 37 per cent of respondents within the previous two years. The proportion of organizations reporting fraud in Western Europe, for example, has risen from 29 per cent to 34 per cent. The likelihood of suffering economic crime grows with the size of a company. Of companies employing less than 1,000 people 37 per cent reported economic crime, while 52 per cent of companies employing more than 1,000 people did so.

---

[1] *Guardian*, 19 June 2003

The average loss to companies was almost US $2.2 million, but almost a third of victims were not able to put a figure on any loss to their companies as a result of economic crime. The financial cost of some economic crime – bribery, corruption and cybercrime – is especially hard to quantify.

Nearly three-quarters of the victims recovered less than 20 per cent of their losses – yet only half of respondents had any insurance against economic crime. The losses are not merely direct financial losses – business relationships, staff morale and brand strength can all be affected. Nonetheless, only 29 per cent of companies had given their boards any fraud related training.

The most widely reported crime was the misappropriation of assets – 60 per cent of companies. But this is not the only major concern for the future – 15 per cent of companies worldwide reported incidents of cybercrime compared with 19 per cent of companies in the UK. The average loss per company worldwide is estimated to be US $812,318. Of companies worldwide, 31 per cent view cybercrime as a key risk in times to come. This increases in developed markets to 38 per cent of companies in North America and 37 per cent of companies in Western Europe. While cyber criminals tend to be selective in their targets, the effects of cybercrime can be extremely severe for its victims.[2]

Hackers

Hackers can be divided into two groups: internal and external hackers. The motivation of hackers can vary between financial gain, political or ideological beliefs, and revenge in the case of a disgruntled employee or dissatisfied customer. What hackers do once they have gained access to a computer system depends on their initial motivation. Their aim may be to steal corporate information, carry out an e-theft, plant malicious computer programs, disrupt the target's computer system, highlight lack of security, or deface the company's Web site, causing damage to its corporate reputation.

It was reported in October 2003 that a teenager charged with offences under the Computer Misuse Act 1990 as a result of his alleged hacking activities had been cleared. The teenager had been accused of effectively shutting down one of America's largest ports as a result of a botched denial of service attack he had launched. The teenager was charged with offences under the Computer Misuse Act 1990. The prosecution alleged that the teenager's target had been a chatroom user who had offended him. The Internet service provider was forced to divert e-mails through intermediary service providers and as a result the server that operated the US port in Houston was bombarded with electronic messages. This caused the server to shut down.

The teenager claimed that a flaw in his computer system had allowed other hackers to obtain access to his computer and plant a Trojan Horse computer program to remotely control his computer. The computer was then used to launch an attack. The teenager claimed that the perpetrator had then edited his log files to disguise his existence. The jury cleared the teenager of the charges.[3]

---

[2] PriceWaterhouseCoopers *Economic Crime Survey 2003*, published July 2003
[3] *Daily Telegraph* 7 October 2003, *The Times* Online 17 October 2003 by PA News

In September 2002, IT security firm Synstar estimated that over 1,000 UK organizations had been cracked into – almost a five-fold increase on the previous year's 225.[4]

In November 2003 it was reported that the Royal Bank of Scotland had been the victim of a denial of service attack perpetrated by hackers. The bank's Worldpay operation was attacked. The server was disabled after being bombarded by bogus requests, which appeared to emanate from computers based in the Ukraine. There have not been any estimates of the losses to clients, which include Vodafone and Freeserve.[5]

In September 2003 it was reported that a 26-year-old computer expert had been convicted of masterminding the UK's largest ever credit card fraud. Over a three-year period, the fraudster, Sunil Mahtani, and his accomplices downloaded nearly 9,000 credit card details from Heathrow Express Railink. These were passed onto a gang of 11 accomplices who forged new credit cards using the details. The scam was uncovered in September 2001, at which point the gang had already stolen £2 million. Had all of the numbers been used it would have made in the region of £20 million.[6] Mr Mahtani was later sentenced to nine years imprisonment and his two associates were sentenced to four years imprisonment for their part in the fraud.[7] Despite the scale of the fraud Mr Mahtani was only ordered to pay back £1,329 as investigators were only able to locate £4.73 which he held in two building societies and a £1,000 share in a car.[8]

Cyber extortion

In November 2003 it was reported that organized gangs of criminals had used the threat of hacking to extort money from companies in the United Kingdom. The organized gangs (thought to be based in Eastern Europe) have been targeting online companies and costing those companies millions of dollars in lost business. The National Hi-Tech Crime Unit is currently investigating how a betting site was disabled. The site later received a threat that it would suffer similar attacks unless it paid thousands of pounds.

■ One UK company was reported to be losing up to £1 million a day in business following attacks.
■ More than a dozen offshore gambling sites have been attacked.
■ Sites have been asked to pay up to US $50,000 to prevent attacks over the course of the next year.[9]

It has been reported that the Russian Mafia are behind this latest spate of extortion attacks. Attacks have been traced to St Petersburg.

In February 2003 Oleg Zezev was convicted following attempts to carry out computer intrusion and extortion in the United States. Mr Zezev had emailed Michael Bloomberg, the

---

[4] Crime uncovered, *Observer,* 27 April 2003,
[5] *Financial Times,* 6 November 2003
[6] Ellen Connolly, Fraudsters duplicated 9,000 credit cards, Times Online, 6 September 2003
[7] Three jailed in major credit card fraud, London Reuters, 9 September 2003
[8] £2M credit card fraudster told to repay only £1,300, Times Online, 10 September 2003
[9] *Financial Times*, 12 November 2003

head of Bloomberg Inc, attempting to extort money from the company in exchange for not revealing to the public that he had managed to hack into the company's computer system.[10]

Netspionage

Corporate espionage carried out by way of the Internet or computer is a growing area of concern for businesses. By its very nature this form of cybercrime is under-reported. A business may not be aware that it is happening or if it does know, may not want to publicize the problem.

The CSI / FBI 2003 Computer Crime and Security Survey has revealed that cybercrime is continuing at a steady pace. Respondents cited their Internet connection instead of their internal systems as the most common point of attack. The CSI report that in the United States US $70,195,900 was lost to theft of proprietary information, the most expensive computer crime, with an average loss of US $2.7 million.

With the advent of the wireless network a new form of snooping has become increasingly common. 'War driving' involves cyber snoopers driving around cities with electronic detection equipment which can be purchased for as little as £200. The equipment scans for open wireless networks. Information passed across the network can reportedly be stored and sold on to corporate rivals. Alternatively the snoopers can obtain free use of the target's network. Computer security firm Trinity Security recently reported that it had carried out a demonstration in which it found 39 wireless networks in London's Square Mile, of which 54 per cent were not using encryption and only one network was fully secured.[11]

In 2002, it was reported that Canal Plus sued NDS for US $3 billion for deliberately sabotaging its business. It was alleged that NDS hacked the security code on the Canal Plus smart card, which gave viewers a choice of different channels. While many companies engage in reverse engineering to examine their competitor's products, Canal Plus claimed that NDS published the security code on the Internet, where international counterfeiters picked it up. In turn, it was alleged that the counterfeiters produced fake smart cards, which allowed users to watch subscription channels free. Canal Plus said this was a deliberate plan to sabotage the business in which it was a market leader.[12] Since the allegations NDS has faced a flurry of similar lawsuits.[13]

It was reported in September 2002 that a Chinese programmer working for the US state-run China National Petroleum Corp. was arrested by federal authorities for allegedly trying to steal software used to map underground oil deposits from a Silicon Valley company. Chinese national Shan Yan Ming was arrested by the FBI after workers at the privately held 3DGeo company discovered him trying to download an expensive, proprietary software program. A California-based company, The Mountain View, sells software

---

[10] Jenny B Davis, Cybercrime fighters, *ABA Journal,* August 2003

[11] Trinity Security sends a wake up call to the City's top businesses, press release, 8 October 2003 [Online] www.trinitysecurity.com; see also article in *The Metro*, 12 November 2003, p 17

[12] Owen Gibson, Set-top piracy court battle renewed, *Guardian*, 30 May 30 2002 [Online] http://media.guardian.co.uk/city/story/0,7497,724664,00.html

[13] Dan Milmo, Murdoch firm ordered to hand over documents in TV piracy row, *Guardian*, 3 October 2002 [Online]http://media.guardian.co.uk/city/story/0,7497,803950,00.html

used in seismic imaging of oil fields. Ming had been at 3DGeo since late April, being trained to use some of the company's software as part of a contract 3DGeo has with the China National Petroleum Corp.

3DGeo said, 'We have security in place and we monitor any kind of activity like this.... As soon as it escalated from being sort of unusual to being threatening activity' the company stopped it and asked Ming to leave. The company said it did not know why the programmer would have been trying to access the proprietary software, which it said costs US $200,000 or more.[14]

Corporate identity theft

It was reported in June 2002 that IBM client security product management representatives had said that as e-business grows, identity theft would be moving into corporate identity, which may result in procurement fraud, industrial sabotage and violation of laws and regulations.[15]

The Internet allows fraudsters to offer bogus credible banking services. It is difficult for the consumer to discern between genuine and fraudulent Internet banks. Fraudsters do not need to go to great expense to dress up their sites as genuine, and will entice victims with a promise of high interest rates. A bogus Internet banking site can be set up offshore, attract funds and be dismantled overnight.

This crime appears to be most prevalent in the United States, where the government recently investigated 16 suspicious banking sites and acknowledged there could be many more sites lying undetected on the Internet. The fraudsters are not content with simply taking their victim's deposits. They also sell their credit card details gleaned from the completed application forms.

In one recent case, three people were charged in North Carolina with fraud and money laundering activities in relation to an Internet banking operation. The bank allegedly operated without a charter and offered an interest rate of 20 per cent. It is said that the bank took over $650,000 from 3,000 customers.

These examples show that there are many fraudulent schemes that use the Internet as their medium. The charges brought by the SEC show that vast amounts of profits can be produced by these scams, which would explain the huge increase over the last year in such frauds. There seems to be no shortage of e-fraudsters, who are prepared to risk criminal sanctions for the vast amounts of possible profits.

It was reported in July 2002 that Euro Kartensysteme, a German credit card handler, was forced to take action in the light of electronic fraud. An estimated 3,000 contracts with online retailers and credit card firms were cancelled. Credit card companies were put under added pressure from a German High Court ruling in relation to illegal Internet and phone transactions. This resulted in a high volume of account closures.[16]

The *Financial Times* reported recently that on top of the 'Nigerian letters' 419 frauds, West African criminals have now begun targeting financial institutions in Britain with a

---

[14] Reuters, 21 September 2002
[15] Troy Wolverton, ZDNet News, 25 March 2002
[16] Tamsin McMahon, Europe Media, 1 July 2002

new range of frauds. The Nigerian fraudsters are infiltrating banks to gather information about their clients to compromise their systems. Others hijack the identities of banks to perpetrate frauds, which has been highlighted by the NCIS in its latest UK threat assessment of serious and organized crime.

Confidential details are passed to accomplices outside the bank who then make unauthorized transfers to drain the accounts. The DTI and the City of London police fraud squad has said that this 'is the most significant trend at the moment.'

In other cases the fraudsters single out bank staff who look vulnerable to temptation and try to corrupt them. The British Banking Association is taking steps to improve the vetting of staff, especially temporary staff employed through agencies. The International Chamber of Commerce encourages banks to speak to their staff about instances where customer information has been misused and to warn them of the consequences.

It is also reported that criminal groups are now setting up bogus Web sites that ape a bank's pages. In 2002, the NCIS alerted South Africa's central bank that someone had put up a fake Web site using its name as part of a scam used to swindle British businessmen out of £130,000. The South African government worked closely with the NCIS to catch the perpetrators.

In 2003, a site called www.barclaysprivate.com was shut down after having been used as part of a wide-ranging fraud, as was www.eurocitibank.com, which had nothing to do with Citibank. Such sites are used to show the intended victims that the promised millions have been deposited in an account that appears to be held at a legitimate bank. In many cases, the victims will be asked to fill in an online application form with their personal details, including the numbers of their real bank accounts and credit cards. Entire bank sites can then be copied, and the confidence tricksters simply redirect search engines to find them.

The Treasury has said it is aware of the issue and is tightening regulations to clamp down on all forms of fraud. It claimed the Financial Services Authority (FSA) was responsible for tackling the problem, an assertion the FSA quickly rebutted, saying it was not responsible for fraud investigation, but rather the wider, systematic issues in banking.

Police and fraud investigators have said banks and other financial institutions still routinely cover up fraud losses and write them off as bad debts rather than risk damage to their reputations. However this practice may not be permitted in the future because UK banks are now under a duty to report suspicious transactions under the Proceeds of Crime Act.[17]

In October 2002 in the United Kingdom, six companies were wound up in the High Court following a DTI investigation that discovered that holidaymakers had been misled into paying thousands of pounds to secure savings on luxury holidays. One of the companies, Travelmasters Limited, falsely claimed to be both ABTA and ATOL bonded and to have originated from a well-known holiday chain 'Intersun'. Clients were also told to go to the intersun.co.uk Web site. In fact, the well-known holiday chain with 80 high street agencies was 'Intasun'. Another of the companies was actually registered as Intersun Limited.

In December 2002, detectives began investigating whether an illegal travel agency had been set up to on-sell flights, having discovered a huge credit card fraud against the

---

[17] Thomas Catan and Michael Peel, *Financial Times*, 3 March 2003

budget airline easyJet in the Liverpool area. In 2001, the chairman of easyGroup threatened legal action against anyone starting a new business with 'easy' in the name as an attempt to capitalize on the name. His fight to protect his brand led him to register more than 9,000 domain names. The name 'easy' is descriptive and therefore not trademarkable, hence the aggressive tactics hoping people would cave in. However he failed with his complaints to the WIPO, the domain name arbiters, against EasyMaterial.com, easy-jet.com and easygetaway.com. A successful action against easyRealestate in passing off is discussed below.

In a new turn known as 'cybergriping', a disgruntled Chase Manhattan customer in New York started a site to complain about errors on his bank account. As a result the bank quickly secured the rights to chasesucks, chasestinks and ihatechase.

In the Seattle protest case, a fake Web site was created on the basis of the official World Trade Organization Web site, in that it was graphically the same but with different contents. For example, the home page announced that the opening ceremony of the Third WTO Ministerial Conference had been 'suddenly cancelled'. The cybergripers even had the gall to place an alert message lower on the page about a 'fake WTO website misleading public', with a hyperlink to the original WTO Web site. The URL, http://www.gatt.org, was carefully chosen with obvious reference to the previous name of the WTO (the official Web site address is http://www.wto.org).

Phishing

It has recently been reported that a number of high street banks have been targeted by online fraudsters. The fraudsters send e-mails, which appear authentic, to customers, inviting them to log on to the bank's Web site and verify their account details including their personal identification number. The Web site to which the e-mails are linked is bogus although it appears to be authentic. This type of fraud is commonly known as 'phishing', and is an example of identity theft. It is already considered to be a significant problem in the United States, Australia and New Zealand. However banks in the United Kingdom have been accused of being slow to warn customers of this new fraud.[18]

It has been reported that the Spanish bank, BBVA, recently discovered an attempt to defraud its customers over the Internet. Several Internet users received an e-mail which purported to be sent by the bank, offering new services and inviting the users to reveal their passwords via a false Web page similar to the real one. The e-mails were sent at about 3 pm but were discovered 10 minutes later. After a few hours the Web site was no longer operational and no clients lost any money as a result of the fraud.[19]

The Federal Trade Commission (FTC) has announced it is cracking down on this growing form of Internet identity fraud. In one particular case in the United States a teenager created a fake AOL member page. The FTC said the youngster ran up US $8,000 in purchases using the credit data he had obtained.[20]

---

[18] *Daily Telegraph*, October 2003
[19] Expansion, BBVA uncovers internet scam, FT.com, 22 May 2003
[20] Jonathan Krim, Online identity theft tactic targeted, *Washington Post*, 22 July 2003

The Fraud Advisory Panel is an independent body of volunteers drawn from the public and private sectors. The Panel's role is to raise awareness of the immense social and economic damage that is caused by fraud and develop remedies. Members of the Fraud Advisory Panel include representatives from the law and accountancy professions, industry associations, financial institutions, government agencies, law enforcement, regulatory authorities and academia.

For further information contact Fraud Advisory Panel, Chartered Accountants' Hall, PO Box 433, Moorgate Place, London, EC2P 2BJ, Tel: 020 7920 8721, Fax: 020 7920 8536, e-mail:info@fraudadvisorypanel.org Web site: www.fraudadvisorypanel.org

Security: the threat from within

There are Mr Disgruntleds, Mr Unawares, Mr Opportunities and Mr Temporaries in every organization. All offer a potential risk to a company's IT system from within, writes Chris Knowles, Practice Leader, Security, Computacenter.

Introduction

Most organizations have a Mr Grumpy, but did you know that you might also have a Mr Opportunity and a Mr Unaware? Many organizations spend vast amounts of money on protecting their infrastructures from an external attack on their security without adequately assessing the likelihood of an internal breach. This means that while many companies have deployed security tools such as firewalls, e-mail scanning and intruder detection, the focus is on preventing unauthorized access, stopping denial of service and preventing viruses and Trojans from getting into the organization. While this provides an adequate degree of protection from outside, it does little to aid in the detection and prevention of the damage that can be done by the 'characters' within.

Profiling your employees

In an ideal world, all of the employees in your organization would be Mr 'Normal'. However, as we are all aware, the world is most certainly not ideal. However through education, policy and appropriate deployment of tools, many Mr Normals can be created

Delivering your technology roll-out, reducing your time to desk.

Since 1981, UK organisations have turned to Computacenter for rapid and risk-free roll-out of their technology estate. Whatever the scope or scale of your requirement, we offer the specialist skills, geographical coverage and best practices needed to ensure your project success – every time. Find out more at www.computacenter.com/services

TECHNOLOGY SOURCING

INFRASTRUCTURE INTEGRATION

MANAGED SERVICES

Computacenter

Transforming IT service delivery

telephone: 0800 617000   email: enquiries@computacenter.com without it appearing as though 'Big Brother' is watching them. So just who are these other characters and what can you do about them?

Broadly speaking, the employees or 'characters' in your company will fall into one of four categories:

■ Mr 'Disgruntled';
■ Mr 'Opportunity';
■ Mr 'Unaware';
■ Mr 'Temporary'.

Each of these characters can pose a significant threat to your organization. The challenge is to recognize them and take an appropriate course of action.

Mr Disgruntled

Mr Disgruntled exists in many organizations. He may well be the person whom you have just beaten to that new position, been put at risk of redundancy, or simply be fed up. Either way, he will have access to many of your corporations systems, some because his job needs him to, others either through lack of security or by his specifically finding out how to get into them.

One of the most well known stories involves a trans-Pacific flight where a message came across the air-ground communication system in the cockpit that 'Four lucky passengers have just won two free tickets anywhere in the world – their seat numbers are …'. The captain of the flight joyfully announced the information, and everyone on board congratulated the four lucky passengers. It turned out that the message was actually sent by a disgruntled employee but in order not to cause a public relations issue, the airline had to deliver what had been promised. The total cost of this incident was over US $100,000.

In this case, it was very easy for the employee to execute simply by sending the message over a terminal that had been permanently logged into a 'group' account. Given the heightened fears over air travel, a different message could have had a far more devastating consequence.

So what can we do about this type of employee? First, good practice dictates that generic log-ins to systems such as group or guest accounts should be removed. This will at least ensure that any potential trouble causer would at least need to log in. Additionally, access should only be provided to systems that are necessary for an individual to use as part of his or her role. Many organizations have deployed intrusion detection systems, and these can be used to identify if employees are trying to access systems for which they do not have authority. However, for a large proportion of these companies, the investment in this technology is wasted. This is because large numbers of log files are generated and very few organizations have the time and necessary skills to go through these and determine what is a genuine forgotten password scenario and what a deliberate attack. In these cases the companies would be better to out-task the monitoring of these files to an external company.

Of course, the employee could quite easily log in as someone else, as there are bound to be many Mr Unawares within the organization.

Mr Unaware

Mr Unaware can be a very damaging specimen indeed. How many of you have security policies in place? Are your employees aware of your policy and kept up to speed with any changes? I was recently presenting to some senior managers in a well known construction company and as part of my preparation, I paid a visit to its Web site. I was extremely impressed to find that the site contained a copy of the security policy signed by the CEO. I brought this up at the beginning of the meeting, and to my surprise none of the people in the room were aware of the existence of this policy! Failure to make your employees aware of policies can also have other negative effects. For example, some prosecution cases against employees using their companies' IT assets for their own purposes, such as the downloading and storage of music files, were dismissed, as the employees were unaware that their actions were against the policy of the company.

In order to prevent this happening it is therefore necessary to ensure that all your employees are aware of the policy. The policy should identify what are the acceptable and unacceptable uses of company resources such as the Internet, and any provided hardware, as well as explaining the consequences of breaking the policy. Of course, the policy does not need to be just a list of the things employees are not permitted to do, it can and should also be used to educate them to protect them from the likes of Mr Disgruntled.

As we touched on before, Mr Disgruntled can quite easily find out information from Mr Unaware and use this to 'steal' his identity. Take for example the recent snack adverts on television which play a game of movie star names. The idea is to put together the name of your pet and your street name to make up the name you would use in films. There are many variations on this, which might include your middle name, your mother's maiden name and so on. Mr Disgruntled will know that for many people these very same names will be used as passwords, and will encourage several Mr Unawares to take part in order to gather information.

Of course many of us use words like these as our passwords so we can remember them. In most companies, there are many different systems we have to log into, and so we use what we can remember and also try not to change the passwords unless we are forced to, because when we do, we very often forget them and need to log calls with our help desks to get them reset. Solutions such as a single sign-on and password self-service can help reduce this pain.

We can also help Mr Unaware protect himself from characters like Mr Disgruntled. As well as Mr Unaware having 'something he knows' such as a password, we can equip him with 'something he has'. This may take the form of a token that generates a number which he can add to password, or a token which he plugs into his USB port, or increasingly, some form of biometrics such as a fingerprint or retina scanner to make sure that Mr Unaware is who he says he is.

Mr Opportunity

Converting Mr Unaware to Mr Normal is one big step in the right direction as far as protecting your environment goes, as is identifying when new Mr Disgruntleds are created. However, just when you think you have it all under control, along comes Mr Opportunity. Mr Opportunity usually has a very good understanding of either your business processes or your IT systems, and most likely both.

One of the most common cases here is when Mr Opportunity sets up as a new supplier on your system. Often this company is registered in Mrs Opportunity's maiden name and the company starts to submit invoices for work completed. Sometimes this is for genuine work, sometimes genuine work but with over-inflated costs, and sometimes it occurs when no work or service has been performed. Often this can be prevented by having a rigorous new supplier take-on process that fully checks out the background of any new supplier, including the names of all directors.

A couple of variations exist on this scheme, which can be more difficult to pin down. The first is where Mr Opportunity gives favouritism to a particular company, such as awarding it contracts or giving it information about its competitors' pricing so it can undercut them, in return for gifts. The second variation, and one which could also be attributed to Mr Disgruntled, is the passing of information to a rival company, again in return for cash or gifts.

To prevent any of these from occurring, not only do we need to limit access to the information to only those who need it for their jobs through the correct configuration of the IT infrastructure, we also need to strengthen our HR policies and new supplier take-on policies to properly vet new recruits and new suppliers. In an October 2003 survey undertaken by Computacenter at the Legal IT Forum, over 25 per cent of the participants stated that they did no vetting of new suppliers and a further 43 per cent relied only on references. This implies that there is a very significant risk of this kind of fraud in these organizations.

In many cases, the tools that have been deployed in order to monitor for inappropriate Internet usage and to prevent virus delivery by e-mail can also aid in detecting Mr Opportunity. Many 'opportunists' set up a Web site in order to give a company an apparently legitimate identity, and Mr Opportunity may be caught uploading information to this site or making changes. E-mail can be screened to see where information is being sent, and alerts raised for those going to inappropriate destinations. Audit trails can also be kept of instant messenger services, and again these can be screened for inappropriate content.

In addition, during the same survey, over 50 per cent of the participants stated that they did not carry out frequent vulnerability assessments. Having a regular assessment will help an organization understand where it has left open entry to systems, and where they have been opened. Using an independent company to do this work is also a good idea. Another well known story details the exploits of an employee in the IT department who when working on night shift opens ports on the firewall so he can play network-based games with his friends. While this does not constitute a financial loss it is both a misuse of corporate equipment and also a serious breach of trust. As with both Mr Disgruntled and Mr Unaware, Mr Opportunity can be in a position carrying a significant amount of responsibility.

Mr Temporary

The final employee type is really a relation of either Mr Opportunity or Mr Unaware and he is called Mr Temporary. Many companies use temporary workers to cover for holidays, sickness or seasonal variations who could turn out to be a Mr Opportunity or a Mr Unaware. Indeed in some sectors, there is a very real threat of industrial espionage and a likelihood that a temporary employee could turn out to be a spy from a rival company. Therefore it is imperative that not only is each new employee vetted to include full details of his or her other business interests and past employment, but also familiarity with the security policy should be a mandatory part of company induction.

Conclusion

While there is no such thing as an ideal world or a perfect system, a combination of strong HR and business policy and user education, aligned with good IT-based practices such as restricting access, checking for unauthorized connections, monitoring Internet access, and configuration management can go a long way toward mitigating the threat of an internal breach.

Computacenter is Europe's leading independent provider of IT infrastructure services. To help our customers maximize the value of IT to their businesses, we offer services at every stage of infrastructure investment.

We can advise customers on their IT strategy, implement the most appropriate technology from a wide range of leading vendors and manage elements of their technology infrastructures on their behalf. At every stage we help them minimize the cost and maximize the business value of their IT expenditure.

Our corporate and government clients are served by a network of branch offices across the United Kingdom, Germany, France, Austria, Luxembourg and Belgium and, through our international partners, at locations throughout the world.

For further information on Computacenter and its services, please e-mail enquiries@computacenter.com.

Cyberliabilities in the workplace

Frank Coggrave, UK Regional Director for Websense, considers how to prevent corporate network misuse.

It is nothing new to say that the Internet is an extremely powerful resource that we have all grown dependent on, yet the very nature of open access reveals a whole host of opportunities for misuse. How can companies ensure that both they and their employees are protected against the numerous legal and security implications that go hand-in-hand with such an indispensable tool?

With just a click of the mouse, company confidential information can leave the building without a trace and land in the wrong hands. Unlike e-mail, where a history log is created, there are many invisible routes for data to leave the network into an unknown world. Where does this data go, and more importantly, who is taking it? Hackers are an obvious malicious threat – and research shows the majority of hackers sit within the organization they are tapping.

So what about the less obvious routes of data leaving the organization? The seemingly innocent act of a user sending data to personal Internet storage sites and Web-based e-mail can be just as damaging. Even if storing on personal Internet storage sites is not intended as a malicious act, it immediately bypasses the secure IT infrastructure that companies have invested in heavily, and brings with it a variety of security issues. When data is stored outside the enterprise, it can be intercepted, distributed far and wide, and can be infected by viruses, malicious mobile code; the list goes on.

Keeping company data protected from emerging security threats is key to the IT health of any company. And as the Internet grows, more threats will appear, and disguise

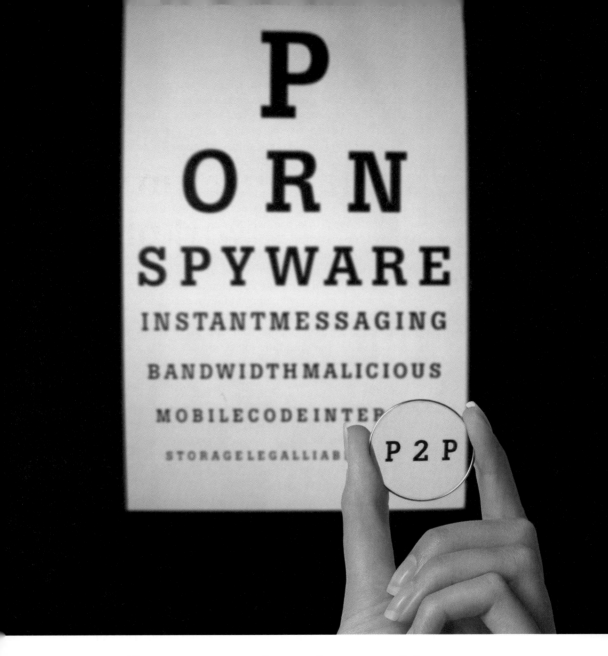

Peer-to-peer is a clear problem.

Take a close look at the serious security, infrastructure and legal liability threats P2P file sharing poses to your organisation. Reduce your risk with Websense Enterprise®. Block access to P2P protocols, sites and applications with the only software that offers end-to-end policy control to effectively eliminate P2P security breaches and other dangers. Stay focused on the P2P solution with a **free white paper** and assess your risks at **www.websense.com/P2P**.

FILTER | PROTECT | OPTIMIZE

themselves to avoid detection. Simply blocking what your company deems inappropriate use of the Internet is one avenue, but it is not always that cut and dried.

One example is instant messaging (IM) software. There are mixed feelings as to whether public IM software should be used in the corporate environment. That said, there are a growing number of companies seeing great value by using this real-time solution. Research shows that one in every five corporate users is using a public IM tool, but steps need to be taken in order for companies not to encounter potentially serious security pitfalls.

There is an option in IM that allows users to turn off tracking, meaning that the IT department has no way of knowing what conversations occur and what attachments are being sent to and from the network via IM. This is not only a security issue, with IM bypassing the corporate firewall, but also a bandwidth issue. Furthermore, if company policy does not allow IM, there is no way of finding out who is using it.

Recent research reveals that three out of every four Internet users access the Internet using a non-browser-based Internet application, such as IM. As this 'door' into and out of the network is open to abuse, not only can company confidential information easily make its way out of the enterprise, but also undetected inappropriate material, viruses, malicious mobile code or spyware could be making its way into the enterprise.

The more popular IM becomes, the more popular route it is becoming to transport such security threats, with reports showing that out of the top 50 viruses and worms in the past six months, 19 used IM and peer-to-peer (P2P) applications – a quadrupling of last year's number. (Source: *Symantec Internet Security Threat Report*, October 2003.)

Blocking access to IM does not suit all organizations, but by simply blocking the ability to send attachments, which may contain anything from viruses to spyware, the security concern is eliminated. There is no reason why anyone should ever need to send work-related attachments via IM – after all, that is what e-mail is for.

Of PCs connected to the Internet, 90 per cent are reported to be infected with spyware. Malicious spyware can infect the desktop, is invisible to the user and transmits keystroke information through a 'back door' out of the enterprise.

Software that blocks spyware from sending keystroke information is essential for any company that wants to protect against its highly confidential information such as quarterly financial results, a new product release or its customer database being electronically monitored without its knowing.

What else gets downloaded onto the corporate network? For most people, home Internet access is slow, and downloading something like a music file will be much faster from the office, so it makes sense that a significant amount of downloads take place in the work environment. Recent research suggests this is a widespread problem, with 80 per cent of surveyed companies reporting employees abuse their Internet privileges by downloading pornography or pirated software. (Source: *CS/FBI Computer Crime and Security Survey, 2003.*) And the problem is still growing. An estimated 5 million people worldwide used pirate sites just in the past 12 months, up from 3 million in June 2002.

Illegal downloads of copyright music has hit the headlines on countless occasions, with the Recording Industry Association of America (RIAA) having sued hundreds of people it accused of piracy. There are currently over 1 billion songs available for download off the Web, with many of these on P2P networks. In the United Kingdom, industry figures suggest an 80 per cent rise in physical music piracy over the past year. (Source: *Recording Industry Commercial Piracy Report, 2003.*)

Downloading music can cause bandwidth and storage issues, but what is of more prominence for corporations is protecting against the downloading of illegally copyrighted software whereby there can be a whole host of legal implications.

There are many P2P sites that have literally any type of software available for download; anything from games and interior design packages right through to accountancy software. P2P sites are growing widely in popularity, with Yahoo! reporting that the number one search term for 2003 was the P2P site 'Kazaa', which even overtook searches for Harry Potter and Britney Spears. Yet with downloading any software from the Web, security issues unfold.

In the United States, copyright owners can collect statutory damages of up to US $150,000 per copyrighted work infringed, as well as legal costs and solicitor's fees. They can also collect damages that can include all of the profits earned by an infringer plus the actual damages suffered by the copyright owner. (Source: *RIAA*, March 2003.)

Obviously, the law varies in each country, but the issues are real throughout. The saying 'prevention is better than cure' applies. The corporate network should not allow software that is in breach of copyright. After all, if employees were using the working day, and company bandwidth, to store music or files that were not work-related, what impact would this have on productivity?

While Internet access has undoubtedly streamlined work processes, it also has opened the gateway to distraction at the click of a mouse. Entertainment, gaming and sports are just a few of the online temptations many workers have trouble resisting at the office. Just consider the following:

■ According to IDC research, 30 to 40 percent of employee Internet activity is non-work-related.
■ Nearly one out of every three companies has terminated an employee for inappropriate Internet use.
■ According to SexTracker, 70 percent of all Internet porn traffic occurs during the 9-to-5 workday.

Employee Internet access is not a black and white issue. As employees work longer hours, they are finding it necessary to accomplish personal tasks online at the office, such as online banking and e-shopping, and appreciate the opportunity for non-work-related Web use. Traditional Internet filters can be inflexible and work by simply blocking or allowing access.

When choosing an employee Internet management (EIM) solution to address Web-filtering needs, the key is balance and flexibility. It is really up to each individual company what parameters are set. These need to be established, and as long as employees are completely aware of the Internet policy, then no misunderstanding should occur.

A solution such as Websense Enterprise has a database of over 6 million Web sites categorized. Companies therefore have the flexibility to cherry-pick whether to block or allow access to each of the 90+ categories for each individual employee, and obtain a report back on Internet use.

So how do you effectively prevent your company confidential data from leaving your building, ensure that the Internet is being used for the right kind of surfing, and that illegal downloads are not taking place? Here are our suggestions:

■ Analyse and report on Internet activity: use the findings to set a suitable Internet policy.
■ Communicate the policy: make sure that all employees have fully understood it.

■ Implement an employee Internet management (EIM) software solution: it is important that the solution is flexible to accommodate departmental requirements and remote working. The solution should manage more than just basic Internet surfing by protecting against emerging threats such as spyware, P2P and instant messaging.

■ Always review and update your policy: ensure it is a live document that reflects any changes in your working culture. A sophisticated EIM software solution should provide detailed reporting that would help you pinpoint any areas of concern.

Figure 1.4.1 A 'hacking alert' from Websense

Websense Inc is the world's leading provider of employee Internet management (EIM) solutions. Websense Enterprise software enables organizations to manage how their employees use their computing resources, including Internet access, desktop applications and network bandwidth. These solutions help improve productivity, security, conserve information technology resources, and mitigate legal liability for organizations. Implemented by more than 19,400 organizations worldwide and preferred by the FTSE 100 and Fortune 500 companies, Websense Enterprise delivers a comprehensive software solution that analyses, manages and reports on employee Internet access, network security and desktop application usage. Websense Enterprise also helps organizations mitigate the problems caused by new emerging Internet threats, such as spyware, malicious mobile code and peer-to-peer file sharing.

To find out more, visit www.websense.com where you can download a fully functional 30-day trial of Websense Enterprise.

The marketing dimension

Protecting a brand through having trusted and secure networks is as good a reason as any to invest in IT security, writes Michael Harrison, Chairman, Harrison Smith Associates.

The single most important aspect of marketing is enhancement – and protection – of the **brand**. This applies equally to the company (Ltd or PLC) and to the public sector (government, local government, agency, whatever) because your clients' brand perception determines where you are in today's world. 'Client' can just as easily be a member of the public utilizing a public service, as a consumer of a product or service from a company.

But this is equally the management board's major concern – the protection and value of the brand is of prime importance. Remove trust in the brand through action or inaction and your stakeholders will very quickly seek your removal – and possibly subsequent housing by one of HM Prisons! Corporate governance applies – very, very specifically. As Turnbull made so clear, this applies just as much to the public sector as the private, and ignorance of the consequences of mistaken policies cannot ever be regarded as a valid excuse.

The most cursory review of what would happen to you if your brand's reputation fell through the floor must emphasize the importance of protecting it (and therefore yourself). But just how much time and energy do you give to this subject? Is this yet another 'must do' item that never gets to the top of the pile – unless something horrific has occurred, in which case it is too late?

Marketing also has a prime responsibility for communications – both external and internal. Therefore if you accept my arguments, not only does there have to be a complete review of your external information communications policy (and therefore everything that goes into enabling it), but there also has to be a total policy concerning the internal marketing of the need for information assurance (protection).

This is a marketing responsibility. Yes, it needs careful interrelationship with 'the IT department', but the recommendations about communication and availability of information can never be an IT decision. Why? Because how on earth can 'IT' know the relative value of every item of information that passes over the networks, and how can it possibly know when something must be kept confidential, whereas something else must be available at any time, whereas yet other items must be protected from any possibility of alteration? IT specialists cannot know – and while the owners of the information should tell them, this cannot be assumed. Therefore the area responsible for (and hopefully expert in) the whole communications issue must take overall responsibility under the guidance and policy set by the management board.

So what is different today? Why should all managers – especially senior managers – take a much closer interest in their information and how it affects their brand? What has this to do with 'online' business, and for that matter, are we all 'online' today so far as this subject is concerned?

My contention is a definitive 'yes'. No organization can pretend that it is not 'online' to some extent, and therefore it can – and probably will – be affected by cyberspace entities that had no part in our existence just a few years ago.

BI (before Internet) life was simple, and marketing life especially so – not that we realized this at the time, of course. Then we had far more control of how we communicated and with whom – and what they were allowed to find out about us. Information was a commodity that we controlled, and in the instances where we lost control we were very unhappy about it, because the responsibility for what happened was normally very easy to identify. But even the loss of information control was usually very limited – leaking one snippet did not automatically lead to other exposures, certainly not to the publication of seriously important details.

The value of information was not recognized anything like as well as it should have been – but the excuse was that the threat to that information was very limited. Okay, a fire could burn the paperwork, and latterly the computer system could go AWOL – but we understood the need to have back-ups and parallel systems, so the danger was still not that bad. We were not connected to what I have described as the 'M25 Information Highway' running slap-bang through the middle of our organizations. We still had 'perimeters' that we could regard as being protected from external threats – and any attempt at breaching them involved actual physical break-in. We knew where we were, and we knew if anything had happened.

What is more, we controlled what anyone else knew about what had happened to us – more often than not including what our own staff knew about it. We had full control of our information; it was our tool to use as we wished (within reason). Now we are all in the Internet age the rules have changed – or more importantly and accurately the lack of enforceable rules is the difference. But we have not made the necessary changes inside our organizations to guard against the 'new challenges'.

While this has a major marketing dimension to it, bluntly this should not be a 'marketing department decision'. Without question it is never an 'IT' decision. We are discussing a major policy change that requires full board approval, and regular and frequent board reviews.

That risk management is a fundamental board responsibility cannot be news, but in this chapter I want to emphasize the importance of the management of this (information) risk, both to the profitability and to the longer-term existence of the organization: *any* organization, of any size, in any sector.

What are the basic threats and opportunities, and why does the board need to understand them and take the overall risk policy decisions? What has this to do with marketing?

The marketing challenges

I have stated that this is neither an IT nor a marketing responsibility – but both of those departments have seriously important roles and responsibilities to bring the need for decisions to the formal attention of the board. Frequently these departments do not work together for the good of the organization as a whole. They do not recognize their joint responsibilities for the organization's most valuable asset, its information.

Marketing should – must – understand the value of every type of information, whereas IT should – must – be responsible for delivering, storing, presenting and protecting every type of information within the policies laid down. But they are not laid down by IT – they should be recommended by marketing, laid down by the board, actioned by IT.

Therefore marketing has a responsibility before the board can make those decisions – marketing has to identify and categorize different 'levels' of information, and be the catalyst to bring together all parts of the organization to agree the proposed rules, and then to obtain formal sign-off by the board.

Within our new 'e'-communicating society we have new tools that provide immense power to the user. But the word 'user' must not be confused with the word 'owner'. There are far too many ways for people to 'assume the role of user' when they have no right – in fact when they are breaking the rules, if not the law. The internal opportunities for 'information theft' today are enormous, and especially in organizations where identity theft can be relatively easy to arrange. The trouble is that this can also apply to external opportunists, sometimes just as easily.

The value and potential brand damage that this information theft provides is many times more costly than the equivalent only a few years ago. This is for two interrelated reasons: information is far more usefully available than it was before (because all users expect and demand this); plus the Internet provides far greater opportunities for that information to be obtained, disseminated and used by people with 'black hats'.

There was always the challenge of the odd rogue member of staff, including the 'temp' (or the cleaner, or whoever) who was not exactly what he or she was supposed to be, but we felt secure from external attack, and an insider still had to take the information out of the premises physically, and was thus more likely to be caught.

So what had this to do with marketing? In those days, almost nothing. Security was seldom used as a differentiator. It is true that 'Safe as the Bank of England' was a saying from the past, but that was all about physical security – and more about the consumers' (or clients') property or deliverable than that of the host organization. Everyone was clear about whether or not they were a 'target'. You could identify your physical defences and contrast them with the value that an attacker might steal (such as cash, valuables and easily disposable items), or you could decide you were just not worth attacking! In retrospect, it was a nice, simple life. So marketing took security for granted, and certainly did not get directly involved, unless the organization happened to be a bank. Even then, 'security' meant one thing only: protection from actual physical loss (from being stolen, copied or destroyed).

Who thought of protecting things from being altered without anyone finding out until too late? Or from being rendered unavailable to your own key personnel for a crucial period of time? Anyway – who considered what negative affects such activities might have on the brand, and in those days would they have been particularly serious?

Today someone can do these things, and thus directly affect your reputation (and your brand) from the other side of the world, without actually meaning to do it! Certainly whether they meant to or not, they have no thought about the damage that they are doing – especially as it is at almost no cost to themselves in time, resources or risk.

The Internet was originally built to allow communication amongst academic groups, known for their preference for sharing information. It was not supposed to be the world's 'trusted business backbone'. So we must take appropriate policy decisions before we continue to trust it with our 'Crown Jewels'.

And the marketing opportunities

As business-to-business, business-to-consumer, and government–public and public–government communications become more and more electronic and online, the need for information assurance becomes more absolute. We need to be re-assured! The organization that can provide that assurance will be our first – and possibly our only – choice. Those that cannot, and those that have been seen to fail, will be blacklisted. We need to know that our confidential information is genuinely protected against all three of the information assurance sub-sets:

- **Confidentiality**: that is, no one else can get at it.
- **Integrity**: that is, it will not be changed, and anything that we are sent has not been changed.
- **Availability**: that is, when it is needed it will be available, instantly if that is the requirement.

Therefore the obvious corollary is that the secure online business will obtain a differentiation that will give it very significant added value. The marketing messages will provide the stakeholders with considerable peace of mind – and therefore extra perception of corporate value. And – this is not a cynical comment – the internal marketing will be easier, especially upwards to the management board, because by creating the secure online business the board's own personal reputation and corporate governance responsibilities are protected.

However, the obvious caveat is that to promise security online, but not to be able to deliver that promise, is a serious mistake – which can be easily made through sheer ignorance of the threat and the vulnerabilities.

The expectation–experience equation

Some so-called 'hackers' carry out attacks just to be able to say that they have got through a specific organization's defences. You may claim to be secure – they may well try you out! 'They' might actually work for you – or have worked for you recently. To have an information assurance management system (IAMS) in place and working properly will provide you with the assurance that you require to make such a claim in the first place. But that is not the reason to have such a system; you must have it in order to conduct business electronically.

You must be secure online. There is no alternative if you want to continue in operation.

Enforcement; regulation; legislation; audit

This is no joke. For too long we have been attempting to operate within totally different communication conditions, opening ourselves up to immeasurable consequences, without a significant change in how we have been 'measured'.

No longer! Auditors and regulators (the FSA, NAO and so on) are becoming far more aware of the financial consequences of failure, and of the questions to ask – and the answers to question!

The government recently created a new department known as the Central Sponsor for Information Assurance (CSIA) – and it has already produced new policy guidelines for the whole of the public sector. It started with central government, moved on to the rest of the public sector – and the next target must be the private sector, for the very obvious reason that we are all interconnected and that we must be more responsible 'citizens', whether individual or corporate. For any organization's marketing function to ignore this would be a very serious mistake – and action is vital.

Become – and be seen to be – a secure online business, or face some very difficult questions from a variety of powerful sources, all under the heading of 'stakeholders'!

Summary

- A company's positive approach to security online will directly affect its marketing positioning and organizational differentiation. It will determine its very future existence.
- Security failure will destroy any organization's reputation, and thus end in total destruction. The consumer and the public will no longer forgive these errors, because they have such grave consequences.
- Information assurance is not a cost, it is a corporate investment that cannot be put off or ignored.
- Everyone is a potential target and no one can afford to ignore this subject. E-business and e-government demand the electronic exchange of ever-more important information, and the 'owner' must demand – and be given – total assurance.
- Marketing should identify and promote the internal and external advantages of having appropriate information security.
- Marketing and 'IT' must work together to achieve a perceived 'trusted status', and take responsibility for creating detailed positioning and differentiation messages for the management board to determine policy – including risk management profiles.
- Marketing must ensure that all communications are written in suitable language for each target audience – internal and external – otherwise the messages will not be understood.
- Finally, the United Kingdom has the 'Protecting Critical Information Infrastructures' initiative where senior management can be better informed about the risks and the solutions available – but in the language of the boardroom and not techno-speak. Frequently it helps the CIO and the other senior management to get these messages from the most senior government and commercial decision makers – and we will do our best to assist! Contact www.pcii-initiative.co.uk for more information.

Michael Harrison, DipM, FCIM is Chairman of Harrison Smith Associates Limited and Chairman, UK of the 'Protecting Critical Information Infrastructures Initiative'.

For further information contact: Michael R Harrison, Chairman, Harrison Smith Associates Ltd, Third Floor, Diamond House, 36–38 Hatton Garden, London EC1N 8EB. Tel: +44 (0)20 7404 5444; Fax: +44 (0)20 7404 8222; Web site: www.hsaltd.co.uk or www.pcii-initiative.co.uk

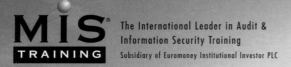

MIS® TRAINING
The International Leader in Audit & Information Security Training
Subsidiary of Euromoney Institutional Investor PLC

Training on your doorstep

On-Site Training

In Europe, Middle East and Africa

Benefits to your organisation:

- Cost Effective
- Time Efficient
- Topical
- Customisation
- Assure Confidentiality
- Hands-On or Workshop Style
- Expert Instructors
- After Class Follow Up

Audit

Risk & Governance

Fraud

Oracle

Peoplesoft

SAP

Unix

Windows

Info Security

Networks

Wireless

IT Audit Core

Sarbanes-Oxley

Outsourcing

For a training consultation or to find out more about On-Site Training please call: Kate Hov
on +44 (0) 20 7779 8292, email: khowe@misti.com or visit our website: www.mistieurope.co

Points of exposure

Broadband

The advent of broadband has opened up a wealth of new opportunities, for both businesses and cyber criminals alike, writes Paul Collins, Head of Customer Marketing at NTL Business.

When the MSBlast 'worm' attack was at its peak, a UK-based security company ran an experiment to find out just how much of a threat it posed. A PC with no anti-virus or firewall software was connected to the Internet; it took just 27 seconds for the worm to infect it.

In a similar experiment, the UK Internet service provider (ISP) PSINet set up an anonymous dummy server to test levels of Internet hacking. It found that its server was maliciously attacked 467 times within just 24 hours of being installed.

Before I am accused of wanton scaremongering, I would stress that these are two isolated incidents and that each was set up with the express aim of proving just how vulnerable a PC connected to the Internet can be to attacks from viruses, worms and hackers. That said, both incidents are pertinent to the subject matter to be discussed in this chapter. Why? Because they illustrate the pervasive and non-discriminatory nature of threats from the Internet. They plainly show that it is not just big multinational corporations and government bodies that are singled out and targeted due to the sensitive and potentially valuable nature of the data they hold.

If a single PC or anonymous server can be breached so swiftly and so comprehensively, so can your business – unless you have adopted the appropriate safeguards. In fact, according to analyst firm Gartner Group, 20 per cent of enterprises will experience a serious (beyond a virus) Internet security incident by 2005. Of those that do, the clean-up costs of the incident will be half as much again as the prevention costs would have been.

The statistics speak for themselves. But the remit of this chapter is not simply to expose the extent of the issue – that it is a serious problem for UK plc has surely never been up for debate. The aim of this chapter is specifically to examine how broadband relates to security, and how companies should review their security policies and safeguards as a result.

Broadband = broader threat?

The simple answer is – it doesn't have to be. With yesterday's dial-up, or 'dial on demand' services, your computer only connected to the Internet when it had something to send, such as an e-mail or a request to load a Web page. Once there was no more data to be sent, or after a certain amount of idle time, the computer disconnected the call. In other words, you chose when you wanted to be online and told your PC to call your ISP, log into its server and use its services – be it e-mail or Web surfing.

Broadband connections, on the other hand, are by definition 'always on' because there is no call set up when your computer has something to send. The computer is always on the network, ready to send or receive data at any time. With broadband – be it via cable, DSL or leased line technology – your PC is connected to the Web whenever it is switched on.

Always on, always vulnerable

While broadband is not inherently more dangerous than dial-up, the chances of an intrusion are higher simply because your computer is online and therefore accessible for longer. And since your computer acts as a gateway to the rest of your network, your entire network can be vulnerable for the length of your online session.

There is also another factor to consider. Each time one computer communicates with another via the Internet, this is done via an IP (Internet Protocol) connection. Each computer connected to the Web has a dedicated 'IP address' – just like a home or business has a dedicated postal address in the offline world. This IP address is unique to that computer, and identifies it from all other computers connected to the Web. In most cases, corporate networks and ISPs economize on the number of IP addresses they use by sharing a pool among a large number of users. This means that your IP address is likely to be dynamically allocated by your ISP each time you log on, giving your computer a different IP address on each call. Since a broadband connection is always on, your computer's IP address will change less frequently than on dial-up, thus making it more of a fixed target for attack. If you are always connected, you are easy to find. In fact, according to a recent Yankee Group report, a broadband connection increases the likelihood of attack fivefold.

All this does not bode well for the increasing number of businesses – particularly smaller firms, typically without the resources to devote to protect systems adequately – that are adopting broadband in ever greater numbers. It serves to highlight the need for businesses of all sizes to carefully select their broadband supplier, and to ensure that the appropriate security measures are in place (more of this later).

Casting the net wider

It is not just the technical capabilities of broadband that we need to consider in this. The very nature of broadband and its ability to exchange more data with more people more quickly have opened up entirely new ways of working, all of which have their impact on a company's security.

Consider, for example, the exchange of a large, complex document such as a new business tender or contractual agreement. In the past, such documents would have been prohibitively large for an online exchange, and would simply have been printed out and sent by recorded delivery. With broadband, however, these confidential and often highly sensitive documents can be sent and received by e-mail in a matter of seconds. Are they always encrypted or password protected? The truth is, not often enough.

Broadband has also opened up the opportunity to communicate with partners, customers and suppliers like never before. The advent of intranets, extranets and private Web site pages means that your data – sometimes even your entire network – is available to more people, more of the time. Add to that the growing number of home-workers, tele-workers and wireless workers, even those who only access their corporate e-mail occasionally, and without the necessary security safeguards your network can start to look about as watertight as a sieve.

The nature of the beast

So we have established that your network could be vulnerable to a security breach, but what would that breach look like, and what impact would it have on your business? The topics of viruses, worms, Trojan horses and spam are covered in some depth in other chapters, so I will not dwell too long on them here. Suffice to say that an unprotected network is to a virus writer like blood to a shark – one temptation too far.

As far as hacking is concerned, thousands of companies are still turning a blind eye – despite the fact that it has firmly entered the Internet mainstream. In previous times, hacking was perceived to be the preserve of hacked-off IT PhDs with an axe to grind. These days, anyone with a broadband connection and a little know-how can find their way into many companies' networks.

According to the CBI, two-thirds of its members have suffered serious cybercrime attacks. Yet only seven hackers have been charged with criminal offences over the last two years. This is due to a combination of weak e-crime laws and the fact that many attacks go unreported: it is as if there's a feeling of shame associated with admitting you have been a victim, and a concern that customers will lose faith in your business or services.

Possibly the biggest question is not 'What do I have to hide?' but 'Who is in control?' An unprotected computer is not just at risk of an incoming attack; it can also become an unwitting accessory to a crime. With access to your computer, an accomplished hacker can quickly establish it as a staging area for the exchange of illegal files, a mail relay for unsolicited commercial e-mail (spam), or a participant in a distributed denial of service attack.

The NetAction Advisory Board has identified five 'A's of security:

Awareness

Your computer is one among millions of other computers networked together. As a broadband subscriber, your computer is generally permanently and reliably connected to the Internet, and your connection is quickly responsive. You have physical control over your machine, and can take informed action to protect your resources and files.

Authentication and Authorization

If you do not want to allow global access to your files, you may need to set log-ins and passwords to limit your computer's users. Authentication means verifying the user. Authorization is allowing that user access to your system. Verifying users of your machine can help you track the activity in files and resources.

Access control

To further limit access to your resources, you may wish to set permissions on individual files. For instance, you may have a text file that anyone can read. This is called global access. Another file may only be read by anyone in a special group that you design. This is group access. A third file may only be readable by you: that is, individual access.

Auditing

Your computer may generate logs that can be important diagnostic tools. For instance, your Web server keeps track of machines that have requested your Web pages:

- machine and domain name or IP address;
- time and date of request;
- page or file requested;
- success or error code;
- number of bytes transferred, and so on.

If you run an FTP server, you also have logs of who moved files in or out. Your security products also produce information logs that can inform you about traffic, system users, and more. In combination with active security products, logs can be a powerful tool to mitigate your security risks.

A marriage of technology and common sense

The same Yankee Group report that claimed companies running a broadband connection were five times more vulnerable to a security breach than those using dial-up also calculated that security breaches would cost UK firms almost £2 billion last year. It estimated that a significant proportion of that cost would be due to broadband, with many firms upgrading without understanding the security risks involved.

So how can firms protect themselves from attack? There are some basic guidelines that all businesses can adopt, ranging from technical solutions to simple common sense policies that will help to keep your business safe online:

■ It may sound obvious, but always turn off your computers and/or modem when not in use. If you are not connected to the Internet, you cannot be a target.
■ Make sure you keep your operating system software up to date. This does not necessarily mean you need to keep buying the latest version. Just make sure that you have installed all available patches for your system.
■ Set up passwords to shared computers on your network, and make them difficult to guess. Good passwords have mixed upper- and lower-case letters, numbers, and characters, and are not obvious. Avoid names or birth dates of family members, or common English words such as 'password' or 'guess.'
■ Do not open e-mail attachments from strangers, and confirm the integrity of attachments even from known sources. Be especially wary of unexpected files ending in .vbs or .exe.
■ Do not volunteer more information to Web sites or strangers than is absolutely necessary. You already leave plenty of information behind in the logs of sites you have visited.
■ Install an anti-virus product to scan both e-mails and Web traffic, and keep your virus definition profiles up to date by visiting the software manufacturer's Web site and downloading its virus update files on a regular basis.
■ Deploy a business-grade firewall product to manage the flow of data both in and out of your network (see box below).
■ Consider using intrusion detection software to monitor for potential threats from outside the organization.
■ Use encrypted e-mail services and programmes whenever possible.
■ In case you do suffer an attack, back up your files regularly. That way, even if your business is hit, you will not lose all your data too.

How can your ISP help?

Selecting the right broadband service provider can be half the battle. If you choose carefully, your provider should be able to offer you advice and consultancy on the best solution to suit your company, and will have a range of firewall solutions for you to choose from.

The most basic firewalls are software-based, and work by setting a series of policies that accept or reject Internet traffic based on IP address, ports or protocols. They have a number of limitations, for example once a particular protocol is allowed to pass, external hosts can use it to establish a direct connection to the internal network, thereby exposing that network to external threats. Software-based firewalls are, however, quick and easy to use and they do afford some level of protection.

At the other end of the scale are hardware-based solutions, which go one step further by acting as a proxy for all applications and performing the data exchange with remote systems on their behalf. They effectively make the hosts behind the firewall invisible to the outside world. Hardware-based firewalls are considered by far the most secure, but are in return more resource-hungry, harder to manage, and can result in slower response times.

Ultimately, there is no perfect solution that will suit every business; the answer will depend on the limits, strengths and weaknesses of your own company. Some solutions need more knowledge, resource and user intervention than others, while those that are the easiest to manage may not provide adequate levels of security for your needs.

Your ISP should be able to help and advise you on this, and may even be able to provide a managed service that enables you to enjoy maximum security without the potential headaches of maintenance and support.

The crucial point to remember is that any solution will be better than none. You may be best implementing a simple product to start with, thereby buying yourself a little more time to research all the options fully before committing yourself to a more advanced solution.

Underpinning all of this must be a comprehensive and comprehensible internal security policy. According to a National Computing Centre (NCC) survey, released earlier this year, the vast majority of employees in UK organizations do not take IT security seriously. This suggests that companies are failing to communicate the business importance of security policies to their staff. The study found that organizations' IT security culture is not keeping pace with their growing reliance on computing systems, with security breaches often leading to severe financial losses and business disruption.

The key lies in making all staff appreciate the issues, and their responsibilities in protecting the business. An awareness of security must permeate the entire organization – from the most junior member of staff to the upper echelons of senior management.

Supporting British business

The Government is committed to making Britain the G7's 'most extensive and competitive broadband market' by 2005, an achievement that is viewed as crucial in enabling British businesses effectively to compete on the international stage. For this to be achieved, it is vital that the continued roll-out of broadband goes hand in hand with an increase in security precautions, to ensure that businesses can enjoy all the benefits of high-speed Internet access without worrying about the potential security risks.

NTL Business is a leading provider of communications solutions to businesses and public sector organizations throughout the United Kingdom. It is the business arm of NTL Incorporated, the UK's largest cable company and Number 1 broadband Internet provider.

For further information phone 01256 752000 or visit the Web site: www.ntl.com

E-mail

An attack on e-mail can stop a business in its tracks, writes Andrew Steggles, Marketing Director, EMEA Nokia Enterprise Solutions.

Business communication is dependent on the speed and efficiency of e-mail. Unfortunately, these benefits attract the undesirable use and attack of corporate e-mail systems. More than 80 per cent of malicious code exploits target enterprise mail because it is a visible and vulnerable target. If a malicious attack brings down the e-mail system, business stops.

The explosive growth in volume of spam traffic consumes system resources and employee productivity. Unauthorized employee distribution of copyrighted or privacy-regulated content exposes corporations to legal liability. Customers, partners, remote employees, mobile workers and IT are all affected.

Protecting e-mail content is fundamental to wired and wireless access to enterprise business communication. IT departments are faced with the challenge to secure e-mail content and confidently embrace new opportunities to extend access to e-mail networks. Organizations need to deploy systems that stop spam, directory harvest attacks, undesirable content, denial of service attacks, third-party mail relay, macro and script viruses, Trojan horses and worms.

Putting spam into perspective

Spam is no longer a nuisance; it is quickly becoming both a potential legal liability and a major productivity drain for corporate IT departments and corporate users alike. Spam not only drains worker productivity and consumes valuable IT resources such as disk storage, CPU cycles and network bandwidth, it can also expose the organization to legal liability because of the offensive nature of some messages. For example, Web-enabled mail clients automatically display the pornographic images of some solicitations.

Spam is also another conduit for unknown viral applications into the corporation, for links to pornographic or objectionable Web sites, and for leaks of sensitive company information. In many cases, senders of unsolicited commercial e-mail (spammers) are resorting to outright criminality in their efforts to conceal the sources of their ill-sent missives, using Trojan horses to turn the computers of innocent consumers into secret spam zombies. A Trojan listens on a randomly chosen port and uses its own built-in mail client to dash off a message to a Hotmail account, putting the port number and victim's IP address in the subject line. The spammer takes it from there, routing as much e-mail as it likes through the captured computer, knowing that any efforts to trace the source of the spam will end at the victim's Internet address.

With e-mail firmly established as the mission critical enterprise application, and the explosive growth in volume of spam traffic, network and e-mail administrators face a sobering challenge: how to ensure the integrity of electronic messaging, and prevent the security exploits that are increasingly introduced through e-mail.

Consider that e-mail accounted for more than 80 per cent of malicious exploits in 2001. Today's exploits are increasing in frequency and sophistication, targeting network vulnerabilities, corporate intellectual property, IT and financial assets, health records, personal identity and liability. The costs of security exploits are staggering – financial theft and fraud, corrupted data, recovery and legal costs, lost productivity, as examples.

Challenges to securing enterprise mail

Traditional approaches to solving the problem fail to deliver the right combination of protection and performance. Traditional desktop anti-virus solutions lack a unified barrier of protection against blended threats and hybrid worms. Manual signature updates at the desktop are expensive to implement and unreliable as they often rely on end user intervention.

Perimeter-based solutions have resulted in numerous hardware and software solutions from different vendors, making it virtually impossible to conduct timely compatibility testing or to deploy these solutions and their updates promptly with sustained confidence. Another approach is e-mail server-based solutions: these often overload these mission-critical servers, resulting in poor reliability and processing performance, as well as the challenge of keeping them up to date.

It is important for a company to protect intellectual property and limit legal liability from offensive messages and copyrighted documents. This can be controlled through policy definition rights. A company can also limit legal liability by preventing sensitive content from leaving or flowing in and out of the network

A policy-setting utility can accommodate privacy and industry-specific regulation.

More than just anti-virus

While security is a top priority for most corporations in Europe, many consider it sufficient to set up a firewall and buy a virus checker. As threats and legal environments change, however, companies struggle to stay ahead of the game. Protecting corporate content while it is stored and transported is a must that most companies consider done when purchasing a virus checker and a firewall, but there is more to security than this. Protecting content and corporate resources – especially when going mobile – will be key in the near future.

Even if a state-of the-art firewall is installed and a company's anti-virus software is updated automatically, they alone do not provide sufficient security. As networks and computing power climb to new heights, so do the sophistication and determination of hackers, crackers and disgruntled employees. In fact, it is easier to harm an organization's most valuable assets – information and content – today than it was a few years ago. So companies need to work harder to stay ahead of the development of new threats, which mean new challenges.

The growth of electronic messaging as a communication medium and the threats of multiple viruses, Trojan horses, worms and spam, combined with the high costs of exploits, demand vigorous techniques and strategies to prevent and protect against security violations. Protecting messages at the Internet gateway can prevent end-user and mail server platforms from infection by Trojan horses, worms and blended attacks.

Traditional approaches to solving e-mail security have focused on anti-virus; new levels of protection are needed to increase the integrity of e-mail messaging through spam prevention, content inspection and virus protection.

Table 2.2.1 portrays the evolution of challenges in securing the enterprise network, and the considerations that need to be taken when choosing the right content security solution to eliminate messaging-borne malicious attacks and reduce administration and deployment costs.

Table 2.2.1 Challenges and considerations in securing the enterprise network

Pre-2000	Today's Considerations
Anti-virus solutions were the de facto standard but became limited in their ability to protect against blended threats and hybrid worms directed at corporate mail networks.	Implement a comprehensive layered approach for complete content security. It should encompass anti-virus and: ■ spam prevention; ■ content inspection; ■ content management; ■ behavioural monitoring; ■ macro stripping; ■ anti-exploit filtering; ■ format vetting.
Desktop solutions were the most widely deployed, but lacked architectural integrity and carried a cost burden due to the challenge of keeping signatures up to date. Point perimeter-based solutions yielded wide variations in vendor software and hardware. Compatibility testing and updates could consume excessive IT resources.	Implement Internet gateway-based solution as the most viable content security alternative available to reduce administrative costs and improve overall system integrity and security.
Security was focused predominantly in wired environments.	Take account of wireless initiatives. Content security will be a key enabler for wireless business environments as enterprises adopt wireless LANs (802.11) and smart phones as they look to the mobile Internet for business advantage and convenience.
E-mail was the only significant form of electronic messaging.	Include plans for protecting SMS, MMS and instant messaging, as well as traditional e-mail.
The only available solutions were software based, delivering limited processing performance with the added headaches and costs of integration and maintenance and support from multiple vendors.	Invest in a purpose-built solution, consisting of industry leading software and hardware and support for ease of deployment and updates, reliability and unmatched performance.

Conclusion

The scope of secure content management extends far beyond anti-virus. Perimeter-based appliances capable of adding a layered approach for hardware, software and security policy are required to complement desktop-based virus protection. Messaging security software can be used to screen messaging applications such as e-mail, instant messaging, SMS and peer-to-peer for spam or other objectionable content. The software is also used to enforce corporate policy by screening for company confidential information and to enforce compliance with privacy regulations. Messaging security also includes secure e-mail.

Messaging security software delivers the capabilities for organizations to protect themselves against e-mail and Web-based threats, meet legal and regulatory requirements, implement productivity-saving policies and manage intellectual property passing through the network. E-mail threats include the circulation of inappropriate images and text, spam and oversized files, loss and corruption of data and breaches of confidentiality. Whereas e-mail scanning merely consisted of a positive list which blocked certain attachments and file endings, modern messaging security solutions intelligently detect, analyse or quarantine incoming and outgoing images, multimedia content, spam and both encrypted, signed and multiple-zipped documents – all based on complex, company-wide e-policies.

Nokia Enterprise Solutions focuses on mobile business devices and providing IP network perimeter security (firewalls and VPN), secure content management (anti-virus scanning and SPAM filtering), and mobile connectivity (remote access VPN and content) solutions designed to help companies mobilize their workforces and increase productivity while ensuring the security and reliability of their networks.

For further information contact Nokia Enterprise Solutions on +44 161 601 8908, e-mail ipsecurity.emea@nokia.com. Full details of all Nokia Enterprise products can be found at: www.nokia.com/ipsecurity/emea

Web security

Worms, spams and phishing – 2003 was a bumper year for attacks on Web sites and the outlook for 2004 does not look much better, writes Suheil Shahryar, Director of Security Consulting Services of VeriSign UK.

Introduction

Web security is more than just the protection of information exchanged between your computer and a Web site, it is also about the security of the computers and information assets accessible via the Internet; and ultimately, it is about protecting your company's business or your private information, often both, from falling into harm's way.[1]

In this chapter, we take a look at some of the key issues relevant to Web security. Our tour includes the following:

- The current state of the Internet – its use and importance.
- Understanding the dangers – why does the Internet need security?
- The state of Web security in 2003 and the key exposures.
- Predictions for the future – what are the concerns?

Parts 3 and 4 of this book provide advice on protecting against these exposures.

---

[1] The words 'Web' and 'Internet' are used interchangeably in this section.

The use and importance of the Internet today

As of January 2003, there were more than 171 million host computers in the world.[2] Many, if not most, have some access to the Internet. Today, the Internet is both a communication highway and a marketplace. Whether it is your company's online order system or your personal e-mail, the Internet is making us more interdependent as well as more dependent on computer technology.

Businesses and individuals are, more than ever, taking the Internet for granted. But, how many are aware of the risks and the countermeasures necessary to mitigate these risks? Certainly not everyone, as we shall see below. The year 2003 has seen new threats coming from the Web, which cost millions of pounds' worth of damage across businesses, large and small. Taking adequate protection against the risks of connecting to the Internet is, therefore, essential for businesses.

Understanding why the Internet is not secure

Computers are not simple, even though at the very basic level, they are machines composed of switches which are either on or off. These have evolved to what are today complex systems. As a result of the general population's demand for more ease of use or more access to computing, the computer, including in particular the operating system, has ever increasing new features, from graphical user interfaces (GUI) to plug and play, which have contributed to this complexity. It is highly likely that the operating system or a complex program will have many errors and will be exposed to risks such as viruses and other threats from the Internet.

While we are going about discovering these coding flaws and errors in well-known operating systems and commonly used programs, the hackers' ability to exploit these vulnerabilities has grown, evolved and flourished. Why? The increasing connectivity due to the Internet has created a situation where the programming flaws can now be exploited remotely to gain privileges on systems without authorization or knowledge of their users. These are the vulnerabilities that are being exploited by hackers, viruses and worms.

The flaws in computing affect us all, from entire economies of the most powerful nations in the world to a single user at home. We are all equally vulnerable to the kid in a garage who can bring down the system or to the virus or worm that spreads through the Internet.

Web security in 2003

2003 was a bumper year for worms, spam, and scams! There were spam and pop-ups littering our Web marketplace, and viruses and worms in the Internet communication grids. According to the CERT, 114,855 incidents were reported in the first three quarters of 2003, which is almost as many incidents as since the start of the millennium.[3]

We will first look at the most reported worms of 2003 and dissect them to get a better understanding of the threats they pose. But before that some definitions may be useful.

[2] Internet Software Consortium, www.isc.org
[3] CERT Coordination Centre, www.cert.org

Worms are usually classed as belonging to the following family of threats that target vulnerabilities in commonly used operating systems, Web browsers and e-mails:

- **Worm:** a program that makes copies of itself from one computer to another, via e-mail or another transport mechanism, leading often to a network slowdown. The worm may also do damage and compromise the security of the computer. Worms can be self-propagating or rely on assistance from the computer user in order to be successful.
- **Virus:** a program or code that replicates by inserting itself or attaching itself to another program, disc or document that supports macros. Some viruses do a large amount of damage as well.
- **Trojan Horse:** a program that neither replicates nor copies itself, but causes damage or compromises the security of the computer. It arrives in the form of a joke program or software of some sort appearing harmless to the casual user.

SQL Slammer Worm

The SQL Slammer worm hit us on 25 January 2003.[4] The worm targets Windows-based systems and exploits vulnerability in database software from Microsoft, called the SQL Server, first identified in July 2002. The malicious code contains a simple, fast scanner to find vulnerable machines by sending a packet of only 376 bytes to UDP port 1434, the SQL Server Resolution Service Port. It spreads very quickly because the UDP protocol requires no authentication and is, therefore, able to send the scans without requiring an answer from potential victims. By sending a large number of packets the worm causes a 'denial of service' on victim machines and affects network availability. Unlike viruses, the worm exists only in memory, so it is not detectable by traditional anti-virus scanners.

The SQL Slammer is the fastest computer worm in history. It took just 10 minutes to spread across the world. As it began spreading through the Internet, it doubled in size every 8.5 seconds. At its peak, which came only 3 minutes after its release into the Internet, it was conducting 55 million scans per second in order to seek out further vulnerable hosts.

The attacking program overwhelmed many Internet data pipelines as it searched for victim computers randomly and aggressively. At least five of the Internet's 13 major hubs were targeted. Significant disruption of financial, transportation and government institutions was reported. It caused network outages and such unforeseen consequences as cancelled airline flights and problems with cash machines. UK companies hit by the worm included Hewlett Packard. Outages or slowdowns were reported as far as Thailand, Japan, Malaysia, the Philippines and India. At its peak on 25 January, the malicious code effectively shut down the Internet in South Korea, the world's most wired country.

It is estimated that SQL Slammer caused approximately £1 billion in lost productivity worldwide in its first week, but fortunately it did not quite break the Top 10 list for the most damaging virus or worm. Sites with firewalls blocking all outbound and inbound traffic to port 1434 from untrusted sources were not affected. Microsoft later released a fix to MS SQL and MSDE for the vulnerability. Fortunately the bug did not contain a malicious payload and did not infect most home computers.

---

[4] The SQL Slammer worm is also known as Sapphire, Slammer, W32.SQLExp.Worm, DDOS.SQLP1434.A, W32/SQLSlammer, and W32/SQLSlam-A.

MS Blaster Worm

The biggest surprise of the year came on 11 August 2003, when the alert community started receiving reports of widespread activity related to a new piece of malicious code known as MS Blaster worm.[5] The worm appeared to exploit a known vulnerability in the Microsoft's RPC DCOM interface. The impact of this vulnerability is critical to any businesses running any modern Windows operating system that allows remote access. It affects every installation of the Windows NT/2000/XP/2003 operating system not protected by additional security mechanisms for access control, such as firewall systems. It is instructive to understand this vulnerability, its history and how this worm exploits it.

Remote Procedure Call (RPC) is a protocol used by the Windows operating system to provide seamless inter-process communication between programs running on a local machine and a remote machine. The Distributed Component Object Model (DCOM) is a protocol that enables software components to communicate directly across multiple network transports, including Internet protocols such as HTTP, the ubiquitous web protocol.

The DCOM protocol uses RPC-enabled ports to listen for activation requests from clients. The flaw exists in the DCOM interface (not the RPC process) and how malformed messages are handled. The malformed message induces a buffer overrun error, causing the machine to fail in such a way that arbitrary code can be executed remotely. To exploit this vulnerability, a specially crafted request would need to be sent to a port configured for RPC functionality. This would provide the intruder with full Local System privileges, which enables it to create new accounts with privileges, install new programs, and view, modify or delete data. It is possible that this flaw existed as an upgrade, patch or update instituted by Microsoft from 1996, when DCOM was first introduced to Windows 95, to the present.

The MS Blaster worm exploits the RPC DCOM vulnerability to gain elevated access where a remote shell on port 4444 is established back to the source. The source then executes a tftp command to pull the binary, msblast.exe, to the target. Once this file is retrieved, the compromised system then runs it and begins scanning for other vulnerable systems to compromise in the same manner. The worm also includes the ability to launch a TCP SYN flood denial-of-service attack against the www.windowsupdate.com Web site, on every day from 16 August until 31 December and after the 15th of every successive month.

The worm has no other destructive payload, but contained a number of interesting strings:

I just want to say LOVE YOU SAN!!
    billy gates why do you make this possible? Stop making money and fix your software!!
    MARB
    MEOW
    MEOW
    MEOW

The RPC DCOM vulnerability was discovered and disclosed on 16 July 2003 by a research group called Last Stage of Delirium (LSD). Microsoft took the LSD disclosure seriously enough to release a patch for the vulnerable systems as the Microsoft Security Bulletin MS03–026 that day! Depending on requirements, sites were encouraged to disable DCOM,

---

[5] The MS Blaster worm is also known as Lovsan, W32/Blaster, W32/Lovsan, and Win32/Posa worm.

but this may also cause undesirable side-effects. At a minimum, sites were told to filter network traffic, by blocking access to all services for port 69, 135, 139, 445, 593, and any other port configured for RPC functionality, as well as port 4444.

Since the release of the MS03–026 Microsoft Security Bulletin, the Internet security community waited guardedly for the release of a worm that would take advantage of this sweeping flaw in the world's most widely used computer operating system. Late in the day (EDT) on August 11 2003, those monitoring system-wide Internet traffic began to see a marked increase in scanning traffic to port 135, the main port of entry to exploit the RPC DCOM vulnerability. Verification soon followed from CERT and the anti-virus vendors.

Several new worms were released over the following weeks, all of them functionally similar to MS Blaster except for their binary names and registry keys. Of these, the Welchia (or Nachi) worm is worth mentioning. This worm uses exploits against the RPC DCOM as well as a Web DAV vulnerability to gain local system rights remotely. The worm then deletes the MSBlast process and applies the Microsoft patch to remedy the RPC DCOM vulnerability. The worm is programmed to delete itself when the system clock reaches 1 January 2004. Despite its good intentions, the scanning technique, by mistake, called up a non-existent patch Web site, which led to the worm generating a significant volume of ICMP host-unreachable messages, causing localized network problems. This forced the US Navy and Air Canada to delay and cancel flights due to disruption in their reservation centres' computers.

It is highly likely that the RPC DCOM vulnerability will exist in the wild, un-patched, for the foreseeable future. The use of the exploit to gain remote access will fade as new exploits become available, and the continued propagation of the existing worms will level off and decline over time; however, as long as vulnerable systems are connected to other computers through the Internet or LAN, this exploit will continue to live on.

Sobig worm

No sooner had business cleaned up after the MS Blaster and the Welchi worms, than a fast-spreading variant of the Sobig virus hit them on 18 August 2003. This was the W32/Sobig.F mass-mailing worm. It has capabilities additional to the original Sobig.A worm, which hit earlier in January, and exploits a weakness in Microsoft's Outlook Express and unsecured local Windows network shares to spread. This time, the damage from the virus was worse.

In the first week, Sobig F had been seen in 134 countries. One of the global ISPs stopped more than 23.2 million copies of the virus in the first three days. Eventually, the anti-virus vendors developed signatures for W32/Sobig.F. Sites were also encouraged to block Internet access to the ports at: 123, 995, 996, 997, 998, and 8998.

The W32/Sobig.F worm is an e-mail-borne malicious program with a specially crafted attachment that has a .pif extension. When it spreads, the virus fakes an e-mail address to hide its origins and regularly changes its form and the subject lines of messages it creates to make it harder to spot. When it infects machines, it harvests e-mail addresses from Outlook address books and net page memory stores. The e-mail messages may appear from random addresses and have a Subject: line such as: 'Re: Thank You!', 'Re: Details', 'Re: Approved' and so on. The worm requires a user to execute the malicious attachment (for instance, details.pif, your_document.pif and so on) either manually or by using an e-mail client that will open the attachment automatically.

The worm also includes code that attempts to contact a list of 20 predefined IP addresses on port 8998/UDP on Fridays and Sundays between 1900 and 2200 UTC (starting at 1900 UTC on 22 August 2003). The worm is believed to have a programmed 'shut down' date of 10 September 2003, at which time it was expected to stop propagating.

Spam

It is not just Sobig that clogged up our e-mails in 2003 – it was a big year for spam or unsolicited e-mails. The scourge of unwanted e-mail is now so serious that it is threatening to stifle the Internet as an effective means of communication. Each time an e-mail-based virus goes around, it collects up e-mail addresses and circulates them, including advertisements for Viagra and so on. Spammers are now turning to new tactics by exploiting these worms to spread their unwanted messages. With Internet relays, chat channels and mail gateways becoming more secure, spammers are hijacking e-mail accounts of innocent users, many of them children, to send millions of messages, using up nearly 40 per cent of global traffic.

The European Commission estimates that spam cost European businesses an estimated 2.25 billion euros (£1.5 billion) in lost productivity last year. To partially protect against the anticipated rise due to the new techniques deployed by spammers, new legislation from the European Union is due to come into force soon banning unwanted e-mail. However, since most spam comes from the United States, China and Eastern Europe, they will be outside the law's reach.

Protecting corporate e-mails from viruses and spam is now a fast-growing managed services industry. Many businesses are having their e-mail vetted before it is delivered to employees to stop viruses striking.

AOL, MSN and Yahoo are considering making it harder to register fraudulent e-mail addresses in bulk. The trio is planning to set up better feedback policies so that their customers can help determine the real identity of the spammers. They are also turning to the courts to try to stop the spammers, under pressure from their subscribers.

Phishing scam

2003 also saw the proliferation of a scam called 'phishing', where e-mails direct customers to fake Web sites in order to extract information. One of the most notable ones was when e-mail fraudsters preyed on online account customers of Citibank, the world's largest bank, on 19 August 2003. Numerous customers received an e-mail, claiming to be from the bank, asking users for their social security numbers. The e-mail said that the terms and conditions of the bank account were changing and demanded consent and verification. The e-mail linked to a Web site that looked like the real Citibank Web site.

On 13 September 2003, a similar scam targeted Barclays customers. This time, the e-mail asked customers for a technical update of their account and took them to a page with a Barclays logo. It then asked for data such as membership number and password. The e-mail appeared to have come from Baltimore in the United States, but the company sending it may not have realized it was hosting the scam. Out of 3.5 million customers who are Barclays online customers, 400 reported this to the bank and a handful claimed to have fallen for the scam. Barclays quickly assured them that their losses would be covered.

According to the National Hi-tech Crime Unit, the occurrence of these scams rose from 8 in 2002 to 40 in the United Kingdom by October 2003. The other notable scams were Lloyds TSB on 24 September, Natwest on 24 October, Halifax on 26 October, and Nationwide on 27 October.

The most prevalent phishing scams in 2003 were, of course, the Nigeria scams, targeting mainly home users and users with pop accounts. Phishing is only the initial stage of a two-tier scam claiming to originate from Nigeria, when the real source is often Eastern Europe. The second stage, known as 'money transfer' or 'job offer scam', involves advertising for British people with UK-based accounts to act as agents to transfer money overseas.

Web threats predictions for the future

Predictions from security experts portend a potentially bleak future for Web security. Some predict that the next big security trend will be real crime. Others predict that we will see destructive political cyber attacks. All indications seem to point towards an increase in malicious activity on the Internet, made possible by the continuing presence of numerous vulnerable systems and processes. Disgruntled employees may act to damage a company's assets, infrastructure or image. Extremist groups or fundamentalists could use a specially targeted worm to disable the critical national infrastructure of a country.

The upsurge of worms is a serious concern for power and oil distribution companies, whose computer systems comprise the critical national infrastructure. Some of their computer systems, known as SCADA systems, are based on Windows. These systems are often not as rigorously patched as the standard corporate machines. As these systems become more inter-connected with corporate networks, governments and corporate security officers are becoming concerned about the possibility of attacks or worms originating from the Internet reaching SCADA systems. The effect of an exposure would be an infowar scenario.

However, it is not doom and gloom for all. Some large global corporations, recognizing that their network perimeters are shrinking fast, with traditional perimeter security barely able to distinguish between friend or foe, are designing radical changes to do away with traditional firewalls and instead hook their computers directly onto the Internet, using it as the primary corporate backbone for business communication! They will need hardened desktops and applications, with a new breed of personal firewalls and strong assurance checks.

OWASP

Regardless of the threats, businesses are likely to deploy more online applications accessible via the Internet. The benefits of the Internet are too great! But so are the risks. The best way to deal with the complexity of these applications is to ensure they are designed, tested and maintained in a secure manner.

An organization called OWASP has specified a set of Web application security standards. In particular, its Top 10 application vulnerabilities are becoming the de facto standard for Web application security.[6] The US Federal Trade Commission strongly recommends that all companies use the OWASP Top 10 and ensure that their partners do the same. The Top 10 are:

■ **Unvalidated parameters:** information from Web requests is not validated before being used by a Web application. Attackers can use these flaws to attack backside components through a Web application.

---

[6] The Open Web Application Security Project, www.owasp.org

- **Broken access control:** restrictions on what authenticated users are allowed to do are not properly enforced. Attackers can exploit these flaws to access other users' accounts, view sensitive files, or use unauthorized functions.
- **Broken account and session management:** account credentials and session tokens are not properly protected. Attackers that can compromise passwords, keys, session cookies, or other tokens can defeat authentication restrictions and assume other users' identities.
- **Cross-site scripting (XSS) flaws:** the Web application can be used as a mechanism to transport an attack to an end user's browser. A successful attack can disclose the end user's session token, attack the local machine, or spoof content to fool the user.
- **Buffer overflows:** Web application components in some languages that do not properly validate input can be crashed and, in some cases, used to take control of a process. These components can include CGI, libraries, drivers and Web application server components.
- **Command injection flaws:** Web applications pass parameters when they access external systems or the local operating system. If an attacker can embed malicious commands in these parameters, the external system may execute those commands on behalf of the web application.
- **Error handling problems:** error conditions that occur during normal operation are not handled properly. If an attacker can cause errors to occur that the Web application does not handle, it can gain detailed system information, deny service, and cause security mechanisms to fail, or crash the server.
- **Insecure use of cryptography:** Web applications frequently use cryptographic functions to protect information and credentials. These functions and the code to integrate them have proven difficult to code properly, frequently resulting in weak protection.
- **Remote administration flaws:** many Web applications allow administrators to access the site using a Web interface. If these administrative functions are not very carefully protected, an attacker can gain full access to all aspects of a site.
- **Web and application server misconfiguration:** having a strong server configuration standard is critical to a secure Web application. These servers have many configuration options that affect security and are not secure out of the box.

Businesses that fail to address the above vulnerabilities are likely to be taking too high a risk against future threats from the Internet.

VeriSign, Inc (www.verisign.com) delivers critical infrastructure services that make the Internet and telecommunications networks more intelligent, reliable, and secure. Every day, VeriSign helps thousands of businesses and millions of consumers connect, communicate, and transact with confidence.

VeriSign's Intelligence and Control^{SM} services for Network Security help customers gain unmatched control and efficiency over their security environments. We are a world leader in managed security services. We design, build, and manage information security and privacy programs for leading companies in the world, through a combination of managed and consulting services. We are a global services company with offices around the world, including the UK and several other countries in Europe.

For further information contact Suheil Shahryar, Director, Security Consulting Services, VeriSign UK, Tel: +44.(0)1582.621211, Fax: +44.(0)1582.461107, 17 Holywell Hill, Suite #6, St Albans, Herts AL1 1DT, www.verisign.co.uk.

Network vulnerabilities

Creating a multi-layered defence structure will create the most secure protection from network vulnerabilities, writes Peter Crowcombe, NetScreen Technologies, Inc.

Basic network security issues have changed very little over the past decade. Protecting the confidentiality of corporate information, preventing unauthorized access and defending the network against attacks remain primary concerns of network security professionals today. What have changed are the precise areas of vulnerability that challenge today's networks – the different levels of trusted users, the sophistication level and quantity of attacks, and the ease with which attacks can be launched. Security professionals and analysts agree that their troubles have only just begun. In fact, the Computer Emergency Response Team (CERT) states that an estimated 83,000 attacks occurred globally in 2002, while in the first three quarters of 2003 alone, nearly 115,000 attacks occurred (up from just above 5,000 in 1999).[1] Attacks that are increasing in number and sophistication are placing networks in an extremely vulnerable position that will continue to be a challenge made worse by several key trends:

- **Ubiquitous access to the Internet**: the availability of the Internet has made every home, every office and every business partner a potential entry point for attack. This ubiquitous access allows sophisticated attacks to be launched against the corporate network by deliberate attackers or unknowingly by remote users logging onto the corporate network.
- **Changing levels of trust**: the different levels of network access that are being granted (remote employees, business partners, customers) are making the network increasingly

---

[1] Source: www.cert.org/stats/cert-stats.html

vulnerable. Remote employees, business partners, customers and suppliers may have different levels of access to corporate resources, and appropriate measures must be taken to protect the corporate network.

■ **Internal attacks**: more troubling and more difficult to defend against are the attacks that are perpetrated from inside the network by employees who have access and ultimately complete control over the network's resources. Internal attacks can range from a nosey employee trying to see how much his or her co-workers make, to a disgruntled employee destroying or stealing proprietary information.

■ **Attack sophistication**: new types of attacks that target application vulnerabilities have been added to the long list of viruses, worms, denial of service (DoS) and Trojan horse attacks that IT departments need to defend their network against.

■ **Wireless LANs – the unseen vulnerability**: the popularity and accepted use of wireless LANs (WLAN) is exposing many networks to security threats. Gartner Dataquest 'forecasts the penetration rate of wireless LAN into the professional mobile PC installed base will grow from 9 percent in 2000 to almost 50 percent by the end of 2003, and it is expected to surpass 90 percent by 2007'.[2] With little or no security on a WLAN, attackers can gain access to the corporate network with relative ease and as a result, may be free to roam the corporate network, inflicting damage or stealing data.

The trends outlined above exemplify how administrators must reconsider their network security architecture to address specific security threats without hindering access. Industry analysts and security experts agree that the key to striking a balance between tight network security and the network access required by employees, business partners and customers is a layered security solution.

Network vulnerabilities

■ **Remote access communications**: in many cases, users who are accessing the corporate network are doing so across a public medium, possibly without the appropriate security measures, which means that all communications are being transmitted in clear text and are susceptible to hackers. The primary solution to this vulnerability is SSL (secure socket layer) Virtual Private Networking (VPN), to include strong authentication capabilities.

■ **Site-to-site communications**: in this scenario, two resources (remote site and main site) that are typically connected to each other via a high-speed connection need to be protected. Potential threats include hijacked sessions, u-turn attacks, compromised PCs, malicious users and attacks originating from one site, yet targeting the other site. To counteract this vulnerability, firewalls and IPSec VPNs should be used. DoS protection is also advisable.

■ **Perimeter security**: fundamentally, as the point where external communication lines enter the corporate network, this is where who and what gets in/out of the network must be controlled. Some of the vulnerabilities threatening the perimeter include hackers trying to penetrate the network, DoS, sophisticated application level and hybrid attacks. Perimeter

---

[2] Source: Worldwide Wireless LAN shipments to grow 73 per cent in 2002, Gartner Dataquest press release, September 2002

firewall/DoS protection (preferably multi-functional to include such features as anti-virus), access control (IPSec) plus intrusion detection and prevention (IDP) layers are advised.

■ **Network core security**: the network's core is the area that contains an organization's most critical data resources, so is vulnerable to unauthorized user roaming, internal attacks launched by disgruntled employees, and application-level attacks targeting specific vulnerabilities. High-performing, properly integrated firewalls, inline but independent IDPs, IPSec VPNs, should all be deployed to protect the network's core.

Layered security to help counteract network vulnerabilities

Overall, the solutions described above should be deployed as a cohesive, layered solution to optimally secure a highly distributed network. The ultimate goal of a layered security solution is to protect the critical resources that reside on the network from today's ever increasingly sophisticated attacks. A layered security solution is made up of multiple layers of complementary security technologies, all working together to provide the required level of protection – if one layers fails, the next layer will cover it. For example, administrators may deploy firewalls, VPNs, anti-virus and intrusion detection and prevention as layers of protection against attacks.

Table 2.4.1   Security layers

Security layer	Description
Firewall	Protects the network by controlling who and what can have access to the network
Denial of Service	Protects against denial of service type attacks
Virtual Private Network (VPN)	Protects communications between sites and/or users with an encrypted, authenticated communications session (tunnel)
Anti-virus	Protects against virus attacks at the desktop, gateway and server levels
Intrusion detection and prevention	Protects against sophisticated attacks such as application-level attacks
Personal firewall	Protects content on personal computers and in turn, keeps corporate networks safe

In addition to protecting network resources from attacks, the need for layered security stems from today's network extending far beyond the walls of the corporate headquarters to where remote users, regional offices, business partners and customers are accessing network resources from their location. This extension of the corporate network is forcing IT departments to treat each of these network entry points as a potential avenue for attack. A layered security solution allows an administrator to apply the appropriate levels of security to protect resources from attacks originating from any location. Layered security is an optimal solution for two reasons.

First, if a security breach occurs, the other security layers that have been deployed can stop the attack and/or limit the damages that may occur.

Second, this allows an IT department to apply the appropriate level of resource protection to the various network entry points based upon different security, performance and management requirements. For example, remote users have lower performance requirements and access to fewer technical resources but still need to protect their PC (and the corporate network) from viruses with anti-virus and from prying eyes with encryption. At the other end of the spectrum, core network security will require higher levels of performance and access to technical resources in order to support the sophisticated levels of security needed to protect the corporate network and business-critical applications.

Most organizations acknowledge that intrusions and attacks are inevitable, and a layered security strategy comprised of multiple layers of complementary security technologies, all working together, helps to minimize this risk by presenting multiple barriers to keep them from penetrating an organization's defences.

Network segmentation and user containment

In addition to various security solutions, network segmentation and user containment can further be used to protect the network against various vulnerabilities. Once thought of as only a perimeter defence security layer, firewalls are being brought into the infrastructure to protect different segments of the network such as finance, HR and engineering. Used internally, firewalls provide additional layers of access control to protect against the organization's sprawling definition of 'authorized user', as well as to provide attack containment. Adding firewalls to the infrastructure enables an organization to protect specific resources, and helps to prevent users from unauthorized roaming and contain attack damages in the event that one occurs. Rather than implementing a separate, physical firewall for every segment, a more cost-effective solution is to leverage virtual firewall functionality and VPNs that can divide the network into distinct, secure network segments.

In the network security world, one thing is certain: networks will remain the target of ever increasingly sophisticated types of attacks originating both internally and externally. Compounding the difficulty associated with protecting the network from new types of attacks is the dramatic expansion of who may or may not have access to the corporate network. These two factors are forcing IT departments to evaluate and implement layered security solutions that are designed to:

■ control who and what has access to the corporate network through robust firewall functionality;
■ protect against denial of service attacks through built-in intelligence and high performance;
■ facilitate secure communications with a VPN so that remote users, business partners and customers can conduct business across the Internet;
■ detect attacks and quickly react, in a preventative manner, to minimize or eliminate any damages that may result from the attack.

NetScreen Technologies, Inc is a leading developer of network security and access solutions for enterprises and carriers worldwide. NetScreen's solutions offer customers multiple layers of network and application-level protection in purpose-built appliances and systems that optimize performance and reduce total operating costs. NetScreen's global HQ are located in Sunnyvale, USA., and in Europe at Victoria House, Cross Lanes, Guildford, Surrey GU1 1UJ, United Kingdom.

More information on NetScreen's products in Europe can be found at http://www.netscreen.com or by calling +44 0 8700 75 00 00.

Wireless applications

Wireless applications can provide many benefits to a company in terms of flexibility and productivity gains but with these come risks, explains Andrew Steggles, Marketing Director of EMEA Nokia Enterprise Solutions.

Mobilizing the enterprise

In today's world, enterprises are capitalizing on mobility to gain business advantages. A large element in gaining these advantages is giving an increasing number of employees mobile access to e-mail, calendars, contacts, tasks and other corporate resources, such as the intranet. The challenge for enterprises is finding a solution that provides secure, cost-effective, usable and flexible access for employees regardless of their geographic location or preferred mobile device.

At the same time, adoption has been slowed by security concerns and less than optimal user experiences. Anyone who has remotely accessed e-mail over a broadband connection will never again be satisfied with dial up.

The rush to mobility can be explained by the growth of new technologies and businesses' desire to stay competitive – mobility offers benefits such as greater access to people and data, improved customer service and responsiveness, and improved productivity. Already, work practices are changing with the increasing decentralization of employees and the growing number of remote and home offices. Technology is making it possible to take enterprises truly mobile by providing an expanding variety and sophistication of mobile devices, connection technologies and mobile content.

Along with the devices, mobile content is also changing from being text only to include multimedia, and is being used differently by employees – evolving from information retrieval to transactions. The proliferation of wireless technologies (including Wi-Fi and 3G) and fixed broadband, combined with sophisticated PDAs and mobile telephones, has meant that the laptop is now not the only method of sharing data with the office while on the move. The requirement for business now is quickly becoming that any device should be able to access any content.

However, as more content goes mobile, so does the threat of data crime. Devices become smaller, yet their functionality and storage capacity increase. This means the smaller things are easier to steal or misplace, while they carry more content and access information to corporate networks. Wireless networks and other wireless transmission techniques (that is, Bluetooth, Wi-Fi aka IEEE 802.11) are largely unprotected and allow for interference, sniffing, easy hacking and so on.

The growing number of mobile devices accessing the Internet is changing the nature of business. IDC forecasts that up to 60 per cent of Internet users will be connecting to the Internet via mobile devices by 2005. The ability for mobile workers to access corporate resources over the Internet is great news for business productivity, but naturally raises a new set of security concerns.

The ability to offer corporate customers security and management capabilities for the mobile infrastructure is critical to the success of any mobile infrastructure initiative. Further, the ability of such software products to scale to demand and interoperate with other network components is essential. Software security and management products aimed at the mobile markets will undoubtedly speed adoption of this technology. However, other factors come into play, including more appealing carrier payment plans and the need for standards to solidify within the mobile and wireless marketing.

Mobile Internet shares the same issues and risks as the fixed Internet, but has additional dangers caused by the nature of its wireless transmission. The fact that users of mobile devices can move from location to location, and network to network, adds another dimension to the security discussion. Other security issues include viruses that could be a possible threat to handsets and to networks, unauthorized accessing of a network, and of course theft of devices. Companies need to consider new ways of authenticating and securing mobile devices, such as PIN codes or user biometrics.

Here is where the story starts to get convoluted for businesses. The IT department steps in and asks: how are we going to manage all these different devices, user profiles and network types? How can we ensure network integrity? And can we do it without running up huge costs?

Securing and managing the devices are the key issues in enabling mobile enterprise. IPSec VPNs have been the tried and trusted security measure used by most companies to reliably secure computers logging into the company network. However, as IPsec VPNs require a client running on the mobile device, an enterprise may be faced with the task of distributing, updating and managing many hundreds or thousands of clients. Without the right management tools, this can add to costs and increases the complexity of the solution – so if an IPSec solution is what the business needs, a tool which keeps mobile devices up to date and eases the management burden of supporting mobile devices is required. But there is another option that is getting enterprises excited – SSL (secure socket layer) VPNs.

SSL VPNs leverage the ubiquity of SSL, which is built into almost every Web or WAP browser. If an appliance is used to authenticate users, restrict access and secure the connection using SSL, access can be given to the intranet and e-mail applications, eliminating the need to install a VPN client for the majority of users. This means the management cost involved with IPSec VPN is avoided, making SSL VPN much more cost-effective for businesses wanting to take their workforce mobile. SSL VPNs also allow a multitude of devices to be supported both now and in the future, and an enterprise does not have to choose a mobile device that has an IPSec client available for it.

This is not to say IPSec VPNs are now a thing of the past. SSL VPNs are perfect for accessing e-mail and Web-enabled applications, which for the majority of mobile workers is all they need. However, some client server applications are not Web-enabled, meaning an IPSec VPN is the best option. Enterprises will have to examine their needs and decide which solution suits the particular application being delivered, and we believe many will use a combination of the two VPN technologies to maintain remote access security.

These technologies provide the basis for secure connections, but simplifying the management of many user profiles, devices, and network types – and doing it cost effectively – requires businesses to select their supplier carefully.

Management software for provisioning IPSec VPN client software to mobile devices on a large scale is key for companies wishing to take this route. Vendor and application independence is also important, as is the expandability of the network product – businesses should not lock themselves into proprietary technology. They need to ensure their investments can cope with future requirements.

Similarly with SSL VPNs, businesses should look for vendor offerings that support many authentication methods and device types, as well as legacy applications. In-built tools that can automatically recognize device type and security settings are vital to simplifying management and ensuring adequate levels of security. For example, logging into the office from a laptop with up-to-date virus definitions and a personal firewall is very different from accessing the network from a hand-held device that has no firewall and outdated virus protection. The access levels for each device can and should be altered accordingly.

With Gartner predicting that by 2007, more than 40 per cent of corporate applications will have some mobility element built-in, planning how to secure, support and integrate mobile devices will be key to enabling a truly mobile workforce. As public Wi-Fi hotspots and broadband access points multiply daily, and new powerful phones and PDAs become affordable and easy to use, it will not just be the travelling business person logging into e-mail from the hotel any more.

Many companies are rushing to embrace wireless networking and install access points without first understanding the security implications. One of the most common reasons for WLAN security breaches is the failure by companies to take any security precautions at all. Wireless networking is great technology and allows great freedom for business, but while pushing a WLAN as a solution, often the security issues are not taken into account, either because companies do not understand the risks or because they think they are nothing to worry about.

This leads to another common security concern, when the corporation attaches the WLAN access points to the network backbone rather than the firewall, meaning everything is broadcast from the backbone – including file transfers, financial information and so on – and it is easy for anyone with the right Wi-Fi equipment and tools to listen in and either read company information, or corrupt data on servers.

Companies need to understand not only how a WLAN can help their business but also what security risks come along with those benefits. The main thing is, the risks are manageable – hardened security technology is available now to deliver strong encryption and flexibility so businesses can take advantage of the great benefits of a WLAN without putting their organization in harm's way. These same solutions can also be used to provide secure remote access over solutions like ADSL, dial-up, hotel broadband solutions and remote WLAN hotspots.

To conclude, a company must understand the importance of technology as a tool to enable business, just as decisions about technology should be made with the overall business objectives in mind – details such as planned expansion, increased numbers of remote workers and the growing number of suppliers needing to access a corporate network should be considered with a long-term view. Security cannot be viewed within a vacuum, and security is no longer just an insurance policy.

Companies are beginning to realize that at one level security is a necessity, and at another it is a very positive infrastructure element. This has been driven by the need for companies to expand 'trusted relationships' with customers, partners, suppliers and channels. In many cases a company's greatest asset is information. The ability to use security technologies to enable greater access to corporate content deepens and stabilizes relationships. These 'trusted relationships' can yield numerous benefits, such as higher transaction rates with greater scalability, lower cost per transaction, and transference of personnel from low-value interactions to a high-value personalized service.

Nokia Enterprise Solutions focuses on mobile business devices and providing IP network perimeter security (firewalls and VPN), secure content management (anti-virus scanning and SPAM filtering), and mobile connectivity (remote access VPN and content) solutions designed to help companies mobilize their workforces and increase productivity while ensuring the security and reliability of their networks.

For further information contact Nokia Enterprise Solutions on +44 161 601 8908, e-mail ipsecurity.emea@nokia.com. Full details of all Nokia Enterprise products can be found at: www.nokia.com/ipsecurity/emea.

Protecting online privacy

Peter Brudenall from Simmons & Simmons takes an in-depth look at the intro-duction of the Privacy and Electronic Communications (EC Directive) Regulations 2003 and what it means for businesses.

As part of the UK implementation of a suite of recent EU legislation designed to regulate electronic communications networks and services across the EU, the Privacy and Electronic Communications (EC Directive) Regulations 2003 (the '2003 Regulations') were implemented in the United Kingdom on 11 December 2003. The Regulations are designed to be more 'technology neutral' than the Telecommunication (Data Protection and Privacy) Regulations 1999 (the '1999 Regulations') which they replace. As a result, the 2003 Regulations broaden the data protection legislation framework from one focused on telecommunications services to one relevant to both telecommunications and new technologies (such as e-mail and SMS). The technology neutral nature of the 2003 Regulations also means that they will be applicable to future technologies that involve the processing of personal data.

Background

The 2003 Regulations implement the Directive on Privacy and Electronic Communications (formerly known as the Communications Data Protection Directive) (the 'Directive').[1] Both

---

[1] Directive 2002/58/EC of the European Parliament and of the Council of 12 July 2002.

the 2003 Regulations and the Directive are derived from the suite of European legislation designed to harmonize Member States' laws in the electronic communications sector. The Communications Act 2003 implements the bulk of this suite of legislation. The Directive, however, is being implemented through the 2003 Regulations.

The old regime

The 1999 Regulations focussed on the processing of personal data in the telecommunications field. One of their principal features was the rules governing the use of unsolicited calls and faxes for marketing purposes, but the rules, on a literal interpretation, were restricted to voice telephony and fax. Indeed the advent of the 2003 Regulations, which deal with other forms of communication, may suggest that there was previously no regulation on the processing of personal data in connection with the sending of marketing via electronic communications. This is, of course, not the case. Data protection laws in the United Kingdom regulated (and continue to regulate) the processing of personal data in connection with the sending of electronic communications to individuals. The over-arching rules relating to the processing of personal data are contained in the Data Protection Act 1998 (the DPA) which will apply where the marketing concerned involves the processing of 'personal data'. 'Personal data' means information relating to a living individual who can be identified either from the data concerned, or from the data plus additional information in the possession of, or likely to come into the possession of, the body controlling the data (the 'data controller').

Compliance with the DPA is monitored and enforced by the Information Commissioner's Office (ICO), an independent supervisory authority reporting to Parliament, which was set up to develop respect for the private lives of citizens and to encourage the accountability of public authorities. The ICO produces guidelines on new legislation when the legislation has an affect on the privacy of individuals.

Marketing via electronic communications was therefore previously regulated by the DPA and the ICO guidance on the DPA (and continues to be so regulated). In addition, in guidelines published in relation to the 1999 Regulations, the ICO indicated that those contacting individuals via e-mail should apply the principles of the 1999 Regulations to unsolicited e-mails. This is despite the fact that e-mail was not expressly referred to in the 1999 Regulations.

In practice, then, the narrow drafting of the 1999 Regulations was broadened by the ICO's guidelines. This resulted in a degree of uncertainty as to the rules relating to marketing via electronic communications. The 2003 Regulations remove a lot of the uncertainty, even if they may be viewed by some as restrictive.

The new regime under the 2003 regulations

Before we deal with the specific rules set out in the 2003 Regulations it is worth noting that under the new regime, the DPA is still relevant. As a result, those making use of electronic means to contact individuals must continue to ensure that the processing of the individual's personal data complies with the eight data protection principles set out in the DPA.

For example, if a company wishes to send a text message to an individual it must ensure that its use of the individual's personal data (such as the mobile number) is fair and lawful (the first data protection principle), and as part of that it must ensure that it has told the individual how the data will be processed. In other words, the company should tell the individual it might send him/her SMS messages, and the purposes for which those SMS messages will be sent.

Within the DPA, section 11 is particularly relevant as it gives the individual a right to prevent processing of his or her personal data for direct marketing. To exercise this right, the individual must give a reasonable period of written notice to the data controller following which the data controller must cease processing the individual's personal data for marketing purposes. If it does not cease, the court can order it to take such steps to comply with the notice as the court thinks fit.[2]

The 2003 Regulations are an extra layer of legislation on top of the DPA. They broaden out the scope of the 1999 Regulations by using fairly broad technology-neutral definitions reflecting those used under the Communications Act. Instead of using terms relevant to traditional telecommunications and voice telephony, the 2003 Regulations refer to 'electronic communications networks and services'. 'Telecommunications' is replaced by 'communications', and the latter is defined as 'any information exchanged or conveyed between a finite number of parties by means of a public electronic communications service'.

Specific changes introduced by the 2003 Regulations

Electronic mail (Regulations 22 and 23)

The problem of spam

According to the European Commission, spam now accounts for more than 50 per cent of all e-mails sent. This results in annoyance for the users whose inboxes it clogs, and reduces productivity in the workplace (according to the European Commission an estimated 2.5 billion euros loss was suffered by EU businesses in 2002) and significantly increases costs of transmission and storage for Internet service providers and network operators. The 2003 Regulations take steps to counter spam e-mailing but at the same time take account of the fact that in business-to-business relationships, marketing by all means (including electronic means) is necessary in order for businesses to effectively promote their goods and services.

The 2003 regulations apply to 'electronic mail'

The 2003 Regulations include new provisions that specifically regulate how businesses may use 'electronic mail' to market to individuals. However, the 2003 Regulations regulate more than the use of just *e-mail* since the definition of 'electronic mail' is very broad. It encompasses 'any text, voice, sound or image message sent over public electronic communications network which can be stored in the network or in the recipient's terminal equipment until it is collected by the recipient and includes ... short message service'.[3]

In other words, and as the Guidelines state, e-mail, SMS text, mobile picture and video marketing messages are all considered to be 'electronic mail'. In addition, the rules also apply to voice-mail or answerphone messages left by marketers. Therefore, there are

---

[2] Section 11(1) of the DPA.
[3] Regulation 1.

stricter obligations placed upon those marketers who make live calls but who wish to leave messages on a person's voice-mail or answerphone, than on those marketers who avoid leaving messages.

The subscriber must 'opt in'

Under the 2003 Regulations, the subscriber recipient of a marketing e-mail must have 'opted in' to the communication being sent by the sender. In the words of the 2003 Regulations the recipient must have previously notified the sender that he/she consents to the communication being sent.[4] This differs slightly from the text of the Directive that states 'prior consent' is all that is required to authorize marketing e-mail. This might have given rise to the argument that those who are already receiving e-mails and have not 'opted out' have implied consent to continued receipt of marketing e-mails.

However, there are two problems with this argument since it is clear that, for the purposes of the DPA, consent requires active communication, and in any event the matter is put beyond doubt by the 2003 Regulations' requirement for 'previous notification', which makes it clear that some active notification on the part of the subscriber is required.

That said, the ICO seems unwilling to take a rigid line on this point. The Guidelines recognize the fact that the new legislation imposes upon marketers a higher standard for data collection than they were obliged to follow before 11 December 2003. Accordingly, for the time being the ICO is taking the view that if mailing lists were compiled in accordance with privacy legislation in force before 11 December 2003 and were used recently, marketers can continue to use them unless the intended recipient has already opted out. (The Guidelines take the view, however, that privacy legislation in force before 11 December 2003 did not permit the sending of unsolicited text/video messages without prior consent.)

The 'soft' opt-in exception

There is an exception to the requirement of consent. The so-called 'soft' opt-in applies to suppliers who obtain e-mail details in the context of a sale of goods or services or negotiation in respect of a sale (suggesting that a concluded sale is not necessary for the soft opt-in to apply). In these limited circumstances, suppliers can send direct marketing of their own 'similar products or services only' to existing customers providing that the addressee is able to opt out of future e-mail marketing easily and free of charge.[5] However, no definition of 'similar' is provided and so this may be problematic, as may be the use of the word 'only' which suggests that a company could not market similar products as well as other products that it might also sell.

The Guidelines, however, adopt a purposive approach to the phrase 'similar products and services only'. They state that the intention of this section is to ensure that an individual does not receive promotional material about products and services that he or she would not reasonably expect to receive. An example given is someone who has shopped online at a supermarket's Web site (and has not objected to receiving further e-mail marketing from that supermarket) who would expect at some point in the future to receive further e-mails promoting the diverse range of goods available at that supermarket.

---

[4] Regulation 22(2).
[5] Regulation 22(3).

Ultimately, as the ICO also points out, if an individual feels that a company has gone beyond the boundaries of their reasonable expectation, that individual can opt out. Accordingly, the ICO's focus will be on failures to comply with opt-out requests rather than suppliers' interpretation of the term 'similar'.

The sender must be identified, and the electronic communication must be identified as marketing material

Spam is further stamped on by Regulation 23 of the 2003 Regulations that prohibits the sending of communications by electronic mail that disguise the identity of the sender and do not include a valid opt-out address.

This builds on the requirements of the Electronic Commerce (EC Directive) Regulations 2002[6] (the 'E-Commerce Regulations'). The E-Commerce Regulations require commercial communications connected with an information society service to be clearly identifiable as such, and for an unsolicited commercial communication also to be clearly and unambiguously identifiable as such as soon as it is received.[7]

In a similar vein, the 2003 Regulations state that, assuming the subscriber has clearly consented to the receipt of messages, each message will have to identify the sender and provide a valid suppression address. This is easy to achieve in the case of e-mail, but not so easy in the case of SMS messages. Nevertheless the requirements must be met and the Guidelines suggest that the following sort of formulation may be appropriate in an SMS message: PHLtdPobox97SK95AF.

Clearly, attaching an appropriate heading to an e-mail is relatively easy but applying a heading to an SMS message is more difficult. None the less, the Guidelines state that 'the practical limitations of standard mobile screens do not mean that marketers can avoid the rules' despite the fact that a standard mobile phone screen can only hold 160 characters.

The Guidelines suggest that a company can give information about the marketing it intends to do before a marketing message is sent or even before the mobile number is collected. For example the information could be given in an advert, or on a Web site where the recipient signs up for the service.

In addition to the E-Commerce Regulations and the 2003 Regulations, marketers must be aware of other regulation and other statutory bodies that restrict methods of marketing. The Code of Practice (CAP Code) of the Advertising Standards Authority (ASA) is particularly relevant to marketing, as is the Code of Practice of the Direct Marketing Association (DMA Code). Marketers should also be aware of regulation specific to their particular industry. For example, law firms must take account of Law Society Rules when reviewing their marketing policies.

When the 2003 regulations do not apply: business e-mail

During consultation on the drafting of the 2003 Regulations a large number of respondents felt that corporate subscribers should not have the same rights as individuals in relation to

---

[6] Directive 2000/31/EC.
[7] Regulation 7 of the E-Commerce Regulations.

electronic mail. Many highlighted concerns that a universal opt-in would be harmful for business-to-business selling.

Consequently, the 2003 Regulations' restrictions on sending marketing e-mails only apply to e-mails sent to individuals, sole traders and non-limited liability partnerships. They do not apply to marketing e-mails sent to employees of companies or limited liability partnerships, since such persons are not 'subscribers' and the rules only apply to electronic mail sent to subscribers.[8]

However, corporate subscribers and individual corporate users whose e-mail addresses include or constitute personal data continue to enjoy protection under section 11 of the DPA as above.

Other new elements of the 2003 regulations

Clearly, the rules relating to marketing messages sent by electronic means will make a significant impact on marketers using electronic mail in the United Kingdom. However, the Regulations also impact on the use of cookies and location data.

Cookies (regulation 6)

Cookies are small data files that many Internet sites automatically upload to a user's hard drive. They are primarily used in helping Web sites recognize previous visitors and in recording users' preferences. Originally, it appeared that the proposed 'opt-in' rule would apply to the use of cookies as well as to unsolicited e-mail marketing messages. However, as a result of pressure from groups such as the Federation of European Direct Marketing (FEDMA), the legislation was drafted in a manner that means that it is sufficient to make the end-user aware that there is a cookie, and what the function of the cookie is.

Regulation 6 requires that a person wishing to use cookies need only tell the individual that cookies are going to be used and how the cookies can be rejected or removed. It also requires that a user or subscriber be provided with clear and comprehensive information about the purposes of the storage of, or access to, the cookie.

The 2003 Regulations do not prescribe the way in which a user or subscriber should be able to refuse the use of a cookie – according to the Guidelines the method is seen as less important than the fact that the mechanism must be 'uncomplicated, easy to understand and accessible to all'.

Regulation 6 is drafted very broadly, referring to the use of an electronic communications network to store information to gain access to information stored in the terminal equipment of a subscriber or user. As with electronic communications above, this is a very wide definition, which is deliberately technology-neutral to allow other future forms of information gathering technology to be collected. Accordingly, although the use of 'cookies' is the principal application of the rule, the definition and future application of Regulation 6 may extend beyond that.

---

[8] A 'subscriber' is defined in Regulation 1 as any person party to a contract with a provider of publicly available electronic communication services for the supply of such services.

Location data (regulation 14)

The 2003 Regulations also deal with the processing of location data, or 'data processed by an electronic communications network indicating the geographical position of the terminal equipment of a user of a public electronic communications service' and this includes information relating to:

■ the latitude, longitude or altitude of the terminal equipment;
■ the direction of travel of the user;
■ the time the location information was recorded.[9]

The processing of location data will enable the provision of helpful location-based services such as a directory enquiries services that are able to use customers' locations to send text or even map details of local amenities. The processing of location data is regulated and can only be processed if the subscriber cannot be identified from the data, or if processing is necessary for the provision of a value added service and the individual's consent has been received.[10]

In this context, a value-added service means any service which requires the processing of location data beyond that which is necessary for the transmission of a communication or the billing of that data.[11] Before consent can be obtained, the communications provider must provide the subscriber with the following information:

■ the types of location data that will be processed;
■ the purposes and duration of the processing of those data; and
■ whether the data will be transmitted to a third party for the purposes of providing a value-added service.[12]

The Regulations do not prescribe how consent should be obtained. However, the Guidelines state that to receive valid informed consent the service provider must give 'sufficient, clear information' to the subscriber. In the light of this, the service provider will not be able to rely on a blanket 'catch all' statement on a bill or Web site. Instead, it should obtain specific informed consent for each value-added service requested and for the marketing of its own electronic communications services.

Subscribers should be able to withdraw consent at any time, and the communications provider should make them aware of this.

Conclusion

It is clear that the 2003 Regulations will have a massive impact on companies in the communications industry. Companies providing communication services will have to ensure that they follow the 2003 Regulations carefully. This will influence their use of – and the way

---

[9] Regulation 1.
[10] Regulation 14(2).
[11] Regulation 1.
[12] Regulation 14(3).

their customers can make use of – electronic mail and cookies. All companies in the EU will have to ensure that their marketing policies comply with the 2003 Regulations, paying particular attention to the rules regarding electronic mail (including SMS and picture messaging) and cookies.

The law will be more restrictive following the implementation of the 2003 Regulations. However, while the 2003 Regulations are restrictive, they also clarify grey areas of the law and provide a framework for the future of the communications industry, which represents a step forward from the old telecommunications regime.

Simmons & Simmons was ranked joint second in the United Kingdom for outsourcing in a recent survey of in-house lawyers by *The Lawyer* magazine.

In 2002 Global Counsel 3000 ranked Simmons & Simmons in the top 10 worldwide for performance in all major practice areas, based on the views of in-house counsel at over 5,000 companies across 74 jurisdictions. Earlier this year the firm won a prestigious Queen's Award for Enterprise in the International Trade category, the only law firm to do so.

For further information contact David Barrett, partner, t: +44 (0)20 7825 4032, e: david.barrett@simmons-simmons.com or Peter Brudenall, senior lawyer, t: +44 (0)20 7825 4346 e: peter.brudenall@simmons-simmons.com

Web site: www.simmons-simmons.com

Protect Your Business From Fraud Attacks!

The continued growth of the online sales channel presents merchants with new opportunities for revenue and efficiency. At the same time, doing business in card-not-present environments exposes you to a greater risk of significant financial loss to fraud attacks.

Improve Profitability, Increase Revenue, and Optimise Fraud Detection!

ClearCommerce Risk Management is the most effective solution available to protect your business against fraud attacks. This powerful solution combines a comprehensive arsenal of fraud detection technologies to provide a flexible decision platform that can easily be customised to your specific business requirements.

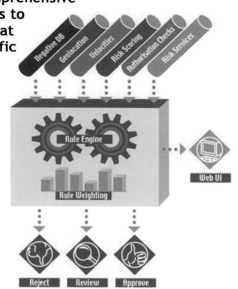

Businesses You Trust, Trust ClearCommerce

Leading companies from various industry segments trust ClearCommerce solutions to safeguard and automate their e-commerce financial transaction processing, including:

Adobe   Apple Computer   ebookers plc

EST   Barclaycard Merchant Services

HSBC Merchant Services   Staples   Yahoo!

Let us help protect your business. Contact us today.

www.clearcommerce.com

136-139 High Street   Egham Surrey   TW20 9HL
01784 430200   email: asmith@clearcommerce.com

2.7

Online payments: safe-guarding against fraud

Identity theft, skimming and general credit card fraud all present risks to an online business. The solution lies in having a range of safeguards in place that suit your particular business rather than any one magic solution, write ClearCommerce.

The rapid growth of online commerce presents businesses with new opportunities for revenue and efficiency. With business-to-consumer online commerce in Europe projected to grow to US $240 billion by 2006, the Internet is set to become a major selling channel for the retail sector.[1] Doing business over the Internet, however, exposes merchants to a much greater risk of losses as a result of payment fraud. Because of the liability policies for *card-not-present* transactions and because of the anonymity, reach and speed that the Internet provides for criminals, fraud prevention has become a necessary component of every e-commerce infrastructure.

Internet payment fraud: a realistic sizing of the problem

The incidence of payment fraud in online retail has been a subject of speculation that has contributed to a widespread concern among both merchants and consumers. Recent statistics provided by the credit card associations put online fraud rates between 0.8 per cent and 0.9 per cent of online orders. The latest statistics obtained from the ClearCommerce

[1] eMarketer report: *Europe E-Commerce: B2B & B2C*, July 2003

Data Consortium show that fraud represents 0.6 per cent of all completed transactions, and 0.8 per cent of the sales volume transacted.[2]

Although these rates may appear within reason, they are in fact more than 10 times higher than those reported for face-to-face transactions (for which Visa reports 0.06 per cent). In addition, as the online sales channel has continued its rapid growth, the absolute losses to fraud have grown in parallel. According to a report published in 2003 by the Association for Payment Clearing Services (APACS), card-not-present payment fraud in the United Kingdom has risen by 33 per cent over the past two years.

Many businesses selling online evaluate the risk of fraud based on published industry averages. Unfortunately, these figures provide a false sense of security by hiding the significant risk of loss associated with how fraud actually happens. It is not, as the averages suggest, a linear problem that grows along with your online sales volume. Rather, sophisticated networks of organized criminals, who attack in lightning fast, multi-million dollar strikes, increasingly target businesses selling online.

Cost of fraud for merchants

Since card issuers classify purchases completed via the Internet as *card-not-present* transactions, online merchants have to pay not only higher interchange rates, but also the full liability for losses due to fraud.[3] Whenever the legitimate cardholder disputes a credit card charge, his or her card-issuing bank will send a charge-back to the merchant, reversing the credit for the transaction. In most cases it is very difficult for the merchant to reverse the charge-back because there is usually no physical evidence available, for example a signature, to challenge it. The true cost of fraud includes several 'line items':

- **Cost of goods sold**: it is very unlikely that the merchandise will be recovered, and the merchant will have to write off the value of the goods ordered.
- **Shipping cost**: the merchant will also absorb the cost of the shipping for fraudulent orders. And because criminals typically request priority shipping, fraudulent orders also carry high shipping costs.
- **Card association fees**: Visa and MasterCard have put in place fairly strict programs that penalize merchants generating excessive charge-backs. Penalties include fees for each charge-back processed, monthly fines, and even termination of the merchant's service agreement in extreme cases.
- **Merchant bank fees**: in addition to the penalties charges from the card associations, the merchant will typically pay an additional processing fee to the acquiring bank for every charge-back.
- **Administrative cost**: every transaction that generates a charge-back involves significant administrative costs for the merchant. On average, each charge-back requires

---

[2] The ClearCommerce Data Consortium is a multi-merchant database containing millions of historical Internet transactions and charge-back data.

[3] Interchange rates for online merchants are, on average, 2.5 per cent of the transaction value, plus an additional 20 to 30 cents per transaction, while bricks-and-mortar merchants typically pay 1.5 per cent of the transaction value and 10 to 20 cents per transaction.

between one and two hours to receive and research the claim, contact the consumer, and respond to the acquiring bank or issuer with adequate documentation.

Need for fraud prevention

One of the most important factors in determining the risk profile of a merchant is the overall traffic experienced by the site. Research data shows that the fraud rates tend to grow with the number of unique site visitors. This is generally due to the fact that high-volume online merchants have highly automated order processing and a human never sees the vast majority of orders. Automation creates an opportunity for criminals to place large numbers of fraudulent orders without being noticed. Online merchants that are just beginning to grow their businesses will experience fewer fraud cases initially, and therefore may underestimate the threat of online fraud. Not having a fraud prevention process in place, however, may expose these merchants to a fraud attack.

One of the main challenges with fraud prevention is the long time lag between the time a fraudulent transaction occurs and the time when the merchant receives charge-back notification. On average, the lag between the transaction date and the charge-back notification is between 45 and 70 days, although over 20 per cent of all fraudulent charges become apparent as much as 100 days after the transaction. This means that if no fraud prevention is in place, one or more criminals could easily generate significant damage to a business before the merchant even realizes the problem.

The unavoidable time gap between the actual fraud event and the charge-back notification requires online merchants to put in place fraud prevention programs right from the start. Without these preventative measures, merchants expose themselves to the risk of unexpected significant losses to fraud and severe penalties from card associations and issuing banks.

How fraud starts

The first step toward effective fraud prevention is to understand how fraud is perpetrated, which greatly helps in appreciating the benefits and limitations of the various prevention tools. Networks of organized criminals, attacking in lightning-fast, large-scale strikes, using increasingly sophisticated tools and techniques, perpetrate a growing percentage of online payment fraud. Their intent is to commit massive theft as one way of financing their operations. Although these criminals design new and more complex schemes every day, they all start with securing a form of payment, typically a credit card, with which to perpetrate fraud.

Account take-over is by far the dominant scheme used by criminals to acquire a form of payment for their illegal activities. Account take-over is described as the unauthorized use of an unsuspecting individual's credit card account number, which in some cases is the only piece of information a criminal needs to place an order. Increasingly, however, criminals are stealing the identity of an innocent consumer and are applying for new credit card accounts in their name. A 2003 report by the Association for Payment Clearing Services (APACS) on UK issued credit and debit cards found that fraud is the second largest contributor to overall identity theft in the United Kingdom.

While the Internet provides a *card-not-present* environment in which to use stolen cards, contrary to consumer concerns, credit card numbers are rarely stolen in cyberspace.

Because nearly all online merchants use secure communication channels when sensitive data is transmitted between the consumer browser and the Web site, the likelihood of a criminals intercepting card numbers during a transaction is extremely small. A greater risk is theft of credit card data from storage on the merchant's Web site. Break-ins resulting in theft of credit card data have occurred at sites with insufficient security, and media coverage of these thefts has heightened consumer alarm at the potential risks of e-commerce. These risks, however, can and are being addressed by implementation of appropriate site security.[4]

Stolen or lost credit cards obviously provide criminals with full access to account information, expiration data and billing name. However, these card numbers typically provide a short window of opportunity since the legitimate cardholder will usually report the accident to the issuer and the account will be blocked. Credit card numbers collected from card imprints, receipts or monthly statements collected in dumpsters give criminals a wider window of opportunity, since the cardholder is unaware that the card number has been compromised until he or she receives a statement from the issuer that includes unauthorized transactions. Newer point of sale systems protect the cardholder by printing out receipts that only include the first and last four digits of the card.

New high-tech tools now commonly used to steal credit card information are hand-held credit card skimmers. These devices can read the card information encoded in the magnetic stripe and store thousands of card numbers that are later uploaded to a PC. Since these devices are easily concealed, an unethical waiter can easily swipe the card while walking between the cash register and the table.

While the methods described above require some form of access to the physical card or paper receipts, others can give criminals access to a card number without even leaving home. Card number generator programs are software tools that can produce hundreds of 'valid' card numbers that criminals can easily generate and then 'test' online. The software generates numbers that are valid with respect to the coding scheme used by card issuers; however the vast majority of these numbers will not correspond to active accounts. Nonetheless, it is relatively easy to test large sets of generated numbers against a target Web site. Once the criminal finds a 'hit', the card is charged up to its limit with fraudulent orders.

Detecting and preventing fraud

While criminals continue to devise new and more sophisticated schemes to compromise credit card information and perpetrate fraud, new tools are available to help Internet merchants to detect and prevent fraudulent transactions. While some of these tools, such as the Address Verification System (AVS) and the Card Verification Values (CVV), have been available for years to *card-not-present* merchants in the telephone and mail order business, new methods have emerged to fully leverage the data richness of Internet orders. These fraud detection tools enable merchants to perform highly automated and

---

[4] For more information on securing your e-commerce site, see the Visa Account Information Security Program (www.visa.com/_gds_mod/fb/merchants/gds/) and MasterCard's Site Data Protection (www.sdp.mastercardintl.com/).

sophisticated screenings of incoming orders, flagging suspicious transactions while the order is being processed in real time.

While none of the tools and technologies can by itself eliminate fraud, each technique provides incremental value in terms of detection ability. Best practice implementations often utilize several, if not all of the tools discussed in this chapter.

Address Verification System

The Address Verification System (AVS) was the first security mechanism supported by credit card issuers for *card-not-present* transactions. AVS validates the billing address information provided by the consumer against the billing address information that the issuer has on record for the account. Specifically, AVS checks the postal code and typically only the numeric part of the street address, and returns a match/mismatch response. An AVS match is not required for a transaction to be approved by the issuer, nor is a transaction that obtained an AVS match response guaranteed against charge-backs. The decision on whether to accept an order based on the AVS response is completely left to the merchant.

Although the AVS response provides useful information for the merchant in determining the risk level of an order, it suffers from several limitations that make it a rather weak screening tool, particularly if used alone. First, AVS has a relatively high failure rate: typically, less than 60 per cent of transactions will obtain a full match on AVS. Second, the vast majority of orders that completely fail AVS are valid: over 98 per cent of the transactions with failure on both postal code and street address are legitimate. Furthermore, AVS only validates the billing address: criminals who obtain billing addresses can still pass the AVS check, and ship fraudulent orders to a different address. Finally, AVS is currently only supported by card issuers in the United States, the United Kingdom and some European countries.

In spite of these limitations, AVS provides some level of protection against a few of the most common account take-over schemes, specifically card generators and credit card skimmers.

Card Verification Value

The Card Verification Value (CVV) consists of a three or four-digit numeric code that is printed, but not embossed, on the back or the front of most recently issued credit cards.[5] The CVV code is also not recorded in the magnetic stripe of the card, which provides protection from skimmers. The merchant can request the consumer to provide this numeric code with the order and submit it with the authorization. The card processor will then validate the code supplied with the number on record for the specific card, and return a match/no-match response. As with AVS, the CVV response is only provided as additional information for the merchant, and a match will not protect the merchant from possible charge-backs on the transaction.

---

[5] The various card issuers use different names to indicate this security feature; CVV2 for VISA, CVC2 for Master Card and CID for American Express.

The purpose of CVV is to ensure that the person submitting the transaction is in possession of the actual card. CVV will not protect merchants from orders placed with actual cards that have been stolen. Furthermore, a criminal who had temporary possession of a card could, in principle, read and copy the CVV code. None the less, fraud rates on transactions with verified CVV codes are reportedly 80 per cent lower than those for non-CVV transactions.

Negative databases

Negative databases are a simple defensive method against repeat fraud offenders, which tend to be the norm, rather than the exception. By building a negative database of confirmed fraudulent orders, a merchant can attempt to link incoming orders to prior fraud. This is typically done by independently matching a number of order elements against the negative database, including credit card number, e-mail address, shipping address and telephone numbers. In some cases information like Internet Protocol (IP) address, postal code and full names can be used in conjunction to provide sufficient evidence that an incoming order might be linked to a known prior offender.

A 'positive database' can also be used to screen out orders originating from 'trusted' returning customers, which for some merchants may represent a significant percentage of incoming transactions. This is particularly easy to do for Web sites that allow customers to create a password-protected user account, which enables a relatively secure identification of previous customers.

Rule-based systems

Rule-based systems provide merchants with a way to leverage prior knowledge about fraud schemes and translate what they have learnt into an automated screening tool. The rule-based system evaluates rich order information, such as billing and shipping address, IP address, e-mail and, most importantly, details about the type and quantity of products being ordered to identify potentially high-risk transactions. For example, orders containing an unusual number of units of the same product, with a next-day delivery request to mail drop address, are quite likely to be fraudulent.

Effective rule-based systems enable business users to rapidly deploy and maintain a possibly large library of rules that are evaluated in real time, as an order is processed. When one or more of the rules 'fires' an order disposition, action is taken: the order is flagged for manual review and approval, or in some cases it is automatically declined.

A limitation of rule-based systems is that they can only help prevent fraud that exhibits certain known characteristics. As a result, rules must be carefully designed and constantly updated in order to track emerging fraud patterns.

Pattern detectors

Pattern detectors are screening filters designed to identify suspicious orders by analysing common attributes in a series of transactions. In many instances, an individual order may not have any of the traits that would indicate the possibility of fraud. By comparing multiple orders placed over a relatively short period of time, 'fraud patterns' can become evident. For example, some criminals now place many small orders, often under different credit cards, instead of one large order, which would be more easily detected by the merchant. Using a pattern detector, a merchant would be able to determine if these orders were placed under the same user account, same e-mail address, or telephone number.

More complex pattern detectors can be used to better pinpoint fraudulent orders while flagging fewer legitimate ones. For example, a detector based exclusively on 'high velocity' will have the tendency to flag not only fraudulent order sequences, but also the legitimate 'frequent buyers'. A pattern detector based on the occurrence of multiple credit card numbers with the same e-mail address, however, is definitively a much more specific indicator of potential fraud than the e-mail address alone.

Pattern detectors can be particularly useful as a defence against credit card number generators. When a generator is used to create and test cards, the merchant may observe a series of orders originating from the same IP address, the majority of which will fail authorization. If, however, the criminal is using a set of valid accounts, generated and tested at another site, then the pattern would be that of multiple orders on different valid cards that share the same initial set of numbers in the credit card account.

IP-based geo-location

The Internet Protocol, or IP, address of the consumer's Web browser can provide critical information for Internet fraud screening. IP geo-location technology can be used to identify, with reasonable accuracy, the originating country of the consumer's order. In most cases, this is the most critical piece of data a merchant needs to potentially identify fraud.

With the emergence of international fraud, in particular with fraud rings based in Nigeria, Ghana, Indonesia, Malaysia and Romania, IP geo-location has become a necessity for effective fraud screening. Often, orders placed by international criminals show little evidence of being destined for a foreign country. Both the billing and shipping addresses are typically legitimate addresses in the country where the merchant is operating. Only by 'reverse mapping' the IP address is the merchant able to identify orders that originate from high-risk countries or foreign-based fraud rings.

Risk scoring

Risk scoring systems combine several of the detection methods described above to produce an overall numerical score that indicates the likelihood of fraud for an individual transaction. The score is typically derived using some kind of statistical model that will weigh and add the effect of dozens of potential individual indicators of fraud. These models are calibrated, or 'trained', using thousands of examples of both legitimate and fraudulent orders to discriminate effectively between the two.

A variety of statistical modelling techniques can be used to build predictive scoring models. All these techniques have in common the ability to 'accumulate evidence' across multiple indicators and can be automatically calibrated on the basis of historical data. Neural network models have the advantage of being able to represent more complex interactions between indicators, and have been extensively and successfully used in credit card fraud detection.

Risk scoring can be based on generic 'industry models' or specialized custom models. Vendor-provided industry models are usually based on a data consortium that gathers data from a network of clients. These models have the benefit of leveraging data from multiple sources, but are also designed on the basis of fraud indicators that can apply across different businesses.

Emerging solutions: payer authentication

The majority of the fraud screening techniques described earlier are essentially based on 'behind the scenes' order verification. None of them answer, with certainty, whether the person on the other end is the legitimate cardholder.

A few years ago a standard called Secure Electronic Transactions (SET) was introduced as an authentication to address Internet fraud. SET required that both the merchant and the consumer have digital certificates in order to authenticate each other during the transaction. Unfortunately, the task of driving adoption of digital certificates on the consumer side was much more difficult than expected and the standard faltered. Indeed the challenge for every 'authentication' scheme for business-to-consumer transactions is to be acceptable to the consumer and have minimal interference during the critical final steps of a transaction 'checkout' process.

New payer authentication schemes are now merging, this time with the backing of leading credit card brands such as Visa and MasterCard, based on a common authentication standard called 3D-Secure. The recently launched Verified by Visa and MasterCard Secure Code programs use cardholder passwords to verify the consumer identity every time the card is used online at participating merchants. This mechanism is essentially similar to the PIN code used by millions of consumers at ATM machines.

The 3D-Secure scheme involves three participants: credit card issuers, merchants and credit card holders. Credit card issuers issue passwords to their card holders and support the authentication process. Merchants participating in the programs are required to install relatively inexpensive 'plug-in' software at their Web site to enable the authentication process. Finally, the card holders need to enrol their cards in the program with their issuing bank, and select a password to be used for online transactions.

If these programs are successful and gain widespread adoption from all parties involved, payer authentication schemes have the potential drastically to decrease fraud on the Internet. As for SET, however, the challenges are not related to the technology itself, but to the willingness of consumers to adopt the tool for making Internet transactions safer. While some merchants have shown resistance in introducing additional steps that may interfere with the checkout process, the majority of merchants appreciate the value of payer authentication and its potential for reducing fraud and making the Internet a safer place to transact for both businesses and consumers. Since these programs are both relatively new, the next 12 to 18 months will certainly provide some critical indication on whether 3D-Secure is posed to become the de facto standard for payment security over the Internet.

Conclusion

Today's best practice approach to fraud prevention is based on an arsenal of automated fraud screening techniques to maximize the efficiency of the order verification process. The first key point is that every fraud detection technique has its limitation; no tool can identify all types of fraud and every tool is best at identifying one particular type of fraud. Only by compounding the benefits of an array of tools can merchants effectively defend themselves from the threat of fraud.

The second key point is that fraud detection tools should be used for automated screening, but only in limited circumstances for automated decision making, for instance, rejecting orders. The reason is that every detection tool will inevitably flag legitimate transactions as suspicious, since fraudulent orders represent only a small percentage of the total. As the result, automatic rejection based on fraud screens is not a viable approach for most Internet merchants, since the risk of declining valid orders is unacceptably high and potentially more damaging than the risk due to fraud itself. Human review is required to make the final decision on whether an order should be accepted or rejected.

ClearCommerce is the leading provider of fraud prevention and payment processing solutions to merchants and service providers in the US and Europe. ClearCommerce software is used by 65,000 businesses worldwide, including customers such as Adobe, Apple Computer, Barclay's, Best Buy, e-bookers.com, HSBC, and Staples. ClearCommerce delivers the most accurate fraud prevention and most flexible electronic payment solutions for credit-card-not-present sales channels.

For more information contact Worldwide Headquarters, 11921 North MoPac, Suite 400, Austin, TX 78759, USA. Tel: 512–832–0132, Fax: 512–832–8901

European Office: Crown House, 136–139 High Street, Egham, Surrey, TW20 9HL, Tel :+44 (0)1784 430 200, Fax:+44 (0)1784 430 201

Online payments: key areas of exposure

Like any opportunity, online payment is a risk if it is not managed effectively. Security is a major part of the online payment process. WorldPay Ltd takes a brief look at some of the key areas of exposure for businesses that accept payments online and discusses how they can minimize their vulnerability.

Securing Internet payment

Retailers are experts in the business of retailing – rarely are they experts in the security of online financial transactions. Rather than build their own online payment systems, therefore, they often outsource these to a payment services provider (PSP) or a bank. A number of specialist processes can be offered by the PSP or bank to ensure that the payments made to the business are secure and that the business is protected from unnecessary exposure to risk. These are described below:

■ **Encryption – keeping card details safe**: this is the process by which the PSP or bank 'scrambles' card data submitted to the company's online shop, to ensure that it cannot be intercepted en route. Encryption is usually achieved through a technology called Secure Sockets Layer (SSL for short), which is now built into most Web browsers as standard (Microsoft Internet Explorer version 3.02 or higher and Netscape Navigator version 3.03 or higher).

When shoppers shop on a site protected by SSL, an unbroken padlock icon or a key symbol appears at the bottom of their screen and the beginning of the site's Web address changes from 'http' to 'https.'

Encryption is the absolute minimum requirement of any transactional Web site and it has been proven to be very effective in preventing data being intercepted en route. According to the Association of Payment and Clearing Services (APACS), fraudulent Internet transactions are almost exclusively the result of the card details being illegally 'skimmed' (copied using an electronic card reader) in a physical environment – the restaurant, the bar, the petrol station – and then used on the Internet thereafter.

■ **Card data invisibility**: some PSPs and banks can accept and process online payments on your business's behalf without at any time communicating the card details to that business; the only thing passed on to your business is the funds. The benefit of this approach is that your business does not need to expose itself to any risk of losing, incorrectly managing or compromising card data – the entire process is managed externally.

■ **Automated fraud detection**: some PSPs and banks can now offer automated fraud detection services as an integral part of their online payment platforms. These services use a number of methods to quickly identify fraudulent buying behaviours, alert the retailer, and prevent the transaction being processed.

■ **AVS and CVV**: your bank or PSP may also offer address verification (AVS) and cardholder verification (CVV, known in its latest form as CVV2) as integral elements of their payment services. AVS checks the card holder's name against the billing address to ensure that there is no mismatch. CVV2 is a three or four-digit number printed on the strip on the back of the card (it is sometimes also referred to as the security code) and cannot be copied by skimming. A card holder who is able to enter the correct CVV2 code is more likely to be in physical possession of the card and therefore less likely to have obtained the card data by skimming.

■ **Authentication**: the card holder's online 'signature': MasterCard and Visa, the world's biggest card companies, have both developed services (MasterCard SecureCode and Verified by Visa respectively) that use passwords to protect ('authenticate') card holders and their online transactions. Card holders are invited to type in their password, via a secure pop-up or similar, when they are buying online. This serves to prove that card holders are who they say they are, and prevents fraudulent use of the card.

In many ways, authentication is the online version of the high street 'Chip and PIN' scheme that will be rolled out in the United Kingdom in 2004/2005 – and it offers a similar degree of protection for both shopper and retailer.

Authentication means that:

■ Cardholders will benefit from the same level of security as when they use a cashpoint – eventually, there will be fewer and fewer online shops where card purchases can be made without the input of the password. Those that do not request the input of the password will lose credibility.

■ Retailers will suffer lower volumes of charge-backs. A charge-back is where a card holder's bank claims the cost of the transaction back from the retailer. This can be because of fraud (someone using someone else's card or card data to purchase goods without the card holder's authority – a problem that authentication, with its password system, addresses very effectively), or because the consumer has challenged the quality

Faster Growth

Sales on the internet have grown by 50% over each of the last two years and are expected to continue growing rapidly.*

Whatever the size and scale of your business today, big or small, WorldPay can enable you to accept payments over the internet as well as by phone, fax and mail. Credit and debit cards, direct-debit and standing-order style payments - even mobile payments. In any language and most currencies.

Part of the 5th biggest bank in the world, The Royal Bank of Scotland Group, we provide safe, secure and flexible payment solutions designed to help you make the most of the internet opportunity.

*Forrester Research

On the Internet

Find out more: call +44 (0)870 742 7001
or visit www.worldpay.com/iod

of the goods or services in some way. Charge-backs expose your business to significant financial risk, so any way of reducing their occurrence should be welcomed.

Data from MasterCard indicates that 'card holder non-authorization' charge-backs (the category into which fraudulent charge-backs fall) represent an increasingly large percentage of all e-commerce charge-back expenses – over 80 per cent in recent years. Visa believes that the use of online authentication will reduce the level of online fraud by as much as 50 per cent – or, in other words, online shopping is about to become twice as safe.[1]

Some PSPs and banks will offer authentication as a standard part of their service, although it will be some time before all card holders' banks support the scheme and all card holders are fully enrolled.

Other risk of fraud

The increasing level of security surrounding online payment has meant that fraudsters have now evolved other means of attempting to obtain sensitive financial information. Currently, a highly fashionable variant of this is the 'phishing expedition.' Here, a fraudster sets up a spoof Web site to look very much like yours and then tricks customers into entering their confidential card details and other confidential information (password, PIN) under a false pretext (such as implying that a recent order that the shopper has placed may not have been processed correctly). The fraudulently obtained data is then used to purchase goods on the Internet or to perpetrate identity theft.

The nature of this fraud is such that ordinarily only the largest retailers (or, more likely, banks) are targeted. Card holders are becoming far more aware of the dangers and are exercising greater protection of their confidential details, but phishing remains a risk nonetheless. It is good practice to reiterate to online customers that they should never divulge confidential card data in the circumstances described above (and, more importantly, that your business would never ask them to submit confidential information in this way).

Phishing activity does not cause the same liability to the retailer as conventional online card fraud does (see Authentication above) – the liability lies entirely with the card holder, who has failed to protect confidential card data. None the less, the spoof sites can be extremely convincing – often using graphics and logos copied from the genuine sites – and so it is easy to see how card holders can be duped.

Proving trustworthiness

Whilst online payment itself is relatively low-cost, creating an end-to-end e-commerce operation (including supply chain and logistics) can be a major investment. This leaves the business exposed to a considerable risk if the perceived trustworthiness of the site is not sufficient to attract the business necessary to amortize the investment.

Major brands have less of a problem in this respect, as their offline brand reputation tends to 'rub off' on their online brand. Smaller and less well-known businesses, however, often need an extra reputational 'shot in the arm'. Online shoppers are not always instinctively

---

[1] www.e-visa.com/security/main.asp

trusting; 30 million adults in the United Kingdom have accessed the Internet, but only 14 million of those – less than half – have actually shopped online.

Businesses should consider investing in a 'trustmark' to help address shopper trust issues. There are several schemes in existence but one of the most manageable and sensibly-priced is Internet Shopping is Safe (ISIS), which is run by IMRG Ltd, one of the e-commerce industry's most respected bodies. For the modest sum involved – at the time of writing, £125 +VAT for a year's listing – it is an accessible and affordable scheme that enables small businesses as well as large to create a collective commitment to honesty and trustworthiness to which online shoppers will attach considerable importance. More information is available at www.imrg.org/isis

In addition, businesses should also clearly display key information on their Web site in order to inspire trust, including:

∎ a complete description of the goods and services offered and details of any guarantee, membership or subscription period offered in the price;
∎ details of the returns/refund policy;
∎ details of the privacy policy – which data is collected, who this information is shared with and how shoppers can opt out;
∎ customer service contact, including e-mail address, phone number and address – so that shoppers can contact the firm directly when they have a query;
∎ delivery policy and prices.

Conclusion

∎ The Internet is a fantastic medium for delivering your company's products/services. Inevitably, there are risks, but if these are properly managed then taking payments online can be a real boost to your business's chances of success.
∎ Be aware that your customers' card details in particular, as well as their names, addresses and other contact details, are highly sensitive and confidential. By outsourcing the management of this data to a bank or PSP, you remove a potentially major technical and legislative headache.
∎ Anti-fraud technologies are constantly evolving in order to progressively reduce the risks to both card holder and merchant. These include Verified by Visa and MasterCard SecureCode, as well as other fraud screening services. All these services reduce the likelihood of the retailer losing significant sums of money by inadvertently sending goods to fraudsters and then suffering a charge-back. The best source of these services is the bank or PSP that handles the payment technology.
∎ Taking payments online is key to successful online trading, but so is trust. Make consumers feel confident that their online shopping experience is safe, and word of your reliability will spread.

WorldPay is the United Kingdom's largest PSP (payment services provider) and is part of the Royal Bank of Scotland Group. It provides payment services for thousands of clients across the world, ranging from sole traders to multinational corporations.

For further information contact WorldPay Ltd, 270–289 Science Park, Cambridge, CB4 0WE, United Kingdom. Tel: +44 (0) 870 742 7000, Fax: +44 (0) 870 742 7009

Web: www.worldpay.co.uk. E-mail: sales@worldpay.com

Spyware in the workplace

Keep an eye on your software, or it will keep an eye on you, writes Frank Coggrave, UK Regional Director for Websense.

Do you know what your company's computers are doing right now? Sure, they are being used to run your business. But what else are they up to behind your back? Are there any other programs running silently in the background, monitoring employee activity and sending confidential information about your company back to other organizations? Unbelievable though it may sound, there's a pretty good chance that this is indeed the case in your company.

According to a recent survey conducted by UK-based security consultancy PanSec, more than 90 per cent of all company PCs are infected with so-called 'spyware'. This is the term given to software that gets installed without the user's permission and which covertly gathers and transmits data about the usage of the machine. A report by IT market analysts The Aberdeen Group claims that there are more than 7,000 spyware programs in existence right now, running on millions of corporate and personal computers.

No computer that is linked to the Internet is immune. A spyware program is not technically a virus so most anti-virus scanners do not attempt to stop it. And spyware does not exploit bugs in Windows, so installing all the latest Microsoft security patches cannot prevent it either. Spyware gets into a PC by being bundled with legitimate products. If you download and install any of the best-known file sharing applications, for example, you have no choice but to accept the spyware that it also installs and through which the free services are often funded.

Once installed, spyware starts monitoring the way that the computer is used and feeding back the information to the Web site operators that sponsored the program's distribution. The site operators want to understand precisely how a visitor travels through their site, and which menu options he or she clicks on. They want to know which other sites are visited, for how long, at what time of day, and which types of adverts get clicked. They want to know which applications are installed on the victim's computer, and where he or she is based (which can be gathered from the user's e-mail address or the phone number programmed into the modem). The spyware distributors then use all this information to present your staff with adverts for products that they hope they are most likely to buy. And the database of usage statistics also gets sold to other marketing companies and spammers.

But does spyware really matter? What does it matter if everyone knows the intimate details of your staff's surfing or shopping habits? Not only is it an invasion of privacy, it can also be a security risk. Do you really want a collection of large marketing organizations to know everything your employees use the Internet for? For example, if staff are researching new products or sending e-mail to potential clients, is it really acceptable for details of such activity to be disclosed to all and sundry?

Poorly written spyware programs can, and often do, cause PC crashes and network slowdowns. Sending all this data back to the database also takes time and consumes network bandwidth, thus slowing down your Web surfing and e-mailing (and costing you money, if you're paying for network bandwidth according to total or peak usage).

And some spyware is particularly malicious. For example a Web site called Lover Spy will, for US $89, send an e-mail to five current or former partners inviting them to click on a Web page to read an online message about how much the sender still misses them. When the recipients install the free program necessary to display the card, it also plants spyware, which records all their keystrokes and passwords and e-mails them to the orderer. It even installs a remote control application allowing the orderer full access to the recipients' computers via the Internet.

Spyware can cost you serious money, too. In the United States recently, an investment broker lost US $40,000 after installing what he thought was a market analysis program but which turned out to be a transmitting his account log-in details to hackers.

Spyware is already a big problem worldwide. In Europe, one in three companies has detected spyware on its network. And the typical spyware program is prolific, typically transmitting 300 items of personal information, totalling some 1 MB of data, from each infected machine every day.

So which software includes spyware? Among the most prolific offenders are the file sharing and swapping sites such as Kazaa, which are used by millions of Internet users to exchange files such as music and videos. The Kazaa software also includes a number of spyware programs that monitor your use of the system and help the company present you with targeted advertising in order to finance the free service.

At present, the legal situation regarding installing spyware without the computer user's permission is a grey area. There is, though, a move afoot in the United States to force software authors to declare up-front if installing their program will also install spyware. Many programs do already do this, but the details are buried in the small print of a long, complicated online licence agreement that most people agree to with a single click and without bothering to read.

How Websense protects against spyware

Websense products provide organizations with preventive measures that automate enforcement of Internet access and software usage policies at the gateway, the network and the desktop, creating a multi-layered solution that complements the existing network security infrastructure. At the desktop, the Websense CPM module finds and stops all spyware and keystroke piracy applications from launching on employees' machines, whether online or offline, enabling organizations to effectively manage employee computer use while mitigating security risks and improving IT resource management. In addition, Websense CPM can easily be installed and managed on all network desktops with a single mouse click directly from the Websense central management console, unlike other security solutions in which IT administrators must manually configure the application on each individual computer.

At the Internet gateway, Websense Enterprise Premium Group III (PG III) database stops these applications in their tracks by preventing back-channel communication to third parties. Through proprietary processes and the company's patent-pending WebCatcher™ technology – by which uncategorized Web sites accessed by employees are anonymously sent back to Websense for categorization and added to the master database – Websense software is able to identify spyware and keystroke piracy servers and block employees from unknowingly sending data to them via back-channel port 80 connections.

Most companies leave port 80 open to handle normal HTTP traffic, allowing keystroke pirates to use the same port. Websense Enterprise PG III blocks these programs from sending potentially sensitive and confidential data back to their host servers. Sites infected with spyware and keystroke piracy applications are added to the Websense PG III database and downloaded daily. Websense continues to block these malignant sources as long as they remain a threat. Once the site is no longer infected, Websense removes the URL from the PG III database for the next day's download.

In addition to preventing the dissemination of valuable corporate data, Websense Enterprise reporting options allow organizations to identify the presence of keystroke piracy applications and other malicious activities on the network. Websense offers free, fully functional 30-day evaluations of both its complete EIM solution and the individual components that allow users to manage and control Websense from separate servers, available at http://www.websense.com/downloads/

If you're worried about spyware on your PCs, here are our top tips for dealing with the problem

■ Software authors often go to considerable lengths to hide the fact that their products include spyware, so it may not be immediately obvious whether there's any on your PC. Check the small print of the licence agreement before installing any freeware or shareware.

■ Get into the habit of uninstalling any software that you do not regularly use.

■ Some of the most common spyware applications include Gator (also known as GAIN), BonziBUDDY and Comet Cursor, each of which is included with many freeware and shareware products. If these products are mentioned within any of the programs you use, your computer is probably infected with at least one spyware tool.

■ Spyware programs are not viruses; so installing anti-virus software does not fully protect you from spyware.

■ Many spyware programs communicate through the same Internet port (80) as general Web traffic, thus making it very difficult to block data transmission using a firewall.

- Check out the privacy policy on the Web sites of the software you use, to find out what they use the collected information for.
- If you are responsible for IT in a corporate environment, seriously consider the use of products such as Websense Enterprise (www.websense.com), which automatically prevents users from downloading and installing programs containing spyware. It will also ensure that any spyware application already installed on the user's PC is unable to run, and thus stops it from transmitting confidential information.

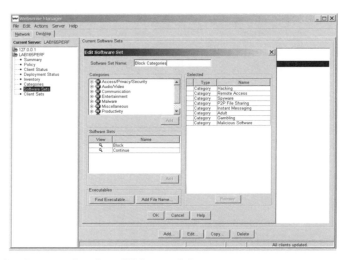

Figure 2.9.1   A screenshot from Websense Manager

Websense Inc is the world's leading provider of employee Internet management (EIM) solutions. Websense Enterprise software enables organizations to manage how their employees use their computing resources, including Internet access, desktop applications and network bandwidth. These solutions help improve productivity, security, conserve information technology resources, and mitigate legal liability for organizations. Implemented by more than 19,400 organizations worldwide and preferred by the FTSE 100 and Fortune 500 companies, Websense Enterprise delivers a comprehensive software solution that analyses, manages and reports on employee Internet access, network security and desktop application usage. Websense Enterprise also helps organizations mitigate the problems caused by new emerging Internet threats, such as spyware, malicious mobile code and peer-to-peer file sharing.

To find out more, visit www.websense.com where you can download a fully functional 30-day trial of Websense Enterprise.

3

Software protection

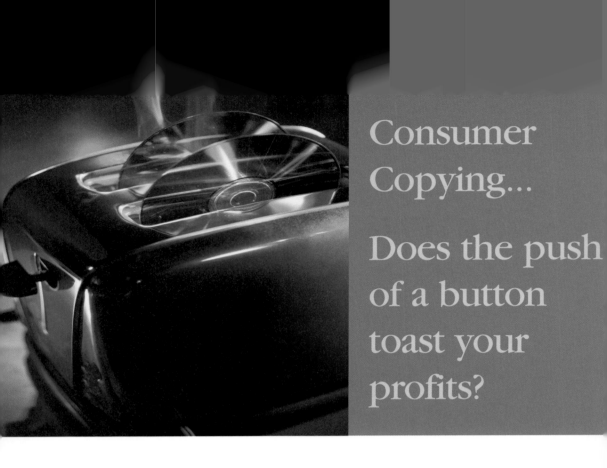

Consumer Copying...

Does the push of a button toast your profits?

It's not just piracy and peer-to-peer copying that costs rights owners millions of pounds and threatens the future value of catalogue releases and pay-per-view revenues.

In a recent analysis of home copying, over 12% of U.K. consumers admitted to copying or trying to copy video-cassettes and DVDs in the past year.

The same study concluded that 80% of consumers who currently owned a DVD recorder had tried to make Pirate copies of DVDs at home. Domestic DVD Recorders look set to increase in sales by over 2000% over the next 4 years.

Macrovision's technology is the only universally implemented copy protection that disables digital recordings to removable media such as DVD-R and D-VHS. When our technology is applied to an original DVD, none of the currently available DVD recorders allow the content to be be copied.

Give your content the protection it deserves. Don't let copying losses outweigh profits. Macrovision can turn that equation around.

A simple call could be worth a lot!

Call us on +44 (0) 870 871 1111 or email us at iodvideo@macrovision.co.uk

Source: Consumer Research Among Home Copiers in the UK – Understanding & Solutions, September 2002

macrovision™

Our business protects your business

www.macrovision.com

Macrovision UK Ltd. Malvern House, 14/18 Bell Street, Maidenhead, Berkshire. SL6 1BR
Tel: +44 (0) 870 871 1111   Fax: +44 (0) 870 871 1161

Intrusion detection

Just because a company does not have a Web site does not mean it is not vulnerable to intruders, writes Arnt W K Brox, of Telenor ASA.

Intrusion detection has become big business on the Internet and, to be honest, it is not surprising. With the profusion of e-commerce Web sites, online banking and other high profile applications, it is understandable that organizations should want to avail themselves of the best possible protection against unauthorized entry. After all, organizations take seriously the threat of physical intrusion, by fitting access control and CCTV devices and employing security guards, so why not take equally seriously the threat of computer intrusion?

But the threat of network intrusion is much wider than those heavily publicized incidents of Web site defacement would have us believe. In fact, it would be a misnomer to imply that this is just an Internet-only problem. In reality, the threat of network intrusion hangs over any organization that possesses a network that is open to the outside world. And, in taking this statement on board, we open up the true dangers inherent in virtually every Internet protocol network. And this, by definition, is virtually every computer network today – used for everything from process industry control to Internet banking and office automation.

Because the byword of every modern organization is connectivity, even those companies that have no direct Internet presence remain vulnerable to hacker attack and intrusion. Just because you do not have a Web site, or equally, because your site does not feature any e-commerce capabilities, does not make you immune to the possibility of someone gaining unauthorized access to your network. Just think about it for a moment. Most organizations running a network have the capability to allow members of staff and even outside contractors to connect to their systems remotely. This makes it easier for workers to connect from home, or while on the move. It also renders the network susceptible to unauthorized entry by third parties.

And there's the rub. Our modern work practices make it essential that we provide a reasonable degree of external connectivity to our networks, regardless of whether we are a bank or financial institution, or even an e-commerce site with sensitive customer data just waiting to be exposed. The fact is, therefore, that virtually every organization running anything other than a perfectly closed loop network is leaving itself open to possible intruder attack.

So what is the answer? One of the most prevalent solutions is the installation of a sophisticated firewall system. Undoubtedly, this can help 'hide' major parts of your system from unwanted attention. But, the problem remains that we still need to provide external connectivity, data communications, Internet access and maybe even voiceover IP for the organization. Inevitably, this means that the firewall will need to be configured to allow access to, and dissemination of, data and information retained within the organization. And all this creates a major problem, because it means that the firewall cannot be used simply to pull the shutters down and isolate the network from the outside world. So the need to communicate brings us the necessity to search for a second line of defence.

This is where intrusion detection comes into the equation. However, because there is no universally adopted definition of what it actually is, it is probably easier to describe the whole concept by reference to more familiar analogies. Think of it as a well-trained guard dog, and you will get the general idea. Now imagine that the rooms in your home represent your network, and the perimeter fence represents your firewall. You need to gain access to the outside world, and equally, authorized guests, visitors and invitees need to gain access to your property. After all, how else would you receive your post, your groceries and have your gas and electricity meters read?

Being the prudent householder, you will realize that there is a distinct possibility that some visitors onto your premises may not be welcome. Now because you have a gate to allow you to mingle with the outside world, and vice versa, this leaves you vulnerable to the attentions of these undesirable individuals – the network equivalent of double glazing salespersons and even worse, burglars. And this is where your trusty guard dog makes its presence heard.

Because your guard dog has been trained to sniff out unwanted guests, it sounds a warning whenever it detects the presence of any unauthorized third party coming through the gate. And this is the basis of intrusion detection. Just as firewalls need open gates in them to enable communication, intrusion detection sits either behind the firewall to warn of unauthorized entry into the network, or in front of the firewall to see who is approaching the gate. However, as you can imagine, not all guard dogs are perfectly trained. Some will happily bark at anything or anyone that approaches your gate, and others will sit down and wait to be patted as the burglar walks past and strolls into your lounge.

So we have a problem. While there are many intrusion detection solutions on the market, some are more efficient than others in the elimination of what we term 'false positives', as well as in the correct identification of unauthorized traffic.

Most intrusion detection systems (IDS) are what are known as signature-based. This means that they operate in much the same way as a virus scanner, by searching for a known identity – or signature – for each specific intrusion event. While signature-based IDS is very efficient at sniffing out known styles of attack it does, like anti-virus software, depend on receiving regular signature updates, to keep in touch with variations in hacker technique. In other words, signature-based IDS is only as good as its database of stored signatures. It is a bit like training our guard dog to watch the front door, but forgetting to tell it to watch the back of the house as well.

Because signature-based IDS can only ever be as good as the extent of the signature database, two further problems immediately arise. First, it becomes all too easy to fool signature-based solutions by changing and obfuscating the ways in which an attack is made. This technique simply skirts around the signature database stored in the IDS, giving the hacker an ideal opportunity to gain access to the network.

Second, the more advanced the signature database, the higher the CPU load for the system charged with analysing each signature. Inevitably, this means that beyond the maximum bandwidth packets may be dropped. So feeds may have to be split and then recombined after analysis, significantly impacting complexity and cost. In addition, it means that the greater the number of signatures searched for, the correspondingly higher the probability of identifying more false positives, especially on smaller and simpler signatures.

Make no mistake, hackers enjoy a challenge, and like to test their software and skills against many of the commercially available IDSs on the market. Because an attacker knows that the IDS will trigger an alarm when it detects certain attack signatures, that hacker will tend to evade the IDS by disguising the attack. For example, hackers are aware that signature-based IDS traditionally has a problem with the complexities of application interactions. This is compounded by the fact that application protocols have become increasingly complex as they expand to provide support for features like Unicode.

Briefly, Unicode allows uniform computer representation of every character in every language, by providing a unique code point or identifier for each character. Unicode is a standard requirement of well-known computer languages such as Java and XML, making it a feature of many modern operating systems. Because signature-based IDS can miss characters written in Unicode Transformation Format, it becomes relatively easy for an attacker to submit a URL containing an exploit that would allow other programmes to be run and files accessed on the host computer.

Of course, this is only symptomatic of a wider issue. Because of the hackers' tendency to continually test and probe, it is only a matter of time before they discover a way around even the most sophisticated signature-based intrusion detection systems. The fact that many signature-based IDS vendors recommend that their customers update their signature databases over the Internet only serves to make matters worse. In fact, this gives any hacker that has the ability to sniff your network connection the perfect opportunity to identify that you are using IDS, and even to ascertain what type it is.

Because of these known problems, signature-based IDS is really only suitable for very basic protection. For any organization wanting to implement a more thorough – and hence safer – solution, I would advocate the use of what we call anomaly-based IDS. By its nature, anomaly-based IDS is a rather more complex creature. In fact, to use our earlier analogy, it is like our guard dog personally interviewing everyone at the gate before he or she is let down the drive. In network traffic terms, it captures all the headers of the IP packets running towards the network. From this, it filters out all known and legal traffic, including Web traffic to the organization's Web server, mail traffic to and from its mail server, outgoing Web traffic from company employees and DNS traffic to and from its DNS server.

Even though this level of filtering significantly narrows down the amount of data to be analysed, anomaly-based IDS can still create large amounts of log data. This is then analysed using database functionality. However, because anomaly IDS sees all the traffic running into the network, there are far fewer places to hide malicious hacker code.

There are other equally obvious advantages to using anomaly-based IDS. For example, because it detects any traffic that is new or unusual, the anomaly method is particularly good at identifying sweeps and probes towards network hardware. It can therefore give early warnings of potential intrusions, because probes and scans are the predecessors of all attacks. And the more targeted the probes and scans, the more likely that the hacker is serious about attacking your network. Equally, the technique is ideal for detecting every new piece of hardware installed on the network. This applies equally to any new service installed on any item of hardware – for example, Telnet deployed on a network router for maintenance purposes – and forgotten about when the maintenance was finished. This makes anomaly-based IDS perfect for detecting anything from port anomalies and Web anomalies to mis-formed attacks, where the URL is deliberately mis-typed.

Some Internet security commentators argue that effective anomaly testing is not possible. They claim that, because the technique requires trained human resources as well as sophisticated hardware and software, the procedures involved simply are not viable. Admittedly, anomaly testing requires more hardware spread further across the network than is required with signature-based IDS. This is especially true for larger networks, and with high bandwidth connections it is therefore necessary to install the anomaly sensors closer to the servers and network that are being monitored. The rationale here is that the amount of data is lessened the closer the sensors are to the application, compared with if they were located close to or at the network backbone. Placing them too close to the main backbone simply results in too much data being detected.

However, none of this detracts from the fact that anomaly testing is a more effective way of detecting possible attacks. In fact, most of the operational criticisms levelled against anomaly-based IDS are equally applicable to signature-based testing. Both methods require tuning, to reduce the numbers of false alerts. This is especially important as the temptation to tune a system too tightly can often cause loss of some of the events of interest that we are hoping to detect. While anomaly-based IDS requires regular updates of the legal traffic definition files, signature-based IDS needs equally frequent updates of the signature database, together with tuning of variables.

Having said that, it is true to say that anomaly-based detection certainly is not the straight-from-the-box solution that signature testing purports to be. Ideally, anomaly testing criteria and parameters need to be configured in conjunction with the organization's own engineers – that is, with the input of IP services and the corresponding network addresses (computers with the IP services exposed to the network they are connected to). Once properly installed, any anomalies detected need to be analysed by trained human operatives. Some may argue that this makes an anomaly-based solution much more of a 'hands on' service than signature IDS. But, looking at the amount of labour involved in nursing a normal signature-based IDS, I would argue that this is not the case.

All this makes anomaly testing much more capable of correctly identifying the basis of a hacker attack than straightforward signature-based techniques. What this does not do, however, is explain what can be done once hacker activity has been detected. Again, this is where anomaly-testing IDS wins, because trained personnel can use a number of analysis techniques to provide customized queries and reports for both technical and administrative staff.

Even the largest enterprises frequently lack the necessary experience for analysing signature and especially anomaly-based IDS. This type of security monitoring often requires a connection to a Security Operation Centre. So, because IDS can only operate as a process, these IP Security centres of excellence have a constant eye towards to the Internet for new and emerging types of attacks. In fact, returning to our analogy, the guard dog has to be retrained constantly, as visitors to the gate may carry different packages or simply dress differently to avoid detection.

All in all, therefore, although the argument goes that some protection is better than none, signature-based IDS really only scratches the surface of what most organizations need to protect against. Because it relies on spotting a duplication of events or types of attack that have happened before, it is rather like leaving your guard dog in the kennel with the door closed. Anomaly testing, on the other hand, requires trained and skilled personnel, but then so does signature-based IDS. And anomaly testing methods can certainly be guaranteed to provide far more effective protection against hacker incidents. It also means that, because of the involvement of the human element, there is a valuable additional tier of defence between your organization and the evils of the outside world.

On 1 September 2003 Proseq was acquired by Telenor ASA, and it is now integrated in Telenor's Internet and Communications department. We still provide the same services as we did before, but they are not a part of Telenor's portfolio under the security banner.

For more information contact Telenor Norway, Snarøyveien 30, 1331 Fornebu, Norway. Switchboard: +47 810 77 000 /+47 678 90 000 Web: www.telenor.no

Contact for security services: Arnt Brox, Product Marketing Manager, tel. +47 911 62 765, e-mail arnt.brox@telenor.com

Firewalls

Firewalls are simply a way of securing your businesses network just as you would secure your home, writes Mark Rogers from More Solutions.

The analogy

I live in a modest house in a normal street. My home has a front door, secured with a Yale lock, and back doors and several windows, all of which can also be locked. It also has a fenced garden with a locked gate. While at home I can see more or less unimpeded through my windows, although passers-by cannot easily see in through the net curtains. My girl-friend and a few family members have keys to the house, and know the code to my alarm. Other than that I have few visitors, including the postal worker who leaves me a never-ending stream of bills and junk mail, and the newspaper deliverer who drops a free local paper through my door once a week. I also have a gardener who visits once a week, and my windows are cleaned every month or so.

I am reasonably happy about this level of security, although I am well aware that there are shortcomings and should anyone have a deep desire to get into my house they will do so.

If I were a computer then I could achieve most of this in virtual terms with a *firewall*.

What is a firewall?

You probably do not care about the security of my house, but if your office network is connected to the Internet you certainly *do* worry that you do not really know who can get in or what they could do if they did. You have probably heard of firewalls, but you do not have time to take a technology degree to work out whether you need one, so let us look again at the analogy.

Your office is your house and garden, and your firewall is what controls the boundary between this and the rest of the world. Striking a balance between security and convenience has many similarities between the two, but worryingly many organizations provide access to their network in ways that would seem cavalier in home security.

Some basics

In theory, at least, my house is secure to anyone who does not have a key. In practice, complete security could not even be guaranteed in a house with no windows or doors (the equivalent of an office network not connected to the Internet). However, while I know that every door or window makes intrusion much simpler, I live in a real world where the benefits in having access to the outside world from my house outweigh the risks, provided that I take reasonable steps to manage those risks.

My front door Yale lock is good at stopping people getting in, and at the same time allows anyone inside to get out without a key. This is similar to many basic network configurations, where access to everything on the Internet is allowed to those on the network, with nobody on the Internet allowed access to the office. This may or may not actually be desirable; if I had small children I would be keen to ensure they could not just leave the house when they felt like it, and similarly there may be certain people who you wish to prevent accessing certain services on the Internet (maybe a blanket ban for some people, or Web browsing but no downloading of movies and games by others). This is a decision based more on personnel management than security, though, and we will return to this later.

In firewall terms, it is common to allow access to the outside world for specific purposes. This is done by applying criteria which must be met in order for access to be allowed, and at a basic level relates to IP addresses and TCP ports. Using a different analogy for a moment, IP addresses are like telephone numbers and TCP ports are like extension numbers; to ring me you need to know both my telephone number and my extension, as without the former you cannot make the call and without the latter our receptionist will not put you through. IP addresses are simply the addressing system used on the Internet, and allowing access to specific addresses is a bit like giving access to certain people.

Returning to the original analogy, appropriately enough the comparison here is between my postal mail and business e-mail. The standard TCP port for incoming e-mail is port 25, and 'opening port 25' on the firewall is the equivalent of having a letterbox on my front door. Unfortunately, it does nothing at this level to ensure that what comes through the port is genuine and wanted e-mail, and this is why firewalls are almost useless at preventing e-mail-borne viruses unless they prevent e-mail altogether. Some firewalls are 'stateful' – that is they do more than just open the letterbox but also check that what comes in them is mail (preventing newspapers or less savoury items passing through), but even then this does nothing to ensure that the mail you receive is mail you want.

Outward bound

Even basic firewalls are able to decide what to do based on the direction data is flowing, and more importantly, which side of the firewall initiated the connection. For example, browsing the Web is clearly bi-directional; your browser 'uploads' the address of the page you want to view, and the graphics and text of the Web page are then 'downloaded' back to the browser for display. Since the connection was initiated by your browser, inside your protected network, it is often safe to assume that data coming in through a connection initiated within the network can be allowed in, unchecked.

On the other hand, if an external device tries to access your computer without a request from you, then the firewall can inhibit the attempted access as being unwanted (most office networks do not usually need to allow any incoming connections at all). This results in a very simple configuration where all un-initiated incoming access is inhibited. However, in practice, this is over-simplistic for all but the smallest networks.

The data transfer capacity ('bandwidth') of the connection between your network and the Internet is finite, and some users can consume disproportionate amounts of this capacity. For example, 'peer-to-peer' (or P2P) protocols allow users to share files with others elsewhere on the Internet with little control or accountability. As well as consuming resources these protocols also allow – even encourage – sharing of copyrighted materials such as film and music files. A firewall, blocking outbound access to the ports used by these protocols, can be an invaluable (if not foolproof) weapon to prevent such abuse. Additionally, many e-mail-borne viruses contain software that, when triggered, makes outgoing connections to pass on passwords or allow external control of the infected PC, so leaving most outbound ports closed brings a degree of protection.

In summary, by acting at the boundary between your network and the Internet a basic firewall can restrict access to certain types of internally initiated connection (such as e-mail and the Web).

What a firewall looks like

Conceptually all firewalls can be seen as a black box with two network ports. One is connected to your local network, the other to the Internet, and their sole job is to monitor and limit the data flowing from one to the other.

There are many firewall vendors such as Cisco, Watchguard and Nokia, each with a range of hardware options to suit a range of medium to large budgets, although comparing the options is beyond the scope of this article.

Also worth considering are the increasing number of PC-based firewalls, often based around the free Linux operating system. All worthwhile firewalls of this type require a dedicated PC (that is they do not run alongside other applications on the same hardware) since any additional software is a potential weak point. These packages (for instance, IPCop and Smoothwall) are ideal for lower budgets since they typically cost little if anything above the cost of a basic PC and provide more than adequate protection for many enterprises.

Some enterprises have areas of their network that need to provide services to the outside world, and therefore need different firewall rules from the network core. Recalling our analogy, this is akin to my garden – an area where security is reduced to allow access to the gardener and window cleaner, but with additional security maintained between the garden and the house. In firewall terminology this is often called a 'demilitarized zone' (DMZ), and it is achieved by having two firewalls, one between the outside world and the DMZ, and another with tighter controls between the DMZ and the core. Some firewall hardware combines these two (or more firewalls) in one box with separate network ports for separate zones.

The weakest link

Securing a network almost always makes life a little more difficult because it restricts the things you can do or the ease with which you can do them. We accept this with home security of course; many a time I have returned home in the rain and wished I did not have to stand out in the cold, fumbling for my keys, but however frustrating it is I would not just leave the house unlocked instead.

If firewalls have weak spots it is usually because humans, who create holes to make life easier without proper regard for their consequences, manage them. They are often a temporary measure 'just to get this working', and temporary fixes frequently become permanent. For example, it is possible to set up secure 'tunnels' into and between networks (for instance, to allow network access to home workers or travelling salespeople). These Virtual Private Networks (VPNs) are efficient and secure methods of allowing external access in a controlled fashion, but they can be complicated to set up compared with just opening a few ports for remote access using remote control software, so the simpler (and less secure) approach gets chosen, offering a relatively easy approach for hackers.

Therefore, an essential part of any security configuration is a routine audit of holes in your firewall. It is a minor task to run a basic scan across the ports of your firewall (from outside your network) to see if any are open, and this should be done regularly (and weaknesses corrected), as it will almost certainly be scanned (and weaknesses exploited) by someone else if you do not. Companies such as ESoft provide subscription services (www.securityspace.com) that can run these scans automatically.

Summary

Conceptually, a firewall is a very simple product that does a very simple job. In practice, the job it does is difficult to achieve, and as attacks get more sophisticated so too must the firewalls; however this is a job for the people who build firewalls, not for those who deploy them.

It is the nature of the job that firewalls do, that results in them being surrounded by jargon and acronyms. If they seemed complicated as a result, hopefully they seem less daunting now.

Now, where did I put my keys?

Mark Rogers is a senior developer at More Solutions Ltd, a company dedicated to designing and deploying software solutions for industry that use the Internet as a communications medium. With many applications involving stand-alone, unattended equipment installed miles from the nearest IT department, security and reliability are essential aspects of their business.

For further information contact More Solutions Ltd, 6 Belgic Square, Fengate, Peterborough, PE1 5XF, Tel: 0845 45 89 555, E-mail: mark@more-solutions.co.uk, Web: www.more-solutions.co.uk

Viruses

While most people are aware of the dangers a virus can present to business, Mark Rogers from More Solutions says that as long as some common-sense principles are applied, any danger can be lessened substantially.

You could be forgiven for thinking that computers are getting more like their owners every year. Few could doubt that they seem to be getting cleverer, and unfortunately, most people are aware that they can also catch the computer equivalent of the common cold. However, while we all know that computer viruses exist, many of us lack knowledge of what they actually are, how they spread, and how to prevent or (if necessary) cure them.

Of course a computer virus is just a piece of software. Gardeners define weeds simply as plants growing in the wrong place, and computer viruses are similar, working like the applications you use every day, but doing things you did not want done. Usually it is simply their presence that is the problem, and the fact that they spread almost uncontrollably using resources not meant for them. Less often, but usually more worryingly, their impact can be more destructive.

Computer viruses are not a new phenomenon, although their methods of propagation have evolved dramatically since Internet use has become widespread. For a virus to jump from one computer to another has always required a transport mechanism, and while the floppy disk was effective a few years ago, the availability of direct connections between computers (with local networks, or LANs), and between those networks (the Internet) has simplified that transport dramatically. Furthermore, the increased power and functionality of computers has made it possible for viruses to do things they could never have done before.

Anti-virus software

Ironically, the increased power of computers and the connections between them is also the biggest weapon in our defence against viruses. We can run anti-virus programs that transparently check every e-mail we receive and every program we run for viruses, without the computing overhead being noticeable. Furthermore, we can keep ahead of virus outbreaks (or, more accurately, no more than one step behind them) by keeping our anti-virus software up to date, again transparently, using the Internet to download updates every few days. Updating your anti-virus software regularly is almost as important as installing the software in the first place.

Anti-virus software is therefore one of the most effective steps every business can (indeed must) take to protect itself from damage. The computer equivalent of immunization will keep most viruses at bay. It is remarkable that many of the viruses still being encountered today were first released months if not years ago, suggesting that many businesses still do not run up-to-date anti-viral software on their networks. However, just as in humans, viruses mutate and new ones are developed (thus being unrecognizable to the software sent to catch them, at least until their updates have arrived). Unfortunately a reliance on software protection alone is at best insufficient, and at worst brings a dangerous false sense of security.

Other measures

Viruses, and their cousins 'Trojans' and 'worms', rely for their spread on certain behaviours of their computer host, its operator, or both. Keeping the computer's operating system and its applications updated ('patched') with security updates can go a long way to limiting the ability of the computer to be an unwitting party to the viral spread.[1]

The operators are a much bigger challenge. Trust is the biggest problem – most people trust (or even fear) their computer in situations they should not. Here are some common approaches designed to trick the unwary operator, all primarily delivered by e-mail:

- Looking like a joke, funny movie clip, screen saver, or similar.
- Appearing to have come from someone you know. (Very often viruses do actually come from people you know, as they often spread by working through address books, so trusting the source cannot be confused with trusting what he or she appears to have sent you.)
- Appearing to have come from some other trusted source, such as Microsoft. A recent trend has been to send fake security patches, cleverly using Microsoft's corporate images and style of presentation in the e-mail to make it look official. Sometimes the sender's e-mail address will give this away, but often this too is 'spoofed' to look like it came from Microsoft.

---

[1] It is unfortunate that updates offered by software publishers could themselves contain weaknesses that are worse than those they seek to fix, particularly when the update is not security-related and perhaps fixes a bug that your organization has not been affected by. Our view is that for a small organization, installing all 'critical updates' is both essential and sufficient; however larger organizations with competent IT departments should assess the individual updates more thoroughly.

Most of these approaches are properly called Trojans, as they are not infectious unless the attached program is run by the recipient, but this is encouraged by their pretending to be something they are not, as with the legendary wooden 'gift' horse of Troy. When activated they deliver some kind of payload, which increasingly includes 'spyware' which monitors your activity on the PC and attempts to collect passwords and credit card details to forward to someone else for their gain (and, inevitably, your loss). They then attempt to send copies of themselves to every e-mail address they can find on your system, by searching your address books and other sources on your PC.

Since it is important to the success of the Trojan that it is not recognized by its recipient, several increasingly ingenious methods of disguise are used. As well as collecting e-mail addresses from your PC, other details such as typical e-mail subjects can be collected and used to make the recipients of the resulting e-mail look more like it really did come from you. At least one even took the step of forwarding a random document from the PC with the e-mail, which could result in sensitive information being leaked to competitors or customers alike.

Potential damage

The biggest concern that many people have is that a virus could damage their PC in some way. In truth, physical damage is pretty much impossible, although formatting the computer's hard disk and deleting all the important data can be pretty devastating to both the individual and the organization he or she works for. As well as taking steps to avoid virus infection and thus avoid this potential damage, it is important that important data be backed up regularly so that its loss is much less significant.

The damage to a reputation that can be caused by sending confidential documents to the wrong people, or the damage to trust and respectability from just propagating a benign virus, are more serious threats to a computer literate business. This, combined with the costs of downtime assessing damage and restoring back-ups, are the real reasons why prevention is much better than cure.

Virus hoaxes

No introduction to computer viruses would be complete without mentioning hoax viruses. Since we have established that the biggest potential threat from a real virus can be to an organization's reputation, it can be true that hoax viruses have the potential to cause real damage to a business despite their false basis.

Hoax viruses usually take the form of an e-mail warning about something that is not a real threat. If they are believed, as they often are, they get forwarded by well-meaning recipients to all their colleagues and friends, often spreading as far if not further than a real virus might.

Some example hoaxes include:

■ Simple lies, detailing serious but non-existent (and often technically implausible) threats. Probably the best known is the 'Good Times' virus hoax, which has been doing the rounds for many years now.
■ Hoax warnings about legitimate programs. A good example is slfnbk.exe, a benign program on most Windows PCs that most people do not use and would not be aware of.

The hoax warns of a serious and potentially damaging virus, and describes how this file is a sign of an infection. People follow the instructions to find that the file is indeed there, and delete it, glad that they caught it in time (and then forwarding the hoax on). If the hoax refers to a program that is genuinely important to the system operation the hoax can cause as much damage as a real virus.

Since these are not real viruses, they are not 'detected' by anti-virus programs. The hoaxes often play on this, describing how the threat is so new that most anti-virus programs will not detect it, thus adding to the urgency with which the hoax gets forwarded.

The 'cure' for hoaxes is remarkably simple, but few people think to use it. Typing a few key words from the hoax (such as 'slfnbk' in the example above) into an Internet search engine such as Google will quickly show plenty of references to the hoax. In any case, anti-virus software writers do not send random warnings around by e-mail, any more than organizations like Microsoft send security update patches out by e-mail. A cool head and a quick check can be the best antidote to many threats.

Many non-virus hoaxes also exist, which can be just as damaging to reputations if forwarded without at least basic checks of their validity. Many claim something to the effect that 'for every person you send this e-mail to, <insert large corporation here> will donate <sum of money> to <very worth cause>'.

Summary

■ Computer viruses can be pervasive and damaging, but most serious problems are easily avoided with preventative action. Up to date anti-virus software and common sense are essential in equal parts.
■ Many viruses do so little that a first scan for viruses can throw up several (even hundreds) which have lain dormant and unnoticed for years, and a panic response will usually do far more harm than the virus itself.
■ However, the most important lesson to learn is that while actual damage to data is a tangible but relatively small risk, the real danger from viruses is the damage they cause to reputations, and this more than anything else is why they cannot be ignored.

Mark Rogers is a senior developer at More Solutions Ltd, a company dedicated to designing and deploying software solutions for industries using the Internet as a communications medium. With many applications involving stand-alone, unattended equipment installed miles from the nearest IT department, security and reliability are essential aspects of their business.

For further information contact More Solutions Ltd, 6 Belgic Square, Fengate, Peterborough, PE1 5XF, Tel: 0845 45 89 555, E-mail: mark@more-solutions.co.uk, Web: www.more-solutions.co.uk

Authentication and encryption

Louisa McCabe of TrustAssured looks in detail at the benefits of authentication and encryption.

As business processes become increasingly computerized and companies use the Internet to work more closely with trading partners, they face new threats to their operations. Authentication and encryption can help your company deal with some of these issues:

- **Theft of proprietary data**: which gives your business competitive advantage – encrypting critical data when stored and in transit, so that only certain users can access it easily, prevents casual theft of proprietary data and makes it much more likely professional attempts to steal proprietary information will fail.
- **Identity theft**: robust authentication processes based on encryption make it harder for malicious individuals to fake identities that fool systems into giving them access, or to borrow the identities of real users.
- **Non-repudiation of transactions**: even if someone has legitimate access to your systems, you want to exercise control over their actions from a business perspective. For your own staff, that means ensuring they do not enter into contracts your company cannot (or should not) fulfil, while you want to be sure that trading partners cannot subsequently deny they placed orders or agreed specific terms. Encryption-based identities can be used to sign electronic documents and transactions, with the same legal status as a signature on a paper document, and to create an audit trail that provides evidence in the event of a dispute.

However, encryption and authentication-based services can be more than a defensive response to new threats. They enable you to change the way your business operates to deliver significant bottom-line benefits. For instance, you can:

■ **Use low-cost but untrusted infrastructure** such as the Internet to streamline business processes, but be sure your systems are protected from accidental or malicious damage.
■ **Develop online collaboration solutions** that allow your employees to work more closely with business partners or overseas colleagues as easily and securely as if they were all in the same office.
■ **Broaden your trade networks**: finding new customers or suppliers on a global basis – by finding partners online, but still be able to create the same level of trust you would look for in a traditional real-world relationship.

Encryption: how it works

All encryption uses an algorithm or mathematical procedure to 'scramble' or encode a message in a particular way. Anyone receiving the message needs to understand how to 'unscramble' or decode the message. A very simple form of transcription is simply to replace each letter in a message by the next letter in the alphabet. Modern encryption solutions are rather more complex, and rely on a key to specify how the message should be encoded. This allows the same algorithm to be used by many different users, but generate encoded messages that are unique to each user.

Encryption can be based on a single secret key that both sender and receiver need to know. However, the process of sharing that key represents a security risk. Most encryption solutions today use a method called public key encryption that allows users to decrypt the messages of others without having to exchange secret keys securely. It works by using algorithms that encrypt and decrypt data using different, yet mathematically linked, keys. One key is 'public' and can be sent out to the people you want to communicate with over an insecure network. The other 'private' key is kept secret and cannot be discovered through knowledge of the public key or its underlying algorithm, except by applying 'brute force' computing power.

If a computer receives a message encrypted with someone's private key, it can decrypt it using that person's public key – and being able to decrypt it successfully also verifies that it was sent by that particular person, since only their private key could have been used to encrypt the message initially. This allows public key encryption to be used for authentication when connecting to systems or services and for legally binding digital signatures. In addition, public key encryption includes a 'checking' mechanism which confirms that messages have not been altered in transit.

In practice, if you want to exchange messages between more than a few users or between users in many different locations, you need some form of public key infrastructure (PKI) to allow you to manage the process of issuing keys to users and sharing public keys.

Authentication: how it works

While public key encryption can provide a technical basis for authenticating a user, authentication itself is achieved in one of three ways, through:

■ something only the user knows;
■ a physical item only the user has;
■ a physical trait unique to that user.

The simplest form of identity verification, which relies on *something only the user knows*, is a user ID and password. The user ID/password combination is extremely cheap and easy to implement, but also relatively straightforward to break or steal. The ease with which user IDs and passwords can be stolen has been shown recently by a number of scams to harvest the IDs of customers of several online banking services. In addition, a simple user ID/password combination only verifies users when they log in or on other occasions when they are asked to re-enter their password. It does not allow users to provide legally binding digital signatures confirming that it was they (and not someone else) who were the originators of a message, approved a document or authorized a transaction.

A more complex form of user ID and password that can support legally binding authentication is a PKI certificate. Certificates are encryption keys and, as described previously, can be used to both secure and authenticate a message.

As with the simple user ID/password combination, the certificate can be simply something that the user knows, although since these keys are typically long, complex alphanumeric strings, it is not practical for a user to remember them. Certificates are therefore typically held on some form of token, requiring users to authenticate themselves through a physical item only they have. Certificates can be implemented purely through software, but there is a risk that a user could be impersonated if someone were to gain access to that user's account on the system in some way.

There are several different forms of token, but the most common is a smart card, since it generally provides the best combination of:

■ **flexibility**: a single card has the capacity to support several different applications;
■ **security**: since the processing capabilities of the smartcard chip allow it to take an active part in the authentication process;
■ **cost**.

The final kind of authentication solution centres on biometrics or checking a physical trait unique to the user, such as a fingerprint or iris print. Biometric systems are expensive to implement, can raise concerns amongst users that they are a threat to their civil liberties, and fingerprint-based biometric systems have already been outwitted by a number of methods for duplicating fingerprints, with or without the knowledge of the user.

Biometric systems are therefore only truly effective when combined with a token or smartcard-based certificate. In these circumstances, the biometrics element usually adds little to the overall strength of the security solution.

The business case for encryption and authentication

Failing to secure data and authenticate users creates risks in many different ways for businesses, such as:

■ **operational risks** if transactions are corrupted or changed while in transit or being stored;
■ **financial risk** in the event of identity fraud, so that bills are unpaid;

■ **reputation risk and damage** to your brand if customer data is misused as a result of a security breach;

■ **strategic risk** if critical proprietary data such as formulae or designs falls into the hands of your competitors.

Any business case for introducing authentication and encryption solutions will weigh these risks against the costs of implementing the solution. The main factors affecting those costs include:

■ **Key strength and processing overhead**: the longer the key, the more difficult it is for a hacker to use brute force to break the code and get access to your information, but the more processing power required to perform the encryption. You should also look at whether you need to encrypt all data or just the most sensitive information. For example, do all e-mails need to be encrypted in transmission or held in encrypted form on the server, or just some of them? A final consideration is that encryption is classified as a military technology by the US and UK governments, which place restrictions on the export of the strongest forms of encryption technologies to certain countries.

■ **How the key is held**: as noted above, users' encryption keys can be held in a number of ways. In the typical commercial scenario, balancing risks and costs almost always leads to the conclusion that a smart-card-based PKI solution is the most cost-effective approach.

■ **Key management and distribution**: considerable effort is required to issue, distribute and manage encryption keys.

In practical terms, companies such as Entrust, Verisign and Baltimore Technologies provide the technical elements needed to implement encryption and create a PKI. However, the strength of the solution depends as much, if not more, on having robust processes for issuing and revoking encryption keys or certificates and verifying them each time they are used.

The process can be broken down into steps managed by three different kinds of organizations:

■ **Registration authorities**: provide background checks on individuals to confirm their identity before they are issued with a certificate.

■ **Certification authorities**: handle the mechanics of issuing and revoking certificates.

■ **Verification authorities**: provide confirmation of the certificate owner's identity as transactions are processed.

It is possible to build your own PKI and deliver all registration, certification and verification services yourself, but it is expensive to create, requires specific and scarce skills to implement and maintain, and a programme of continuous development to update it in line with the latest technical developments and threats.

You could work with some of the managed services suppliers who have sprung up to offer one or two of the three steps outlined above. However, a robust process and PKI which will allow you to reap the full benefits of authentication and encryption depends on three factors which a single organization will struggle to implement by itself, even with this support:

■ Someone to act as the guarantor of that certificate. The kind of self-certification offered by many PKI-based products and by most certification authorities (who cannot offer registration authority services) is about as valuable as someone offering you a membership card for a local gym as proof of identity, whereas a guarantor-backed certificate is equivalent to a credit card or passport.

■ A set of rules for issuing and revoking certificates and for checking them each time they are used – and a standards-based process and infrastructure for applying those rules.

■ Support for global operations with any partner, current or potential. The real returns of encryption and authentication come not from deploying locally with existing trading partners but from using PKI to facilitate low-risk trade with people you have never dealt with before.

There are few organizations that can provide all these aspects of the certificate management process. A lead in this area is being taken by the banks, which have traditionally provided trust services to businesses. The availability of end-to-end managed PKI services from providers such as RBS TrustAssured allows companies to provide smart-card-based certificates for their employees and trading partners in an extremely cost effective fashion.

Conclusion

Large and small businesses alike will increasingly find their trading partners looking to introduce encryption and authentication solutions to secure online transactions and allow trust to be created between online trading partners. The benefits will be great, and the costs and management challenge of meeting these requirements do not need to be painful.

The Ministry of Defence, with the assistance of Cap Gemini Ernst & Young, has implemented the Defence Electronic Commerce Service, a secure portal that allows suppliers to bid for contracts and make use of a collaborative environment that supports joint working on specific programmes.

The MoD deals with thousands of suppliers, who provide everything from toilet rolls to tanks, in transactions worth in total several billion pounds each year. DECS will allow the MoD to cut its procurement costs by 20 per cent, as well as deliver improvements in design time, risk reduction and lifecycle costs.

Suppliers authenticate themselves when connecting to the DECS service by using ChamberCard, which provides them with a digital identity held on a smartcard. ChamberCard is being provided by TrustAssured from the Royal Bank of Scotland (RBS) and the British Chambers of Commerce. The British Chambers of Commerce provides the branch network where suppliers can present their credentials to obtain a ChamberCard, while TrustAssured's fully managed service provides the processes and technical infrastructure to issue and revoke ChamberCards and validate them each time they are used.

TrustAssured provides the services that enable you to conduct business cost effectively and securely over the Internet. With TrustAssured you can take confidence in the knowledge that a major global bank is providing a service that enables e-commerce to operate within a secure and trusted environment. The key to this is the provision of unique digital identity credentials; these eliminate the fear of dealing with unknown counterparties over the Web.

Our end-to-end managed service, based on public key infrastructure (PKI), asks users to authenticate themselves each time they connect to your online systems. Once online, our service allows them to conduct business securely through, for example, the authorization of transactions or the signing of documents with legally binding digital signatures.

For further details contact Louisa McCabe on 020 7672 6775 or louisa.mccabe@rbs.co.uk or visit: www.trustassured.co.uk

Digital signatures

ID cards maybe a hot topic of debate in the United Kingdom but in Belgium they have taken the concept a step further with the introduction of the e-ID card, driven by the technology behind digital signatures, writes Johan Sys, General Manager of GlobalSign.

As e-mail increasingly is substituted for the use of letters and faxes, and as commercial transactions on the Web become increasingly important to organizations, the need for secure communications grows to the same extent, especially with spoof attacks, interception of transmissions and other hacking methods becoming more widespread and getting more 'intelligent' every day. So, if the Web is to achieve its true commercial potential, it is important that the right technological infrastructure is in place. Public key infrastructure (PKI) enabled by cryptography provides a secure basis. PKI is the technology behind digital certificates and digital signatures.

What digital signatures are

Like the signature you use on written documents today, digital signatures are now being used to identify authors/co-signers of e-mail or electronic data. Digital signatures are created and verified using digital certificates. To understand what digital certificates are, we need to take a closer look at *cryptography*. Cryptography is the science of transforming information anyone can read (in plain text) into information not everyone can read. In this process, information is coded (encryption) to stop information from being read or altered by anyone but the intended recipient. It may be intercepted, but it will not be intelligible to someone without the ability to decode (decrypt) the message. Encryption and decryption require a mathematical formula or 'algorithm' to convert data between readable and encoded formats, and a key.

There are two types of cryptography: symmetric (or secret key) and asymmetric (public key). Symmetric key cryptography is characterized by the fact that the same key used to encrypt the data is used to decrypt the data. Clearly, this key must be kept secret among the communicating parties; otherwise the communication can be intercepted and decrypted by others. Until the mid-1970s, symmetric cryptography was the only form of cryptography available, so the same secret key had to be known by all individuals participating in any application that provided a security service. However, this all changed when Whitfield Diffie and Martin Hellman introduced the notion of *public key cryptography* in 1976.

In such a system, in order for two parties to exchange information in a secure fashion, each participant requires two keys: a public key and a private key. If one key is used to encrypt a message, then only the other key in the pair can be used to decrypt it. Although the keys of the public and private key pair are mathematically related, it is computationally infeasible to derive one key from the other, so the private key is protected from duplication or forgery even when someone knows the public key. Therefore, it is safe to openly distribute your public key for everyone to use, but it is essential that your private key remains closely guarded and secret. The public key can be used to verify a message signed with the private key, or encrypt messages that can only be decrypted using the private key. If someone wants to send you an encrypted message, they encrypt the message with your public key and you, being the sole possessor of the corresponding private key of the pair, are the only one who can decrypt it.

How are digital signatures created and verified?

To create a digital signature, the signer creates a 'hash', an algorithm that creates a unique shortened version of the message, and then uses his or her private key to encrypt the hash. The encrypted hash is the digital signature. If the message were changed in any way, the hash result of the changed message would be different. The digital signature is unique to both the message and the private key used to create it, so it cannot be forged. The digital signature is then appended to the message, and both are sent to the message recipient. The recipient recreates the hash from the received message, and then uses the public key of the original sender to decrypt the hash included in the received message. If the two hash results are identical, two things have been verified. The first is that the digital signature was created using the signer's private key (assurance that the public key corresponds to the signer's private key) – no one is pretending to be or masquerading as the signer. This verifies the *authenticity* of the signer, and the signer cannot claim to have not signed the message. The second is that the message has not been changed: this verifies the *integrity* of the message.

The role of a certificate authority (CA)

A digital signature is created using a digital certificate, which binds a public key to an individual or organization. The binding of a public key to an individual or organization is certified by a trusted source, typically a certification authority (CA). A CA is a trusted authority that issues and manages digital certificates. A CA uses a PKI to perform the life-cycle management of digital certificates. These certificates typically include the owner's public key, the expiration date of the certificate, the owner's name, and other information about the public key owner. CAs may also be involved in a number of administrative tasks such as end-user registration, but these are often delegated to the registration authority (RA). The role of the RA is to verify the identity of the person or organization that attempts to register.

Legal framework

Digital signatures can be compared to the traditional hand-written signature that has been used for centuries to do business. The only difference is that the transactions take place via a new medium, the Internet. Therefore, new laws have to be implemented to reflect this new reality.

The use of digital signatures is supported by recent legislative actions that provide credibility to the concept of electronic signatures and recognition to the need for such a capability. Both the US E-Sign Law, (passed in 2000) and the EU Digital Signature Law (passed in 2001) are examples of this trend.

Using digital signatures in your business

One of the most crucial questions in any business transaction is the identity of the entity with which the transaction is being conducted. Historically, personal relationships, face-to-face contract signings, notaries, and third-party counsel are used to help establish trust in this most important aspect of conducting business. As the reliance on paper shifts to electronic transactions and documents, so must the reliance on traditional trust factors shift to electronic security measures to authenticate our electronic business partners, customers and suppliers before engaging in the exchange of information, goods and services. Similarly, the need for confidentiality and confidence in the integrity of exchanged information is critical. Extending this list of security services, there may be further need to establish the non-repudiation of agreements, and to digitally certify and securely timestamp transactions.

Digital signatures support all these security services. Let us take a look at some applications in different vertical markets that can benefit from the use of digital signatures:

- **Financial services**: payment authentication for stock purchases, access control for online banking, digital notary of loans.
- **Insurance**: digitally sign quotes, authenticate online payment of premiums, version management of documents.
- **Government**: electronic ID-cards, automated and electronic response to RFPs, secure messaging with the government.
- **Industry**: digitally sign electronic contracts, linking procurement systems in an automated way, access control for business partner to online applications, establishing a Web presence.

The PKI market

In the late 1990s, market analysts predicted a bright future for digital certificates. The market for PKI – the technology needed to generate certificates – would become the fastest growing segment in the IT security space. Reality was different, though. PKI projects did take off, but most of them never got beyond their pilot phase. As a consequence many PKI vendors ran into financial problems, and some even went out of business. The PKI market has not delivered on its promise because the implementation and maintenance of an in-house PKI requires highly specialized internal staff. After all, PKI is a combination of very specific technologies, infrastructures and practices.

What companies and governments want are digital certificates to secure their communications and applications. They do not necessarily want the hassle of implementing and maintaining a complex PKI infrastructure. Some companies in the IT security market have realized this, and have come up with an alternative model: the so-called outsourced PKI solution. This means that companies that want to implement digital certificates today have three choices to get these certificates:

- purchase certificates from a public CA such as GlobalSign or VeriSign;
- operate a private CA, meaning the company has to purchase and implement its own PKI;
- go for an outsourced PKI solution, offered by companies such as GlobalSign and Ubizen.

The first alternative is a good solution if, for instance, a company wants to provide its employees with digital certificates to sign confidential e-mail communications. If a company wants to deploy certificates across different applications, involving both internal and external parties, or if it wants to be a CA itself, it will have to choose between the last two of these three options. The main parameters related to the decision between these two options are time to market, size of population, application, interoperability, financial and human resources, legal framework and more.

For early implementers of PKI with huge budgets and sufficient IT and administrative capacity, deploying an infrastructure on an in-house basis was most appropriate. However, as PKI attracts increasing interest from a larger number of large and medium-sized companies and organizations, the case for outsourcing PKI becomes favourable. Outsourced PKI solutions provide a multitude of benefits for business. Although the underlying idea is to transfer the burden of implementation and management of the PKI solution to a service provider, there are undoubtedly important strategic and financial advantages in outsourcing trust as well.

Electronic identity cards are on their way

So far digital certificates have typically been used as part of projects in the private sector, that is, securing e-mail communication within a company, securing access to a specific Web server, or securing a VPN connection. With the rise of electronic identity cards this will change dramatically. E-ID cards will make sure that the public at large will get digital certificates in a very user-friendly way. The certificates will simply come with each e-ID card.

In 2003 we have seen one of the first large-scale rollouts of e-ID cards in Europe, namely in Belgium. The BelPIC project will provide each Belgian citizen with an electronic identity card over a period of five years. The Belgian electronic identity card comes in an ID1 (bank card) format, displays a photo, some basic identity information, a signature of the cardholder and incorporates a microchip. The microchip on the e-ID card holds the same data as the physical card but is, in addition, equipped with two key pairs and their related digital certificates, articulated by a private PIN code. One certificate is used for secure identification, the second for electronic signing.

The e-ID card, safeguarding the traditional purposes of the former identity card, will give Belgian citizens simpler, faster and more secure access to administrative procedures. As such, over time, citizens will have access to numerous e-government services and be able to vote electronically, submit tax returns online, communicate changes of address, obtain civil records, declare household employees, and declare births or manage birth certificates. In addition, as the e-ID cards are based on referenced standards, they can also be used to access other than e-government applications requiring a certified identity. It is interesting to note that for this large-scale project the Belgian government has opted for an outsourced PKI solution (provided by subcontractors Ubizen and GlobalSign).

GlobalSign is Europe's leading certificate service provider offering digital certificates and co-sourced PKI solutions. GlobalSign's digital certificates allow individuals and businesses to secure e-mail communication, to conduct fully authenticated and confidential online business and to set up trusted software distribution. GlobalSign also offers CorporateRA™, an out-of-the-box co-sourced PKI solution and a unique service called RootSign™, for corporate certification authorities that do not have their root certificate embedded in popular browsers. GlobalSign's public root key is embedded by default in all major Internet applications such as e-mail clients and browsers. Consequently, GlobalSign certificates are globally accepted and are not limited by any application, geographic area or business sector. Furthermore GlobalSign is one of the few certification authorities in the world that attained the WebTrust accreditation level.

For more information contact Johan Sys, General Manager, GlobalSign, Tel: +32.16.287123, E-mail: johan.sys@globalsign.net, Web: www.globalsign.net

Biometrics

Biometrics might seem to be in the realm of science fiction, but as Clive Reedman and Bill Perry from Emerging Technology Services write, it is actually very much non-fiction and can add a very non-fictional layer of security to a company's bottom line.

Biometrics is the automated identification, or verification of human identity through the measurement of repeatable physiological, or behavioural traits. In general terms identification means the search of a biometric sample against a database of other samples in order to ascertain whether the donor is already contained in, or new to the database.

Verification refers to the 'one to one' comparison between a sample and another to ask the question, 'Are you who you say you are?' The majority of access control applications utilize verification techniques, rather than attempting searches of databases, which could compromise accuracy and raise costs. The one major exception to this is iris recognition, which is nearly always implemented in a 'one to many' scenario.

The benefits of biometrics

Look at it this way. Security is now usually based on either 'something you know' or 'something you have' or a combination of both. Take the example of a cashpoint card. You *have* the card and you *know* the PIN number. However, the card may be lost or stolen, or your PIN may be stolen by stealth, or simply because it is written down and kept with the card! Maybe the 'something you know' is a password, but how many of us have multiple passwords, and how many of us write them down and leave them where they can be found? How many costly calls to IT help desks are concerned with forgotten or compromised passwords? How many employees are 'clocked' in and out by friends when they are actually somewhere else, or permit their passwords to be used by others? The integrity or quality of data entered to, or extracted from, systems is often trusted implicitly. However, how can anybody using that data rely on it unless they can be sure who it was that entered it, or manipulated it? For instance is a 'signed' e-mail actually to be trusted if all that is required to sign it is a password, used to release the appropriate key(s)? Can you be sure that an unauthorized person who may have access to the required passwords at the receiving end cannot read an encrypted e-mail? What real trust do we therefore have in the data audit trail?

Traditionally, security of data and the trust in data relies on the use of 'something you know', for instance, a password, or PIN and/or 'something you have', such as a smart card. Used in combination, a reasonable level of security may be possible. However, there remain a number of risks associated with the use of the 'have' and 'know' scenarios.

Figure 3.6.1

Biometrics adds a 'something you are'. Can you leave your fingerprint, face, voice and so on at home in the morning like you can your office pass? Can your iris be stolen? There lies the prime advantage of a biometric. It is part of you and is not therefore easily compromised. Consider also the issue of 'non-repudiation'. I could claim that I had lost my cash-point card before money was withdrawn, or that somebody had found my computer password. However, it is hard for me to claim that somebody had copied my iris pattern!!

Table 3.6.1 Security methods

Method	Examples	Properties
What you know	User ID	Shared
	Password	Many passwords easy to guess
	PIN	Forgotten
What you have	Cards	Shared
	Badges	Can be duplicated
	Keys	Lost or stolen
What you have combined with what you know	Cashpoint card and PIN	Shared PIN compromised
Something unique to each user	Fingerprint	Not possible to share
	Face	Repudiation unlikely
	Iris	Forging difficult
	Voiceprint	Cannot be lost or stolen
	Signature (dynamic)	

How biometric systems work

All biometric systems work in much the same way. A sensor (camera, microphone and so on) captures a physical or behavioural characteristic. The 'image' is then converted to a numerical code (template) using a proprietary algorithm. The data is often then compressed for transmission within the system, which may be self contained, or spread over two continents! The extracted feature data is either then stored, or compared against other numerical codes created during the 'enrolment' process. The result of the comparison is an automated decision (see Figure 3.6.2). This may be, 'does this person have access to the building', or 'can this person be logged onto a computer network?' However, the range of applications is vast and spread throughout all areas where data integrity and security are issues. Remember though that in some applications, security is not the reason for implementing a biometric system. Occasionally it is purely to provide a measure of convenience to the end user, such as perhaps a task-oriented computer program, which normally requires a number of key presses to change 'modes'. A biometric may relieve the user of the need to remember how to navigate complex menus, or may make the use of 'hot desk' scenarios simpler, as for all intents and purposes the data network can recognize exactly who is logging into a given terminal, without the need for that person to remember passwords or carry any cards.

Although the vast majority of feature extraction and search algorithms are proprietary in nature, international standards for biometrics are beginning to emerge. These standards are mainly focused on the need to make biometric systems more interoperable across differing vendor platforms. It is unlikely and possibly unrealistic to expect vendors to give up their proprietary code in favour of global interoperability. However, the effort is now focused on how to achieve the goal of large-scale acceptance and adoption of biometrics without undue damage to the commercial base. In general, this can be achieved in a number of ways, particularly the specifying of data interchange standards that specify how images should be transferred across diverse systems. Given a good quality image of the biometric trait, such as a face, finger or iris, it becomes possible for most data to be encoded by any suitable biometric system.

The International Standards Organization (ISO) has an active program through Standards Committee 37 (SC37). To develop the standards the work was divided into six distinct working groups, and convenors were appointed. These groups are:

- WG 1 Harmonized Biometric Vocabulary (do we speak the same language?).
- WG 2 Biometric Technical Interfaces (how do we transfer data?).
- WG 3 Biometric Data Interface Formats (what form does the data need to be in?).
- WG 4 Profiles for Biometric Applications (what are we trying to achieve?).
- WG 5 Biometric Testing and Reporting (how do we ensure the system works well?).
- WG 6 Cross Jurisdictional and Societal Aspects (what are the legal and social imperatives?).

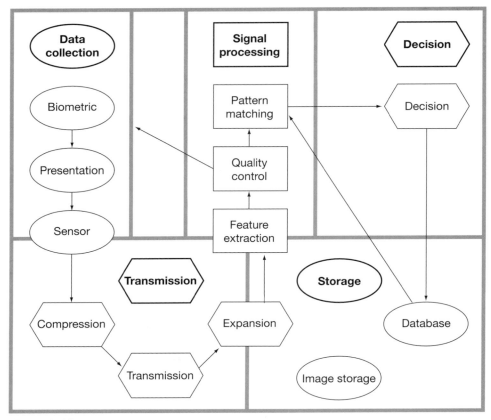

Figure 3.6.2

How biometrics is relevant to e-business

Reliable user authentication is becoming an increasingly important task in the e-business world. It is one of the cornerstones of transaction security, and linked intrinsically to confidentiality, integrity and non-repudiation. The consequences of an insecure or untrusted authentication system in a corporate or enterprise environment can be catastrophic, and may include loss of confidential information, denial of service, and data integrity being compromised.

The established techniques of user authentication, which involve the use of either passwords and user IDs (identifiers), or identification cards and PINs (personal identification numbers), suffer from several limitations. Passwords and PINs can be acquired unlawfully by direct or indirect observation. Once an attacker acquires the user ID and the password, that attacker has total access to the user's resources. In addition, there is no way to positively link the usage of the system or service to the actual user, that is, there is no 'real' protection against repudiation by the user ID owner. For example, when a user ID and password is shared with a colleague there is no way for the system to know who the actual user is, and it is consequentially extremely difficult for any organization to institute criminal charges or internal disciplinary measures. A similar scenario arises when a transaction involving a credit, debit or charge card is conducted over the Internet. Even though the data being sent over the Internet may be protected using secure encryption methods, current systems are not capable of assuring that the rightful owner of the card initiated the transaction.

It is also of course important to note that the source of a great number of criminal attacks on systems emanate at the administrator level, or amongst those who have an element of control of the data system above that held by the general user. Indeed, 'shop floor' data users are less able, or likely, to attack the system simply because existing security policies prevent them doing so without expending a great deal of effort in the attempt. A biometric access control system adds a level of assurance that those persons with access to the control of system configuration and security are themselves subject to another layer of security and audit. Consider how often computer rooms themselves are left relatively insecure because anybody with the appropriate card, or knowledge of a door code, could enter them.

With the emergence of multiple new services on the Internet, a great deal of importance is now being placed upon the personal and commercially sensitive information transmitted over open public networks and stored on often shared commercial servers. Security techniques such as PKI are becoming more and more the order of the day. However, these security techniques only ensure that the correct, authentic digital certification is being used during the transaction. There remains the assumption that the correct person is actually using that certificate *and* that he or she has the authority to do so. Biometrics is the only technical solution that is able to closely couple the actual person to the authorized transaction, ensuring that the complete circle of authenticity, confidentiality, non-repudiation and trust is evident.

Biometrics, as a technological solution, has been slow to attract the interest of the general public and large corporate bodies alike. To a great number of people it is still viewed as 'science fiction' and not really for this world. They could not be more wrong. Biometrics not only provides the capability of filling a large hole in the transaction security world, but also offers various other solutions to common business process challenges. It should also be remembered that process efficiency always results in a cost benefit for the business. Estimates of just how much it costs individual businesses to deal with forgotten or compromised passwords vary considerably, from a few pence to many pounds. A biometric solution can alleviate this burden and subsequent cost by a considerable amount, releasing IT staff's time to perform other duties and reducing the overall costs of IT system management. Large systems integrators quote return on investment as being within months rather than years.

With the ever-increasing use of wireless technology in the office, roaming laptop and mobile phone environments and Internet based, secure e-commerce brings a new challenge to secure identity authentication. As mobile e-commerce takes off, and the value of transactions increase, secure user authentication will become ever more important.

Today, anonymous transactions permeate modern life. People misappropriate the identities of other people, giving them access to that person's money and everything else. With biometrics, once you are identified by your biometric, whether it is a fingerprint or iris scan or another unique identifier, you can use it everywhere as proof of your identity. Biometrics is the key, not a password or knowledge-based system.

Emerging Technology Services is technology and vendor-independent, giving the customer the satisfaction that any system we recommend is focused on their requirements and not pure technology, but the business application of technology. Only ETS offers a complete 'end to end' service to customers, from requirements analysis, awareness training, installation, administrator training, user enrolment, through to full service support and technology refresh.

For further information contact Clive Reedman and Bill Perry, Emerging Technology Services, Tel: +44 (0) 1604 660125, e-mail: bill@ets.uk.com, Web: www.ets.uk.com

Digital rights

As the entertainment industry has discovered, the digital revolution has brought many challenges in the fields of copyright and distribution, however with the right systems in place it can address these issues and bring more opportunities, writes Macrovision UK's Marketing Manager Simon Mehlman.

Every company needs security – for its own premises and, critically, for its products. In the days when all products were physical in nature, requiring manufacture and delivery in physical terms, this was a relatively straightforward process. Designs needed protection through copyrights and patents, and the security of the goods themselves was a matter of physical protection.

The introduction of the digital age has blown that model apart, and the entertainment industry is striving to manage these high technology, value-added product sectors. To do this, companies need to understand the issues of copy protection and how they relate to the opportunities provided by Internet distribution and unauthorized copying.

At a legislative level, the Copyright Directive is in the process of implementation and has already been implemented in a handful of European countries including Germany and the United Kingdom. One of the primary goals of this legislation was to provide a legal framework to protect the rights of content owners in order to enable them to define and protect their intellectual property from unauthorized copying in the digital age.

The catalyst for the development of adequate legal and technological protection measures has been the proliferation of copying devices and the rising adoption of broadband. Once the CD burner became commonplace the genie really was out of the bottle, and the rapid take-up of DVD recorders and cheaper broadband Internet access has only exacerbated this issue. Without adequate protection, there is little to prevent the mass duplication and unauthorized distribution of digital products – which include all software, music, movies and computer games.

Without strong and timely action, the producers of the digital content are hugely vulnerable and the impact on revenue can be catastrophic: to anyone who doubts the damage that unlimited copying can do, the music industry provides a salutary lesson. The music industry initially delayed far too long in facing up to the problem of illegal copying, with music CD revenues falling significantly for the last three consecutive years. The impact on sales and revenue has made this issue a high-profile debate within the media.

The music industry is now addressing the issues of unauthorized copying and distribution, and has started to implement protection on CDs and in some cases, provide a licensed download service via the Internet. Copy protection of CDs has evolved to permit users to store their tracks on hard disks and even export these files legitimately to MP3 devices that respect the rights of the content owners. Products such as CDS 300 from Macrovision will enable record label publishers to permit a set number of 'protected CD burns' to allow users to create their own compilations; to the consumer this means that copy protection no longer means that users are bound by functional restrictions in how they choose to enjoy their music. The most effective copy protection technologies are designed to be transparent, and added value through enriched content is far more likely to be added to protected CDs than those left unprotected.

If the music industry provides a graphic example of the potential problems of unauthorized digital distribution, however, it also reveals the huge opportunities open to content owners for new and imaginative delivery methods, marketing initiatives and revenue-raising opportunities. All of these are entirely dependent on the existence of a range of really effective protection systems. Enabling the sharing of legitimate content provides a tremendous opportunity for the entertainment and software businesses – but only if the legitimacy of this content is preserved. The traditional terminology for technology to achieve this has involved phrases such as copy protection or, more recently, digital rights management. Both of these, however, carry an impression of containment and limitation, whereas in reality protecting the content properly opens up huge new avenues for the use and distribution of content. A more accurate term would be digital rights *enablement* (DRE), reflecting the wider role that this technology is now playing.

The really big breakthrough in the distribution of all types of digital content – both business software and entertainment products – will be effective and legitimate mass distribution via the Internet. The Internet is already widely used for the distribution of music files (both legal and illegal), but the distribution of software, movies and games is still in its infancy. Restrictions to growth include the limited access to broadband in the United Kingdom and a lack of broad content. However, the United Kingdom is catching up fast, and broadband access is estimated to reach 26 per cent of households by 2006, with business access building even faster.

The opportunities that broadband access provides for the fast delivery of digital products are significant – but content owners are only going to capitalize on them if their products can be protected adequately both during delivery and during use at the consumer/customer site. Companies need to ensure that a single sale does not mean that their content is subsequently available on the open market for anyone to download and use.

Content owners are increasingly using copy protection and digital rights enablement products both for straightforward delivery and for innovative marketing strategies. The possibilities for 'trial versions' of software or computer games, for example, present immediate opportunities for proactive marketing. The right type of digital rights enablement provides access to products for a limited time period or number of uses and then simply disables them when the trial period is over, leaving the customer with the option of buying the product, often by downloading a new licence via the Internet.

For business users this application has clear appeal – presenting the opportunity for their customers to try software systems before committing to potentially significant investment. More sophisticated DRE solutions allow for flexible payment terms, allowing customers to pay for software in relation to its usage and to receive automatic updates and add-ons to the software they use. This type of functionality may also simplify the registration and payment systems that currently protect business software use.

While most business users are accustomed to observing the copyright of content owners and can recognize the benefits that DRE can provide, the consumer market is a more difficult market to develop. Here, the issue of developing innovative added-value products is overshadowed by the task of winning the hearts and minds of a demanding public who vary greatly in their technical ability. It is not always the sophisticated technology that wins market share but the better marketed and usually simpler to implement solutions that earn a place in the home.

The two threats: piracy and home copying

The illegal 'pirating' of content is nothing new, and the international trade in pirated CDs, videos and DVDs is a widely recognized problem, with international law enforcement agencies working hard to retard its growth and limit its impact on legitimate business and revenues. However, research also shows that the impact of home copying is just as serious – with legitimate businesses losing as much revenue to the home copier as to the large-scale duplication operations.

Different industries have approached these issues in different ways. The movie industry really grabbed the nettle at an early stage by implementing effective protection of videos while that technology was still new. The result is that it is completely clear to all users that it is illegal to copy the content, and there is no expectation that copying is an entitlement.

As any new form of distribution has come into the market, the movie industry has implemented protection measures for each new route. Thus pay-per-view movies and DVDs have effective protection measures in place, and the industry is currently developing better ways to support legitimate distribution of movies over the Internet. It is only because such protection has been developed that the proliferation of distribution methods has been possible – clearly the content owners in the movie business will only allow their products to be distributed if they are confident that it is safe to do so, and the provision of a varied and high-profile range of content entirely depends upon this confidence.

The music industry, as mentioned before, suffered by not implementing copy protection measures earlier in its digital life. The industry has had to cope with a legacy of copying which had created the expectation in the consumer's mind that copying was not an illegal act.

Within the PC games industry, effective copy protection has evolved past the point of simply requiring that an original CD be present for the game to function. It is now possible to program a degraded functionality into illegally copied versions of protected software. Consumers who use such copied games may find that resources in the game are no longer available or that, progressively, their progress is slowed or made more awkward. Game publisher help desks are already informed as to which 'bugs' are in fact clear evidence that the user is using an illegal copy of the game. This technology is referred to as 'silent alarm' and is embedded into PC games already on sale.

The recent European Copyright Directive is making the attempt to clarify what is protected by copyright law and what rights a consumer has to access and disseminate digital content. Just as significantly, the Directive (which came into force in the United Kingdom at the end of October 2003) also makes clear that it is illegal to manufacture, sell or promote devices whose main function is to circumvent copy protection coding on products. Meanwhile, in the United States, record companies are using punitive legal sanctions to prosecute individuals who copy content illegally.

These legislative moves give welcome support to businesses trying to protect their products, but can also be a PR problem. A 'softer' approach is to use offers that exploit digital rights enablement features to encourage legitimate purchase in the first place. Computer games companies, for example, are experimenting with increasingly sophisticated methods of distributing 'tasters' of games that enable the user to try the concept and then provide a very simple order process through which the game can be purchased. Legitimate users can then automatically receive upgrades, new versions or extended functionality.

If new distribution models are to be exploited to the full, then clearly all those involved in the creation, marketing and distribution of content need to work together to ensure that new marketing possibilities are fully exploited. We see new partnerships and affiliations springing up all the time as traditional publishing and distribution models are superseded. In every case, an agreement needs to be reached on the type of DRE that is to be implemented.

A good example of this cooperation arises in the movie industry. Digital set-top boxes and DVD players provide the latest routes into the home for most movies. In order to provide protection to films being played, both the film content and the player need to have the relevant protection installed. Providing this secure distribution platform has required the movie producers, distributors and the manufacturers of set-top boxes to work together to produce a seamless protection system. Macrovision itself has provided its own technology for over 110 million digital set-top boxes worldwide, including 98 per cent of those used in the United Kingdom.

New technology is also being developed to meet the needs of integrated home entertainment systems. The challenge here is to experiment with new DRE solutions that allow multiple uses of movie products on different systems – TV and PC – around the home without losing control over the ownership of the content. Flexible rental models are being developed that will allow such usage, and the cooperation of the equipment manufacturers is actively sought to produce the best solution.

As always, new methods of accessing and distributing content (of any kind) will create both challenges and opportunities. Fundamentally, content owners need an assured revenue stream in order to allow them to continue to invest in new product development, and for them to make their most valuable content available through new distribution routes. DRE can provide this security where it is implemented in an effective and timely manner, and can therefore create an environment where experimentation, innovation and creativity can thrive, driving revenues forward.

Macrovision Corporation (Nasdaq: MVSN) develops and markets electronic licence management, digital rights management (DRM) and copy protection technologies for the enterprise software, consumer software, home video and music markets. Macrovision is headquartered in Santa Clara, California, with international headquarters in London and Tokyo.

Macrovision has copy protected over 3.5 billion VHS videocassettes and, in the last four years, one billion DVDs. Its copy protection technology is embedded in over 50 million digital set-top boxes including over 98 per cent of those used in the United Kingdom. These statistics and the company's extensive user base, which includes the Hollywood studios, the UK satellite television and cable industry, and the major PC games publishers, make Macrovision the world's leading copy protection provider for video, PC games and PPV television. Macrovision is now repositioning itself more as a rights management solution company, and has developed and acquired patented technologies that provide DRM solutions for rich media (video/audio) delivered via IP (Internet), software and Audio CD/DVDs.

Macrovision has developed a complete end-to-end DRM solution to support the distribution of rich media over a variety of distribution channels, including Internet Protocols (IP). This solution is called MacroSAFE. It is a multi-layered solution that enables video and audio content owners, software vendors and service providers to securely distribute their content to consumers and businesses – to enable them to maximize their revenue opportunities through new and cost-effective distribution channels. MacroSAFE is an enabling technology. Users can get access to quality media and publishers have access to a wide range of business models: purchase, rental, subscription, time-restricted playback, number-restricted playback, pay-per-view, video on demand, trial, free, and super distribution.

For more information contact Macrovision UK Ltd, Malvern House, 14–18 Bell Street, Maidenhead SL6 1BR, Tel: +0870 871 1111,Web: www.macrovision.com

License at will

Creating new business models from your current software portfolio is not as difficult as you may think: over 2,500 suppliers of software have already utilized electronic licensing to create new flexible distribution and pricing solutions. Macrovision UK's Marketing Manager Simon Mehlman explains their benefits.

From its origins in the fight against software piracy, when it was promoted as a means to help honest software users ensure that their licence usage did not exceed the terms stated and agreed within the software license, electronic licensing has evolved into a platform offering a raft of solutions that enable software users to close the gulf between what they pay for and what they deploy. It acts as a means of accountability to both software providers – to ensure that they charge only for what is necessarily used – and networked or stand-alone users – to ensure that they use only what they have paid for. Electronic licensing has come of age.

The Business Software Alliance (BSA), an organization set up to promote safe and legal use of software, estimates that software piracy is currently costing around US $11 billion in lost revenue, representing approximately 10 per cent of total software sales. Much of this revenue is lost not through professional pirates but through 'honest users' who purchase their software – but then exceed their licensed usage.

The BSA offers a series of guidelines for directors, saying that 'a good software policy will not just protect you against the risks inherent in using illegal software – it can also help you work more efficiently.' It claims that:

> Effective software policy will make sure that employees have exactly the software they *need*. This will remove the waste of providing expensive software to employees who do not need it and ensure that no expense is incurred through employees lacking in software that would improve efficiency.

Policy can also improve your software planning and control, making it easier to identify and control any software upgrades and any related training requirements. This will provide you with a better understanding of total IT costs and usage. Finally the implementation of effective policy will reduce time wasting and errors: you can ensure that all employees work on compatible systems and file all documentation in a sensible and easily accessible manner.

These guidelines could not provide a stronger argument for the case of electronic licensing. This series of technologies provides a directly accountable system that allows you to know precisely what software you pay for, what you need, for whom and whether you are using what you are paying for – and removes the risk of piracy suits.

Software piracy is a criminal offence for which penalties include an unlimited fine and even custodial sentences – and companies are responsible for the actions of their employees. From sending unsuitable e-mails through to using illegal copies of software – even 10 people using an application licensed for five is a serious offence – electronic licensing provides systems that automatically enforce license terms and prevent piracy using secure product activation.

For stand-alone users, the licensing is relatively simple. Exceptionally flexible solutions are now available that enable software and hardware vendors to protect their offerings and profitably manage licences throughout their lifecycle. With this protection in place, developers and vendors can securely price, package and deliver software products any way their customers want to buy them, via any digital medium to be 'unlocked' and/or 'activated' in a controlled way and used by the customer. The most effective of these products can accept payment and unlock products via the Web, by phone, fax or e-mail, allowing customers to go from initial purchase to full use without even leaving their computers. The registration of the product that is generated as part of the purchase process then means that the customer is eligible for all accompanying technical backup and guarantees.

While this provides a solution for stand-alone applications through the use of additional modules, it also offers the business network a more robust and scalable system for the use of network-enabled software via a file server. Any system that offers a network and stand-alone must be easily managed across the breadth of its usage and – ultimately – user-friendly.

Users of electronically licensed software can ensure that they comply with agreed licence terms as stated in a centrally held 'licence file'. This licence file can be updated or modified to allow their customer access to 'agreed' modules, and can be used to control the number of networked users allowed to access the software at any one point in time to the number stated within the software licence terms agreed with the vendor. The rights to access additional modules can be amended with a new licence file, creating a flexible and scalable system. This provides software vendors with a means to create customer-specific software builds without the expense of redeveloping a software application; new pricing models are enabled.

Whenever an application that is licensed in this way is accessed for use over a network, two actions take place: first a check is made to ensure that the software usage is within the terms listed inside the licence file and second, an authenticated log file is updated with a user ID and a date/time-stamped entry. This log file is then analysed for licence usage management.

The information generated by this control mechanism can then be used to look at more flexible payment structures such as a pay-for-use system. Clearly if usage is monitored this closely, customers can be billed only for the access or the individual functions that they use.

This is not only a licence compliance mechanism, then, but also a product that offers added value to the user. Any system that tracks licence compliance also necessarily tracks usage data – and it is in this application of technology that electronic licensing has become a quintessential product for today's networked business, in the form of 'utility computing' or 'usage-based licensing'. Utility computing can be applied most effectively when the software developer embeds code within the software that allows usage to be logged by time, by user and even by specific software component used.

Many variants of this system can be worked out to suit the customer's requirements, but a popular one is to base a monthly payment schedule on anticipated usage. Provided actual usage remains within accepted parameters, customers benefit from predictable costs, based on their own level of use. Once usage changes the costs are renegotiated.

Usage-based licensing provides end-users and software vendors with the ability to monitor actual software usage patterns and bill or audit based on this usage data. This means that you quite literally only pay for what you use – and that you have an effective and usable knowledge of who within your company needs which software, so you need never again pay for packages you do not need or overpay for the use you require.

Clearly this utility model is very attractive to software users, allowing smaller companies to benefit from software they may not be able to afford on a traditional pricing model and to see a clear relationship between use and cost. Where usage levels are being scrutinized this closely, customers are able to attribute costs to their individual departments in direct proportion to their usage levels, which can be invaluable in terms of internal accounting.

The pay-per-use system, therefore, is a flexible, accountable process that can be viewed as a positive asset by both user and provider. Rather than simply an inhibitor, preventing illicit use or copying, it is a facilitator, allowing users much greater control over the costs and application of the software they use.

In addition to this, software licences can now be initially deployed and licensed (purchased) over the Internet. The creator can now also offer the user freedom of choice to, for example, buy, try, rent, license, sample or test the product. This freedom of customer choice, at the click of a button, endows businesses with a far greater choice and flexibility than ever previously enabled. This has already revolutionized the way in which entertainment software is supplied, and is now being applied to more and more business technologies, removing the need to store lots of boxes and instructions: software purchasing, installation and monitoring can all be digitally managed.

A universal licensing platform takes the complexity out of software licensing and enables the very latest electronic licensing solutions. A single integrated platform can help software publishers to increase product revenues and reduce licensing costs, while delivering greater convenience and value to end-users. This technology's modular design and adherence to industry standards reduces business risk and protects technology investments. Modular platform architecture means that new capabilities can be added easily whenever needed. Adherence to industry standards ensures that systems interoperate seamlessly, making implementation of a licence management solution simple and safe.

Another feature of universal licensing is the capacity to provide automatic upgrades and new packages, delivered directly to their users. Whereas now for an upgrade to be implemented the original packaging often needs to be sought out from cupboards and filing systems, with a product enabled by such best-practice technology the upgrade can be sent directly, not to the IT staff or the MD to be passed along, but straight to the computers of its primary users. This is yet another example of the enabling capabilities of electronic licensing products.

It has never been seriously debated that software vendors have a right to protect their product from illicit copying. What has been slower to develop is an interpretation of protection systems that allows them to be used for the benefit of the customer as well as the vendor. With the kind of flexibility that is now available, and with licensing technology companies applying their expertise and imagination to promote new business models and create still more efficient and effective solutions such as Macrovision's FLEXnet, electronic licensing looks set to form the future of business software management.

Macrovision Corporation (Nasdaq: MVSN) develops and markets electronic licence management, digital rights management (DRM) and copy protection technologies for the enterprise software, consumer software, home video and music markets. Macrovision is headquartered in Santa Clara, California, with international headquarters in London and Tokyo.

Macrovision has copy protected over 3.5 billion VHS videocassettes and, in the last four years, one billion DVDs. Its copy protection technology is embedded in over 50 million digital set-top boxes including over 98 per cent of those used in the United Kingdom. These statistics and the company's extensive user base, which includes the Hollywood studios, the UK satellite television and cable industry, and the major PC games publishers, make Macrovision the world's leading copy protection provider for video, PC games and PPV television. Macrovision is now repositioning itself more as a rights management solution company, and has developed and acquired patented technologies that provide DRM solutions for rich media (video/audio) delivered via IP (Internet), software and Audio CD/DVDs.

Macrovision has developed a complete end-to-end DRM solution to support the distribution of rich media over a variety of distribution channels, including Internet Protocols (IP). This solution is called MacroSAFE. It is a multi-layered solution that enables video and audio content owners, software vendors and service providers to securely distribute their content to consumers and businesses – to enable them to maximize their revenue opportunities through new and cost-effective distribution channels. MacroSAFE is an enabling technology. Users can get access to quality media and publishers have access to a wide range of business models: purchase, rental, subscription, time-restricted playback, number-restricted playback, pay-per-view, video on demand, trial, free, and super distribution.

For more information contact Macrovision UK Ltd, Malvern House, 14–18 Bell Street, Maidenhead SL6 1BR, Tel: +0870 871 1111,Web: www.macrovision.com

4

Operational management

Developing a culture of security in the workplace

Every employer should consider taking precautions against security breaches. Peter Brudenall of Simmons & Simmons looks in detail at the risks involved and what can be done.

After the events of 11 September 2001 in the United States, US White House officials presented a sobering assessment of US preparedness for cyber attacks. They called for a new 'culture of security' in relation to information technology, in which everybody in and outside of the commercial world was to play a part.

The culture of security was described as a 'new way of thinking'; a voluntary rather than a regulatory change to the way information technology was used and secured. The Federal Trade Commission of the United States drew analogies to the responsibilities individuals take for their own safety in their everyday lives: 'we already take safety precautions in order to limit risks in our everyday lives. We wear our seat belts. We lock our houses when we leave. We need that kind of risk-minimizing thinking with our computers, and we all have to get involved'.[1]

The importance of operating within a culture of security is now recognized across the world. In the European Union, the European Network and Information Security Agency (ENISA) was set up in November 2003 by the Information Security Commission. At the time, Errki Liikanen, the European Information Society Commissioner, said that 'trust and

---

[1] 'Creating a culture of security', remarks by Commissioner Orson Swindle, Federal Trade Commissioner, at Privacy 2002: Information, Security and New Global Realities Conference.

security are crucial components in the Information Society and by establishing ENISA we continue the work to create the culture of security.'[2]

The risks for an employer operating outside a culture of security

Taking safety precautions to protect information systems is of particular, though clearly not exclusive, significance within the commercial world. Companies of all sizes, providing any product or service, are at risk of security breaches. If a company uses a computer at all, it is exposed. There are threats from outside and inside the business. These range from a hacker defacing the business's Web site, to e-mail-borne viruses, or to the employer facing liability for defamatory e-mails sent by an employee.

Defamatory e-mails are a risk because employers can be responsible for the actions of their employees where employees act in the course of their employment. This is known as vicarious liability. Consequently, offensive e-mails written in the workplace can result in claims for sex, race or disability discrimination, all of which carry unlimited compensation in employment tribunals. It is a problem that can easily arise in organizations that have a heavy traffic of internal e-mails, and a recent example involving a law firm led to sex and race discrimination claims. Following the resignation of his African-American secretary, a solicitor sent out an e-mail during the recruitment process for her replacement saying, 'Can we go for a really fit busty blonde this time?'

Another case shows how far the employer's vicarious liability can extend. E-mails were sent by staff at Norwich Union regarding rumours falsely suggesting that Western Provident was in severe financial difficulties. Western Provident believed that these messages could be used by Norwich Union to obtain new business and to damage it in the marketplace. It instituted libel proceedings seeking to hold Norwich Union responsible for the actions of its employees in sending defamatory messages through its e-mail system. Immediately after issuing proceedings Western Provident obtained a court order for the preservation and delivery of hard copies of the allegedly defamatory e-mails. Later, Western Provident obtained a further order allowing it to search Norwich Union's e-mail records. The case finally settled with Norwich Union paying Western Provident Association the sum of £450,000.

Other risks from inside the business include disgruntled employees, or possible mistakes by IT staff which enable users to access the wrong information. All of these are very real risks that an employer must consider before developing its culture of security.

The building blocks of a culture of security

There are practical steps that an employer can take to develop a culture of security within a company. A straightforward and comprehensive monitoring policy, together with a statement explaining it, staff training and management of operating systems, will help to protect an employer against some of the risks detailed above.

---

[2] As reported by the BBC on Friday 21 November 2003. See bbc.co.uk.

Monitoring communications systems

Monitoring the communications of staff is at the crux of a culture of security in the workplace. A well drafted monitoring policy can, and should, meet a number of objectives such as:

- Educating employees.
- Setting guidelines for what is, and what is not, acceptable use of the company's e-mail and Internet systems. Clear guidelines should be set out which go beyond the simple ban on 'offensive material' and define in more detail which websites are not appropriate to access or what the appropriate content of e-mails should be.
- Helping to ensure misuse does not occur.
- Minimizing risks.
- The basis of a defence if misuse does occur.
- The basis upon which to discipline or dismiss employees if necessary.

Data protection

However, before drafting a monitoring policy the employer must be aware of the impact of data protection legislation on the monitoring of staff communications. The Information Commissioner's Employment Practices Data Protection Code (*Guidance on Monitoring at Work*) (the Code) highlights the relevance of the Data Protection Act 1998 (the DPA) to this area. The Code acknowledges the need for monitoring staff communications, which it describes as a 'recognised component of the employment relationship', but states that: 'this must be balanced against an employee's right to privacy in the workplace'.[3]

The DPA is based on eight fundamental principles. One of the principal concerns of an employer should be to ensure that the processing complies with the first principle of the DPA. This requires that the organization have a justification in place for the processing of employees' data. Under the DPA, processing is drafted broadly to include obtaining, recording or holding information or data, or carrying out operations on the information or data. The two likely justifications are either that the employee has consented or that the monitoring is in the legitimate interests of the company and does not prejudice the rights and freedoms of the individual.

However, as the Code points out, obtaining consent from employees is problematic. The Code says consent must be 'freely given, which may not be the case in the employment environment'.[4] The Code also points out that consent can be withdrawn at any time.[5] An employee may well have very little real choice.

Since the company is therefore likely to have to rely on the legitimate interests justification, the Code advocates that the company undertakes an 'impact assessment' before monitoring takes place to assess whether the adverse impact of monitoring can be justified by the benefit to the employer and others. If an impact assessment is carried out and the criteria under the Code are held to show that the monitoring is justifiable, then monitoring can be carried out without consent of the worker being required.

[3] The Code, p 19
[4] The Code, p 19
[5] The Code, p 19

The Regulation of Investigatory Powers Act (RIPA) is also very relevant to the monitoring of staff in a culture of security. RIPA's intended purpose is to ensure that the interception of communications is done in accordance with certain basic human rights. The activities it covers include the interception of communications and therefore any monitoring of employee e-mail or telephone conversations.

Under RIPA, the unlawful interception of data is unlawful and could lead to criminal and civil sanctions against the employer. However, a communication can be lawfully intercepted if an exception applies. It can be intercepted where both the sender and the intended recipient of a communication have consented to the interception, or it can be intercepted under RIPA and the Telecommunications (Lawful Business Practice) (Interception of communications) Regulations 2000 (the Regulations).

Under the Regulations, interception of a communication (that is, a telephone conversation or e-mail) in the course of its transmission is lawful provided that: the interception is carried out for one of the lawful business practices set out in the Regulations (as listed below) and the company has made 'all reasonable efforts' to inform every person who may use the telecommunications system that the interception may take place.

Monitoring or keeping a record of communications relevant to the business are lawful business practices under the Regulations in the following circumstances:

■ in order to establish the existence of facts (for instance, keeping records of transactions carried out);
■ in order to ascertain compliance with regulatory or self-regulatory practices;
■ in order to ascertain or demonstrate the standards that are or ought to be achieved by persons using the system in the course of their duties (for example, quality control or staff training);
■ in the interests of national security;
■ for the purpose of the prevention or detection of crime;
■ for the purpose of the investigation or detection of the unauthorized use of the communications system;
■ ensuring the effective operation of the system (for instance, monitoring for viruses, backing up and forwarding e-mails to their correct destination); and
■ monitoring communications to determine whether they are relevant to the business.

The Code sets out certain suggestions as to what data protection features employers might want to integrate into a policy for the use of electronic communications. These include making clear the extent and type of private use that is allowed for the Internet and e-mails, and setting down the purposes for which any monitoring is conducted, the extent of the monitoring and the means used.

The Code makes it clear that simply telling staff that e-mail or Internet access could be monitored may not be sufficient. Employees should be left with a clear understanding of when information about them is likely to be obtained; why it is being obtained; what the information will be used for; and, if the information is to be disclosed, to whom it will be disclosed. The monitoring statement should detail this information and be updated whenever significant changes are made, such as the introduction of additional monitoring.

The monitoring statement should be integral to the general monitoring policy: all employees should know where it is to be found and should be reminded of it periodically.

Education of staff

Having a well-drafted policy is important, but clearly there will be no culture of security unless the policy is followed. It is a good idea to include employees in the decision process from an early stage when a monitoring policy is being considered. They are more likely to follow guidelines if their needs have been considered.

Employers must also not turn a blind eye to transgressions of the policy. If there is a breach of security, the employer must be consistent both in terms of the monitoring and any misuse of the company's technology systems. A fair disciplinary procedure and a right to appeal are important parts of a monitoring policy.

Employee training sessions should be held where e-mail and Internet use are discussed, in addition to emphasizing the consequences for the business and its employees if misuse occurs. Regular reminders of the rules and standards may be necessary through more training sessions or e-mails to all employees. The training sessions could also stress the alternatives to using e-mail or company telephones for matters that are confidential to the employee, such as doctor appointments or family matters.

A final option to protect a business is to consider libel insurance against the risk of defamatory e-mail.

Ensuring that operating systems support the culture of security

There are further practical protective steps concerning daily contact with the outside world that an employer can take. One is encryption – of e-mails that are being sent out, of data stored on laptops and perhaps also sensitive data stored on servers. Encryption would mean that information accessed unlawfully was meaningless to anyone who obtained it. Laptops and PDAs are a particular risk without encryption because they are more easily lost or stolen. They should be secured completely. A software lock can be used which requires an ID and password to be entered before the system can be used. This allows everything to be encrypted so that if, for example, the laptop is broken into, no information can be taken.

The importance of confidentiality should be flagged up to employees. Information is key to a business, and loss or unauthorized disclosure of information to third parties can have very serious repercussions.

Where there is no express or implied contractual obligation of confidence regarding information in the hands of employees, a duty of confidence may still exist. To protect the business, employees should be asked to sign confidentiality agreements as part of their contract of employment.

Confidentiality notices on e-mails

A confidentiality notice is a useful addition to e-mails. The notice tries to say that the content of an e-mail is confidential and should be read only by the intended recipient. For obvious reasons, the message should be put at the top of the e-mail – if it lurks at the end of the e-mail, the notice will only be read after the message it refers to. Confidentiality notices have a certain value but it is worth remembering that there is no legal authority concerning these notices in e-mail communications. Where such notices are added to every e-mail, it is possible that the court may find that their ubiquity dilutes their importance.

E-mail disclaimers

An e-mail disclaimer is another option for an employer. This can appear beneath the message but, more so than with the confidentiality notice, should be used with caution. There are no legal authorities on e-mail disclaimers as yet. However, guidance on disclaimers generally suggests that disclaimers of the type that effectively warn a recipient not to rely on the content of an e-mail will be of no impact. Of course, in warning a recipient not to rely on the content of the e-mail, a disclaimer may also alienate its recipient if used. Certainly, e-mail disclaimers should be used carefully.

Firewalls and filters

A firewall protects information systems by only allowing access to and from the internal systems to the outside world through a single point. This is commonly known as the 'network gateway server', and data following through the server will be filtered for known viruses and spam. These can help to keep unwanted visitors at bay.

When using firewalls and filters it is essential that adequate security is put in place to prevent attacks from hackers. Failure to do so can result in a breach of the DPA if personal data is revealed without the consent of the person it describes. The results could be commercially devastating: if confidential data concerning a client were to be hacked from the system of a law firm, for example, and used against the client, the liability of the law firm would be massive.

Virus protection is also important for identifying the viruses on the network as soon as they appear, so in effect being a dynamic and continuous monitoring, as are *browser controls* to monitor the use of the Internet and therefore its misuse. The controls can include the number and time of use and also what is being browsed.

Physical security

A final point for an employer to bear in mind – and one that is rarely considered when talking about information technology security – is physical security. It is very important to maintain physical security because it is far easier to get into an office and take paper from a desk by just following somebody through a security barrier ('tailgating') than it is to access that business's information technology systems.

Conclusions

To develop a culture of security in the workplace, an employer should:

■ **Protect against internal risks**: this can be done through the monitoring of staff communications within the parameters of data protection legislation. A monitoring statement should be drawn up and staff educated about monitoring and its impact on them. The employer should respond to all breaches of security in a consistent manner, and adhere closely to the monitoring policy.

∎ **Protect against external risks**: steps should be taken on the operation of the systems: employers should review their own business and consider implementing encryption, firewalls, filters, confidentiality notices on e-mails, e-mail disclaimers (although these should not be applied indiscriminately) and virus protection. Physical security within the office should also be an important consideration.

Simmons & Simmons was ranked joint second in the United Kingdom for outsourcing in a recent survey of in-house lawyers by *The Lawyer* magazine.

In 2002, Global Counsel 3000 ranked Simmons & Simmons in the top 10 worldwide for performance in all major practice areas, based on the views of in-house counsel at over 5,000 companies across 74 jurisdictions. Earlier this year the firm won a prestigious Queen's Award for Enterprise in the International Trade category, the only law firm to do so.

For further information contact David Barrett, partner, Tel: +44 (0)20 7825 4032, e-mail: david.barrett@simmons-simmons.com, or Peter Brudenall, senior lawyer, Tel: +44 (0)20 7825 4346, e-mail: peter.brudenall@simmons-simmons.com. Web site: www.simmons-simmons.com

Security as standard

By emphasizing management systems, the British Standards Institution is hoping to help companies improve their security from the inside out.

'Walls have ears' – this slightly surreal cautionary wartime note was one of the first warnings about confidentiality that most of the British public had ever heard. But it presaged an imperative that was soon accepted by almost every organization in every country in the world – the need for caution, thoroughness and foresight in avoiding the leak of business-critical information to enemies or competitors. In three decades the battlefront has moved from the waste bin and the pub to IT, telemetry and corporate governance.

Of course, the stakes are now so high that information security has spawned a whole industry – and a rewarding one. But different organizations have approached it in different ways, perhaps because matters of confidentiality and security are discussed only 'on a need to know basis' or perhaps because the technology of espionage and counter-espionage is so precious it is kept close to the chest; and perhaps because bosses and IT managers do not like to deal with outside authorities on matters so intimate.

Varying standards of security equipment are permissible. You get what you pay for – and, anyway, there are British standards (BS) and international standards (ISO) to cover product and service quality, aren't there? But what about best practice in the organizations that wish to be protected? How do they know they are following the right approach? Equally important, how can their suppliers and customers be reassured that their own confidential information and trading secrets are not being misused?

Establishing the standards

Towards the end of the last millennium the British Standards Institute knuckled down to establishing an information security standard. Following extensive consultation with industries and organizations all over the world, it developed BS 7799 Part 1, Information Security Management – Code of practice for information security management, and BS 7799 Part 2, Information Security Management – Specification for information security management systems.

BS 7799 promoted protection for intellectual property, in the same way that material goods are traditionally protected. It reminded us of how important a business reputation can be to customer confidence and ultimately to profits. Among its benefits, the promotional material listed 'fewer crises' and 'less risk of litigation'.

An Audit Commission survey of 900 UK organizations revealed that half of the public sector organizations interviewed and a third of private sector companies had been affected by IT fraud or abuse. The professional world was quickly coming to the conclusion that a simple lapse in information security can damage an organization's credibility, reduce customer confidence, and ultimately damage profits.

The whole point of establishing standards is to promote the widespread standardization of working practice; so it was inevitable that such a significant business issue was recognized to be a universal problem – one demanding a worldwide standard. Thus, it was only a matter of time before the British standard BS 7799 Part 1: 1999 became the internationally recognized ISO standard ISO/IEC 17799: 2000, Code of Practice for Information Security.

In the few years between the development of the original BS 7799 and the ISO/IEC 17799 standards, there had been a sea change in BSI's philosophy: the institution recognized that standards alone could be viewed as prescriptive and restrictive – that is, if there were not the working practices in place to meet the relevant criteria, the standard would be perceived as little more than a set of rules.

The new enlightened view was that what businesses need are management systems – in short, the structure, philosophy and working methods that inherently meet the values defined by the standard. This led to the development and release of BS 7799–2: 1999 and subsequently to the release of the revised standard BS 7799 Part 2: 2002 – Information Security Management Systems: Specification with guidance for use. Part 2 of BS 7799 then becomes a basis for the organization's own information security management system (ISMS).

By emphasizing management systems, BSI was more able to help organizations to improve their efficiency from the inside out, whereas an emphasis on standards meant change from the outside in. BS 7799–2: 2002 introduces a better way of working, based on a management system that, with its inbuilt facility for constant improvement, is self-perpetuating.

Nowhere was there a greater need for consistent, focused working patterns and management practices than in the field of information security. It is a field in which care and attention have to permeate throughout the organization – from the CEO to the casual cleaner. This was a management system that could not afford to be the concern solely of the quality manager or the CEO or the IT manager – it demanded commitment from everyone in the organization.

Both the BS and ISO/IEC standards address the issues related to conventional paper-based information systems, analogue communications, digital communications and IT-based information systems. It is worth noting that the original BS standard was conceived during the hysteria of the 'dotcom bubble' – it was, rightly, perceived that the speed and prevalence of e-mail and other digital communication posed a phenomenal risk to information security. Data was travelling faster and further than ever before, and could readily be copied and compressed into ever-smaller media.

What the international standard covers

So what does the ISO/IEC 17799: 2000 document address? It provides guidelines on how the various controls that are identified in BS 7799–2: 2002 Annex A can be implemented by an organization developing an ISMS. Although it provides detailed information on these controls, it should be remembered that end users are advised to use the controls as appropriate to their business, and to identify and implement other controls that they may determine to be more suitable to their business. However, wherever possible the ISO/IEC 17799: 2000 document should be used in parallel with, and as a supporting document for, any registration or compliance statement to BS 7799–2: 2002.

An ISMS, as defined in BS 7799–2: 2002, must cover all of the following:

- **Management responsibility**: including management commitment, and resource management.
- **Management review of the ISMS**: including review input, review output and internal audits.
- **ISMS improvements** including continual improvements, corrective actions and preventative actions.
- **A security policy**: a document that demonstrates management support and commitment to the ISMS process.
- **Security organization**: a management framework to implement and sustain information security within the organization.
- **Asset clarification and control**: an inventory of assets, with responsibility assigned for maintaining security.
- **Personnel security**: job descriptions for all staff, outlining their security roles and responsibilities.
- **Physical and environmental security**: a definition of the security requirements for the premises and the people within them.
- **Communications and operations management**: a method of ensuring that communications operate within secure parameters.
- **Access control**: network management to ensure that only authorized people have access to relevant information, and to protect the supporting infrastructure.
- **Systems development and maintenance**: to ensure that IT projects and support activities are conducted securely, using data control and encryption where necessary.
- **Business continuity management**: a managed process for protecting critical business processes from major disasters or failures.
- **Compliance**: evidence of the organization's commitment to meet statutory or regulatory information security requirements, for its clients, employees and relevant authorities.

Most organizations will already have some of these in place, but few will be doing everything. BSI client managers are experienced in working with companies to evaluate their current system's merits, and in guiding them through the steps necessary to develop their management system to the point where it can be registered under the standard.

BSI have developed client service into a fine art – they can arrange training schemes to train clients' staff, they can provide written and digital training materials for self-study and they arrange regular seminars all over the country to introduce thought-provoking and informative angles on BS 7799–2: 2002 and other management systems.

Through its intimate relationship with businesses all over the world, BSI has learnt very graphically that standards – and, indeed, management systems – are not an end, but merely a means. But to what?

Benefits

The benefits are expressed as 'benefiting the bottom line' – that is, supporting the private sector objectives of efficiency and profitability – although clearly non-profit-making organizations stand to benefit in other no less valuable ways. When you consider the health, education and police services, it is obvious that BS 7799–2: 2002 could be even more relevant to the public sector.

The direct and indirect benefits of operating a management system based on BS 7799–2: 2002 include:

■ improved employee motivation;
■ increased efficiency;
■ better use of time and resources;
■ cost savings;
■ increased competitiveness;
■ increased customer satisfaction;
■ confidence throughout the supply chain;
■ fewer crises;
■ less risk of litigation;
■ wider market opportunities;
■ increased profits.

And there are further advantages. BSI point out that once an organization's ISMS is registered to BS 7799–2: 2002, it is in a good position to integrate this system with a quality management or environmental management system, to create an integrated management system.

Conclusion

This chapter began with the slogan 'walls have ears'. It should end with the slightly more sinister message that 'knowledge is power'. Over the years, successive boardroom coups have demonstrated that information has a tangible value and a very powerful influence over the fortunes of organizations and individuals.

In today's broadband, satellite communication world, ISMSs should not need much selling. The need for them is obvious – you cannot be unaware of how much information flows to and from your desktop, your department, and your domain.

While the threats are often invisible, it is reassuring that the solution is tangible and accessible. BS 7799–2: 2002 and its supporting document ISO/IEC 17799: 2000 are logical, practical to implement and easy to sustain. Are you going to go for it? Mind who you tell, or it will be all round the building …

BSI is a group of complementary businesses, all working to the same vision of support for business improvement and trade worldwide. We believe in the universal adoption of best management practices, reduction of risk throughout the trading process and the harmonization and acceptance of standards by consent as a means of achieving economic prosperity.

For further information contact: BSI Group, 389 Chiswick High Road, London W4 4AL. Tel: +44 (0)20 8996 7720; Web site: www.bsi-global.com

Countering cybercrime: risk management

Taking adequate steps to improve an organization's risk management in terms of cybercrime is no longer simply desirable; it is imperative, write The Fraud Advisory Panel's Cybercrime Working Group.

The combined code

In July 2003 a new version of the Combined Code was issued. The preamble to the Combined Code states:

C.2 Internal control: main principle

The board should maintain a sound system of internal control to safeguard shareholders' investment and the company's assets.

The Code provides that a company's board of directors should conduct a review of the effectiveness of any system of internal control on at least an annual basis. The company should take steps to establish a formal and transparent arrangement for considering how they should apply the financial reporting and internal control principles.

This includes ensuring that an independent audit committee is established. One of the roles of the committee is to ensure that the company's internal financial controls, internal control and risk management systems are reviewed.

Adequate procedures to deal with cybercrime is a part of the risk management system that needs to be in place and reviewed on an annual basis.

Turnbull guidelines

Non-compliance with the Turnbull Guidelines can result in management of a company being held liable and accountable for their failure to effectively carry out risk management and adequate checks of control processes.

Provision D2 of the Turnbull Guidelines states: 'The board should maintain a sound system of internal control to safeguard shareholders' investment and the company's assets.'

Provision D.2.1 states: 'The directors should, at least annually, conduct a review of the effectiveness of the group's system of internal control and should report to all shareholders that they have done so. The review should cover all controls including financial, operational and compliance controls and risk management.'

Provision D.2.2 states: 'Companies which do not have an internal audit function should periodically review the need for one.'

Data protection

Anyone who stores information about another person, be it for a commercial or other purpose, has a duty to maintain that data in accordance with the principles of data protection. This means that as well as the requirement that the data stored is accurate and not stored for a period of time longer than necessary, the data must be kept secure.

This will require businesses to take steps to ensure that their computer systems and operational functions comply. The DTI provides a business standard benchmark called BS 7799 (now adopted as ISO 17799) for businesses and organizations attempting to comply with the Data Protection Act and other IT security issues. This is a common-sense standard that every business should measure itself against even if it does not apply for full accreditation.

Liability of directors

Directors may, under the Turnbull Guidelines, find themselves in breach of duty to the company and, consequently, the shareholders for failing to carry out the correct risk management procedures and controls in respect of cybercrime.

Directors owe the company a number of fiduciary duties due to the position they hold within the company, including a duty of good faith and duty to act with due diligence. They also owe duties of professional competence depending upon the terms of a director's service contract.

In the event that a company loses a substantial amount of money to a cyber-criminal it may be unable or find it not commercially viable to pursue the fraudster. In that case a company may be obliged to look to the director responsible for the implementation of risk management for redress. If the director has failed to act with due care in respect of a foreseeable risk, this may result in the company seeking to establish that the director was liable for breach of duty of care and to recover damages from that director.

Liability of accessories

It is important to appreciate that the person who has committed the fraud may not be the only person against whom a remedy can be obtained. There may be other people involved in committing the crime and therefore equally accountable. For example, in the case of cyber laundering, a firm may become liable by virtue of the principle of constructive trusteeship, depending on whether it was at any point in receipt of laundered funds.

It is as a result of the principle of liability of accessories that banks and others used as a conduit by money launderers may find themselves becoming secondary victims.

Following the Electronic Signatures Regulations 2002 it is now possible in certain circumstances to pursue an action against a certification service provider that guarantees the veracity of a digital signature, where that guarantee is reasonably relied on by a person and that reliance causes loss.[1] If one of the prescribed circumstances exists and a duty of care is thereby established, the onus is upon the certification service provider to show that he or she was not negligent. It would usually be the task of the party alleging negligence to prove that the other party was negligent.

Lawyers and accountants who have been involved in setting up any scheme may also be legitimate targets.

Therefore, depending on the particular nature of your business, there are multitudes of different ways in which a business can incur liability for the cyber crimes of a fraudster.

The key to avoiding liability for money laundering is to 'know your customer'. Firms should take action in support of anti-money-laundering measures in order to comply with legal requirements and protect their corporate reputation. Evidence of identity and beneficial ownership of a company should be sought, and a higher level of due diligence undertaken where there are:

∎ numbered or alternative accounts;
∎ high-risk countries involved in a transaction such as those appearing on the Financial Action Task Force's list of non-compliant jurisdictions;
∎ offshore jurisdictions;
∎ high-risk activities;
∎ public officials involved.

Reviewing policy and procedure

Many firms will carry out financial controls, audits and assessments. The Turnbull Report places greater emphasis on the need for assessment of risk and operational controls. This means that senior management are required to review the procedures applied to risk management and control on an annual basis and decide which areas are lacking in such controls. Essentially they will have to start carrying out an internal audit of operational risk. The business benefit of this is that it can be stated on annual accounts and could lead to greater trust by customers.

---

[1] Statutory Instrument 318/2002

In order to effectively review policy and procedure in terms of operational risk management, companies should be reviewing their Internet strategy and the related risk management issues at board level. In particular it is advisable that companies and organizations appoint one director to oversee the area where business strategy warrants this level of supervision, attaching responsibility for operational risk in relation to cybercrime to this individual or his or her department. This has the advantage of reducing the risk of criminal and civil prosecution of directors or the company for failure to comply with current standards and regulations, and may well reduce long-term fraud losses. It may also reduce the chances that the company is rendered liable for receiving laundered or fraudulently obtained funds under the doctrine of constructive liability. However the fight against cybercrime must be fought on all company levels. It is necessary to establish policy and procedure that applies to everybody in the business.

Cybercrime policy statement

A policy statement and settled working practices should be published by the board to ensure that all employees know the standard required of them and the company stance in relation to cybercrime. Such a statement needs to be explained to every employee, and should ideally be included in contracts of employment, supply and outsourcing agreements.

The policy statement should be clear about the action that the company will take in the event that an act of cybercrime is detected. The statement should clearly express the company's policy towards cybercrime and its determination to deter fraud generally.

It should be made clear that the company:

- will investigate and report to its local police or other appropriate authority any suspected acts of cybercrime;
- will assist the police in their investigations and prosecution of a cyber-criminal if appropriate;
- will take civil action where possible and recover assets that have been stolen or pursue a cyber-criminal for damages;
- expects employees to report any incidence of cybercrime of which they are aware, and assumes that each employee, irrespective of his or her level of seniority, has a responsibility for reporting cybercrime;
- will treat internally perpetrated cybercrime as seriously as a cybercrime perpetrated by an outsider;
- has particular procedures that should be followed in the event that a cybercrime occurs.

The DTI report says the increase in cybercrime is partly because companies give employees access to the Web and their own work e-mail addresses. It may also be of merit to include guidelines and company policy statements in relation to employee Internet and e-mail use in employment contracts. For example, these might highlight the danger of opening e-mails with attachments from unknown sources, list sites that are prohibited from use, or explaining company policy in relation to Internet and software piracy (another common form of cybercrime).

Managing the prevention, detection and prosecution of cybercrime

Cybercrime management should be dealt with throughout the organization, and the importance of employee awareness should be emphasized at all levels.

Cybercrime needs to be treated as a business risk, and an organization therefore needs to carry out a risk management assessment procedure to ensure that the steps taken to prevent cybercrime are effective in relation to the practices peculiar to that organization. Anti-cybercrime procedures should be tailored to match the type of business in which an organization is involved. For example, an e-tailer is more likely to be concerned with establishing the identity of the individual attempting to carry out a *card-not-present* transaction to make an online purchase, as this type of business is more prone to the risk of identity theft and credit card fraud. The fraudster is more likely to be an outsider. A business-to-business company trading online may be more concerned with establishing procedures and controls that reduce the risk of e-procurement fraud, and may wish to employ fraud detection methods such as data mining, or require procedures for the making of e-tenders. In the case of e-procurement fraud the fraud is far more likely to be perpetrated by an insider, and as such the methods of detecting the fraud need to reflect this fact.

Risk management of the threat of cybercrime should be approached as follows:

- Identify the areas within the business that are most vulnerable to cyber-attack.
- Establish the controls that they already have in place to address these risks.
- Identify any further controls that may assist in reducing the risk.
- Monitor pre-existing controls to ensure they are being implemented effectively.
- Assess the controls to account for any changes or developments made in the operation of the organization.
- Ensure that procedures and controls are workable and supported by a sufficient level of resources.
- Establish a regular review procedure.

Whistle-blowing policy

All organizations should establish a culture of cybercrime awareness, and part of doing so is to ensure that employees know that whistle-blowing is a necessary part of the fight to prevent cybercrime. Employees should have available to them a simple procedure for reporting any suspicion that cybercrime is taking place. This may include an internal e-mail address to send details to, or a hot line to enable an employee to report his or her complaint quickly, and if desired, anonymously.

It should also be made possible for the employee to report to management in different departments or management with no direct responsibility for that employee, given that the employee may fear that his or her direct manager is somehow implicated in an act of cyber-fraud. It should be made clear to employees that all reports will be treated as confidential and where they are made in good faith the employee is normally protected under the Public Interest Disclosure Act (PIDA) 1998.

This is particularly relevant to incidences of cybercrime where, as discussed earlier, a good proportion of the problem arises from the unlawful conduct of insiders and employees. The objective of PIDA is to ensure that employees can inform their employers of wrongdoing within an organization without fear of repercussions, allowing problems to be identified and resolved in as little time as possible. The repercussions referred to cover different types of detriment that an employee may suffer after having made such a disclosure, including a denial of a promotion or training opportunities, or of facilities that the employee would have been offered had it not been for the disclosure.

An employee is protected by PIDA if he or she makes a qualifying disclosure of information that he or she reasonably believes (and the employee can show that he or she reasonably believes) tends to show that one of the following offences or breaches have been, are being or will be committed, irrespective of whether the employee is later shown to have been incorrect:

■ a criminal offence;
■ a breach of a legal obligation;
■ a danger to health and safety of any person;
■ environmental damage;
■ intentional concealing of information that demonstrates that any of the above has occurred.

The disclosure is protected if the employee makes a qualifying disclosure either through his or her employer's internal whistle-blowing procedure, or by making the disclosure to another person whom the worker reasonably believes to be solely or mainly responsible for the relevant failure.

The employee must also make the disclosure in good faith.

A worker may also be protected if he or she makes a disclosure in good faith externally, though there may be additional conditions that need to be complied with, depending on the circumstances and to whom the disclosure is made. For example if the information relates to a fraud the employee might be protected in reporting to the Serious Fraud Office, or in the case of an offence relating to the environment, the Environment Agency.

Where a company does not have the resources to set up a whistle-blowing mechanism internally, it is possible to outsource the service. For serious cases of cyber-fraud it is possible to report to the National Hi-Tech Crime Unit.

What to do when cybercrime is detected

It is necessary to maintain a procedure for dealing with any report of cyber-fraud. The procedure to be implemented will vary depending on the size of the business and the scale and seriousness of the cybercrime being investigated.

A firm may wish to appoint one person as responsible for investigating the cybercrime. This person will in turn be responsible for researching the best methods of investigating a specific type of cybercrime. They may also be given responsibility for assessing the in-house skills available for investigating cybercrime, for example whether the firm has anyone with the computer science skills to enable electronic evidence to be detected and preserved. It will also be necessary for that person to establish contacts with specialist lawyers and investigators.

Damage mitigation is another issue that must be addressed by the firm. It should be decided how it is possible to stop a particular cybercrime from happening again, and whether improved techniques of risk management are necessary. It must be considered how the firm intends to secure and gather the evidence without alerting a criminal. The firm must address the question of how it intends to deal with a suspect, and when it should contact the relevant authorities such as the National High Tech Crime Unit.

As with all frauds, it must be considered when it is appropriate to inform the public that a cybercrime has occurred, bearing in mind the damage that such an announcement can have on a business compared with the value of the crime itself.

If an organization does intend to prosecute a cybercrime it must bear in mind the following:

- speed;
- strategy;
- surprise.

Money is transferable by one e-mail, telephone call or fax. It is therefore vital not only that any investigation/analysis is conducted in utmost secrecy, but also that action is taken before the fraudster has an inkling that he or she is being investigated. At the very earliest opportunity, an analysis should be carried out to assess:

- whether there has been any fraud;
- the extent of the fraud;
- whether it is viable to try to recover the losses sustained.

To do this it may be necessary to examine the computer server logs and individuals' computers. There is a list of 'Do's and Don'ts' at the end of this chapter aimed at helping prevent otherwise vital evidence needed for civil recovery or criminal action from being destroyed.

Third party disclosure as to assets and whereabouts

The English courts provide invaluable assistance to a victim, in that in certain circumstances they grant orders that enable the victim, without notice to the fraudster, to discover:

- the extent of the fraud;
- who is responsible; and
- who was involved in the commission of the fraud and therefore could be liable as well.

The court would for example grant orders against third parties who have been unwittingly involved in the fraud, whether such fraud has been committed electronically or in the physical world. For instance, the court will require disclosure of relevant information by an Internet Service Provider or a bank through which money stolen from the victim has passed. Such orders for disclosure can be combined with what is called a 'gagging order' that prevents the party giving disclosure from notifying the fraudster. Breach of such an order will amount to contempt of court, which is punishable by prison.

Once the extent of the fraud has been assessed, decisions need to be taken whether it is commercially sensible (and whether there is an obligation) to pursue the fraudster and if so, to what extent. No victim, however large or small, should fail to assess the significance of publicity, given the fact that it has been the victim of fraud which is often caused by inadequate security measures or lack of judgment.

Recruitment, training and personnel policies

Insiders and employees perpetrate the majority of financial crime. Cybercrime is no different. It is therefore essential for organizations to take appropriate steps to ensure their computer and physical security is adequate. Personnel should be carefully vetted. References should be checked, and this includes temporary staff. The procedure for vetting and checking should become more stringent when employees are promoted to greater positions of responsibility, and the greater the amount of personal, financial or sensitive data to which the employee is privy.

Employers should consider multi-level security, including biometrically fingerprinting employees and implementing similar security procedures of this nature to ensure that employees are only permitted access to an appropriate level according to their role or seniority. Access levels should be reviewed on a frequent basis.

Employees who leave a firm (for any reason) should immediately be removed from the security clearance lists, and any access to an organization's database should be removed. Security lists should regularly be reviewed to ensure that those who do have access should have access, and whether access is necessary to the level permitted.

Employers should consider the use of monitoring e-mails and communications in order to prevent fraud and other forms of cybercrime, where it is warranted.

Collaboration with government agencies and professional advisory bodies

Organizations should consider collaborating with governmental and professional advisory organizations to report how they manage information security and cybercrime threats, and work with suppliers and users to coordinate information on incidents. This will assist businesses in plugging the knowledge and information gaps, assessing where risk management procedures are lacking and where a business's vulnerabilities lie.

In connection with this, organizations may find it of great assistance to collaborate with government and industry advisory bodies to produce educational materials on the nature of cybercrime, why it has posed a problem for their particular business and how they have obtained information and guidance on the subject.

Ultimately, reviewing existing and producing further guidance on basic information security requirements and good risk management practice to combat cybercrime could be used to produce a Superhighway Code. This would ideally take into account BS7799, organizations established by the Information Systems Audit and Information Control Association, and also the work of the IT Governance Institute in the United States.

The aim is to eventually raise general awareness among industry, accountancy and the legal professions of the law relating to cybercrime and its effective precaution.

Compliance

No procedure or control is effective unless it is properly implemented throughout an organization. Regular checks must be undertaken in order to ensure that all necessary controls are being adequately implemented by employees at all levels, short-cuts are not used in such a way as to dilute their effectiveness, and that these controls remain effective in the light of changes in the law or in the development of the organization's business.

Do's and don'ts for computer based information

Computer evidence or data is fundamentally different from, say, paper evidence. Just the act of turning on a computer can change a whole series of dates and times and invalidate its use in a court or tribunal. Therefore, a few basic principles need to be followed when dealing with potentially valuable computer evidence.

Do:

- fully assess the situation before taking any action;
- isolate the computer so that it cannot be tampered with;
- record where the computer is based and all who had access to it;
- consider securing all relevant logs (for example, building access logs, server logs, Internet logs) and any CCTV footage at the earliest opportunity;
- call in IT security staff or external consultants as appropriate.

Then ask the relevant expert to:

- disconnect the relevant computers from your network;
- restrict remote access;
- take an 'image' copy of the computer.

Don't:

- alert any potential suspects;
- call in your own IT support staff (they often change evidence inadvertently);
- turn on the computer if it is switched off;
- turn off the computer if it is switched on;
- make a copy of the computer;
- examine electronic logs without first ensuring that they are preserved elsewhere.

The Fraud Advisory Panel is an independent body of volunteers drawn from the public and private sectors. The Panel's role is to raise awareness of the immense social and economic damage that is caused by fraud and develop effective remedies. Members of the Fraud Advisory Panel include representatives from the law and accountancy professions, industry associations, financial institutions, government agencies, law enforcement, regulatory authorities and academia.

For more information contact the Fraud Advisory Panel, Chartered Accountants' Hall, PO Box 433, Moorgate Place, London, EC2P 2BJ, Tel: 020 7920 8721, Fax: 020 7920 8536, E-mail: info@fraudadvisorypanel.org, Web site: www.fraudadvisorypanel.org

Countering cybercrime

Peter Brudenall of Simmons & Simmons assesses what should be done to reduce the effects of cybercrime.

Introduction

The security of information technology (IT) and management of data will be a key area of risk for business in the foreseeable future. On both sides of the Atlantic, the legal profession is paying greater attention to the liabilities that companies and individual directors face if they fail to manage adequately the security of their systems or data, or are unable to prevent their systems being used to attack third parties. The accidental release of customer data, for example, has already led to significant claims being made against major companies, leading to negative media attention and the loss of consumer revenue.

However, despite ongoing concerns about global terrorism, the denial of service (DoS) attacks against 13 of the Internet's core servers during 2002, and the problems caused in 2003 by the SQL 'slammer' bug, the recent MyDoom virus, the evidence is that there is still a considerable disregard shown by businesses to the issue of IT security. Less than a third of UK businesses have a documented security policy, and only 27 per cent spend more than 1 per cent of their IT budget on information security. There is clearly a significant lack of awareness to the risks posed by an IT security breach.

Accordingly, businesses will need to substantially increase the attention paid to IT security. With perhaps the exception of financial institutions, healthcare groups and other regulated bodies, it is fair to say that most businesses spend paltry sums protecting their corporate networks. Many firms simply do not understand the cost of a security breach, and what the impact may be on reputation, customer loyalty or revenue. In any event, increasing the budget for IT security may become a requirement of conducting business in many jurisdictions. There are already signs that government regulation in this area will increase dramatically in Europe, the United States, and in the Asia-Pacific region.

As the threat from cyber-terrorism, computer viruses, malicious hacking and technology failure increases, so too will the risk that legal action will result from a failure to implement minimum standards of security.

Risks to computer systems can be anything from defacing a corporate Web site to sabotaging an electricity distribution system. Each of these risks is associated with business risks. If, for example, a business incurs a serious virus infection, the costs that may be incurred will relate to:

- loss of e-mail gateway;
- loss of data;
- fall in productivity and wasted staff time;
- loss of opportunities;
- costs associated with repairs and remedial action.

There may also be damage to brand or professional reputation. When a security incident occurs, the need to be able to respond quickly and effectively is vital in order to minimize what may be some significant costs. Knowing the main vulnerabilities of IT systems will be necessary in order to plan such contingency measures. A comprehensive risk assessment is therefore essential. Once identified, the necessary personnel can then put together plans to reduce the risks that are likely to have the greatest impact on the organization's assets.

Objectives of IT security

Malicious attacks on data will threaten the core elements of trust and reliability that underpin your IT business systems. Threats to confidentiality, integrity or availability of data will render data unreliable and have serious business, and possibly legal consequences.

Data confidentiality

A key objective of security is confidentiality: ensuring that information is kept away from people who should not have it. For some industries, such as health care and finance, privacy and the confidentiality of personal data is now a regulatory issue. The US, European, Canadian, and Australian governments have all legislated privacy controls to varying degrees. When an IT system is accessed by an unauthorized person, or in an unauthorized way, the confidentiality of data is put at risk. An attacker may snoop, eavesdrop or intercept communications. Software for cracking passwords or other hacker scripts is freely available, and unsuspecting people may be tricked into divulging confidential information.

Data integrity

Another key objective of security is integrity: assuring that the information stored in the computer is never contaminated or changed in a way that is not appropriate. The basic ways to maintain the integrity of data are to keep it away from those who should not have it, and to ensure that those who should have it can access it.

Data availability

A third objective of security is availability: ensuring that data stored in the computer can be accessed by those people who have the right to access it. This is a broad subject addressing things such as fault tolerance to protect against denial of service and access control to ensure that data is available to those people authorized to access it. A DoS attack, for example, targets data availability by flooding the communication link with excessive packets precluding all other traffic. Such an attack disrupts e-mail operation and Web site transactions. A recent example of a DoS attack was the attack that flooded all 13 of the root servers of the Internet Domain Name System (DNS).

Data non-repudiation

The technologies used for the objectives of confidentiality, integrity and availability can also be used to achieve another objective of security: non-repudiation. This allows for the formation of binding contracts without any paper being printed for written signatures. Non-repudiation has valuable goals: assuring that messages received from the person whom the message claims actually sent it and that the message has not been altered in any way in transit. This also usually provides for the ability to prevent users who send messages from denying that they were sent.

Principles for best practice

What are the 'appropriate' IT security measures that businesses should be taking? Although such measures will change over time, and it is important to stay current with what constitutes best practice, the following represents a general guide as to what is required.

Threat and vulnerability assessments should be performed regularly

Some companies have been doing threat and vulnerability assessments for years; others are yet to introduce any program to assess cyber risks. In light of the ongoing risk of terrorist attacks, and the well-documented risks to computer systems, it is clear that assessments should be as common as other types of better-known security assessments, such as theft.

Accordingly, it is suggested that organizations consider that:

■ Critical infrastructure providers might now be attractive to terrorist organizations.
■ Those companies that do not manage 'attractive targets' may need to prepare for business disruptions.
■ They must contemplate the ways in which such an attack may occur.
■ They carefully assess vulnerabilities by hiring corporate or government agencies to conduct an 'attack and penetration' of their own networks. If successful, they can convince management that their systems can, in fact, be exploited.
■ They deploy network assessments, which are more thorough than an attack and penetration.

Information about threats and vulnerabilities should be shared

As systems have become more complex, securing them has become increasingly more difficult. The challenge for the security community has been to ensure that computer users are notified when vulnerabilities are found, and that fixes are implemented. Information exchange is seen as key, and is considered a central plank of the US Government's National Strategy to Secure Cyberspace. However, there is an understandable reluctance on the part of commercial entities to reveal security flaws in their own systems. Once a company has been exploited, such public exposure can cause customers and investors to lose confidence, adversely impact equity markets and create the risk that other crackers will view the organization as vulnerable, thus inviting additional attacks.

Effective security policies and procedures should be implemented

Robust security policies and procedures are the pillars upon which security is built. While it is almost certain that regulators will insist on security issues being given more prominence in light of recent terrorist activity, there are already a number of excellent industry-led international standards regarding security (for instance, ISO 9000, BS 7799) with, as indicated above, the likelihood of more being developed with the input of the major industry players. Companies should identify gaps between their own corporate standards and these industry-wide best practices, but recognize that they may need actually to go beyond what is set out in the standard. Certainly terms and conditions with service providers managing your data should specify compliance with the appropriate standard.

Computer security should be assessed and upgraded continually

Threats must continually be reassessed as the world changes, because neither technology nor security is static. Computer security and upgrades must also be assessed continually. On the technology side, some of the considerations are that new vulnerabilities may be discovered in older products, so installing patches may be required. Old products may be upgraded, and new products deployed, thus introducing new vulnerabilities into a network.

Business changes may also require computer security to be reassessed. For example:

■ Outsourcing critical functions may give contractors privileged access to an organization's computer systems. Remember also that legislation may dictate certain terms to be added to contracts, particularly if personal data is being managed or transferred out of the country.
■ Entering into a joint venture may cause two organizations to connect their networks.
■ Offering new applications to customers (for example, online shopping or e-banking) may create links between the public at large and an organization's internal systems. So each business change affecting the information infrastructure creates a need to reassess threats, to identify new potential vulnerabilities, and to take proactive steps to minimize risks.

'Round the clock' monitoring should be deployed

Computer security experts generally agree that most computer crimes are neither detected nor reported. This is often because many computer crimes are not self-evident. When a hacker steals a computerized customer list, the original remains in place, available to the owner, and it may not be immediately apparent that anything has been taken. Employing monitoring that is as close to 24/7 as possible is becoming standard.

Security incident response plans should be developed, and coordinated with overall contingency plans

An organization's ability to detect and respond quickly to simulated attacks should also be tested. While some investigations may be conducted merely to assess damage and restore the security of the attacked system, the primary goal should be to develop the evidence necessary to assign responsibility and take legal action.

Before such testing can be done, an organization should review and document the following:

■ incident management policies, procedures and plans (including staffing, tool requirements and escalation procedures);
■ processes to log network activity in the event of an attack;
■ evidence collection and maintenance procedures.

Cyber security incident response plans should be closely coordinated with physical contingency and disaster recovery plans, especially since future cyber attacks may be linked with physical attacks. These plans should address ownership of an incident, escalation procedures, physical and electronic evidence handling procedures, coordination with law enforcement and media relations.

Educate customers

Educating your customers is also important to minimize the risk of identity theft or the unauthorized accessing of personal data. For example, suggesting to customers that they use different passwords, avoid common passwords and then change them frequently, can contribute greatly to decreasing the chances of unauthorized transactions occurring.

Simmons & Simmons was ranked joint second in the United Kingdom for outsourcing in a recent survey of in-house lawyers by *The Lawyer* magazine.

In 2002, Global Counsel 3000 ranked Simmons & Simmons in the top 10 worldwide for performance in all major practice areas, based on the views of in-house counsel at over 5,000 companies across 74 jurisdictions. Earlier this year the firm won a prestigious Queen's Award for Enterprise in the International Trade category, the only law firm to do so.

For further information contact David Barrett, partner, Tel: +44 (0)20 7825 4032, E-mail: david.barrett@simmons-simmons.com or Peter Brudenall, senior lawyer, Tel: +44 (0)20 7825 4346, E-mail: peter.brudenall@simmons-simmons.com; Web site: www.simmons-simmons.com

Bibliography

Information Assurance Advisory Council (IAAC) (2002) *Protecting the Digital Society* IAAC, Cambridge, UK (March) [Online] www.iaac.org.uk

Lewis, J (2000) Security strategy must focus on business issue of managing risk, *InternetWeek*, 831, Manhasset; 2 October, p. 41

Witty (2001) *The Price of Information Security, Strategic Analysis Report*, Gartner Research, 8 June, Note no: R-11–6534

Centralized security management

Zuhamy Colton of Indicii Salus considers the benefits of centralized management.

Security is vital to businesses as a risk management tool. Risks can take many forms and affect organizations in many ways – access to a restricted resource, disclosure of confidential information, modification of information in transit between sender and receiver, the sender pretending to be somebody else and so on. Gartner Group estimates that hackers attack more than 200 UK companies every day, and according to the Department of Trade and Industry, 51 percent of companies suffered a data abuse incident in 2002, with each attack costing on average £30,000. Cryptography, specifically encryption and digital signatures, can be used to reduce many of these risks. It is a powerful tool used to secure communications and ensure the confidentiality, authenticity and integrity of a message. Yet the use of cryptography introduces new problems. In order to understand the importance of centrally managed cryptographic technology, one needs to understand the different types of cryptographic keys used and the effects of managing these keys.

Cryptography uses keys (large numbers with appropriate mathematical properties), in order to secure information. There are two types of keys, symmetric and asymmetric. A single symmetric key is used for both protecting a document (a procedure that involves a mathematical transformation of information into apparently meaningless gibberish, called cipher text) and recovering the original document. Symmetric keys are mainly used to ensure the confidentiality of information, and must themselves remain known only to individuals with rights to recover a protected document.

Asymmetric keys on the other hand, come in pairs (called public and private) and have the property that what one of the pair protects only the other of the pair can recover.

Therefore these keys can be used to ensure not only the confidentiality of documents but also their integrity and authenticity.

Private keys must be kept secret. Public keys can be distributed freely, but it is important that the connection between public keys and user identities is maintained, since otherwise an attacker could substitute its own public key for that of another user and trick other users into protecting documents for it instead of the intended recipient. This can have devastating effects for an organization.

A private key is used either when digitally signing a document to prove whom it came from or when retrieving protected information received from another person. The person holding the private key is the only person that can turn the e-mail/file from completely unintelligible text into a legible document.

The public key is used either when verifying the digital signature on a document or (using the recipient's public key) encrypting for the recipient, and is given to anybody who wants to send encrypted information to the user.

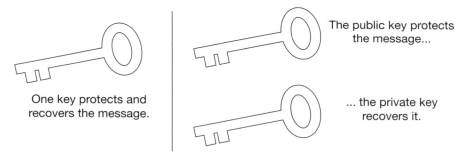

Figure 4.5.1   Symmetric and asymmetric cryptography

All keys need to be managed and protected (from both theft and substitution), which can become a costly and panic-inducing experience to organizations, especially when all conventional solutions force end users to manage their own keys. Effective key management is fundamental to the success of any crypto-based security infrastructure. Poor key management renders the security system obsolete and is an economic burden on an organization.

Client-centric versus server-centric: comparative key management functions

When most of the work involved with managing the keys is performed on the client machine by the end user, this is called a client-centric system (or device-centric); this means users store their own private keys and everyone's public keys on their devices and each of these has to be secured. In contrast, a server-centric system is where public and private keys are stored on a central server. All users access their keys via this central server, instead of having direct access to them on their devices.

These different architectures have radically different consequences and associated costs for the management of keys. In the case of a centralized system the cost is reduced in many ways: perhaps the most palpable is not having to secure the private keys on every device, only the server.

Key generation or regeneration

Good security practice dictates that keys are only used for one purpose. Users need to have separate key pairs for encryption and signing. This means each user will have several public and private key pairs. These must be generated with mathematical properties before a user can use the system.

In a client-centric system, key pairs are typically generated by performing an operation on the user's own personal device using the client-centric software. This may be done by the user, assuming the software is easy enough to use or the user has sufficient knowledge to do so, or by a system administrator performing the operation on the user's device. Either approach is time-consuming for either the user or the internal IT resources of your organization.

In a server-centric system, key pairs are generated by an administrator on the central server and are stored on that server. This step is completely invisible to ordinary users. The administrator can easily generate keys for hundreds of users without having physical access to their personal devices, therefore saving the organization time and money.

It is important that the machine where the key pairs are generated should not have been compromised, or an attacker could steal them as they are being generated. A server is a much more difficult target than an ordinary user machine, making a server-centric system safer.

Key distribution

In order for two users to communicate securely, they must have access to each other's public keys. In a client-centric system, users must either exchange public keys amongst themselves or must send their public keys to a central administrator who will then distribute a list of public keys to all users. The client-centric software may provide facilities to automate this process to some extent, but since users keep public keys (their own and other people's) on their personal devices, some user involvement in and understanding of this process is inevitably required, and once again the process is time-consuming. In a server-centric system, all public keys are held on the central server, so users can easily access them with no additional effort.

Key protection

In a client-centric system, by definition, private keys are held on the users' devices. They are usually protected with a password, but (particularly if a user has chosen a weak password) anyone who can get access to the device can copy the private key and attempt to guess the password. Devices used directly by users are often relatively easy to get access to; many employees will have physical access to other employees' devices such a laptop or PDA, which are even more easily accessed since they are routinely taken off the company premises.

In a server-centric system, the keys used for encrypting and signing are held on the central server and never leave it. Users and their personal computers never have the private keys in their physical possession, so it is impossible to steal a key by stealing a device. The worst that can happen is that an attacker is able to authenticate to the server-centric system as one of its users, which temporarily allows use of the user's keys via the server, but once the problem is discovered the administrator can immediately prevent access to the keys.

Key revocation

If an attacker acquires access to a user's private key or compromises the protection of the public key, even temporarily, other users must be notified so that they stop using the corresponding public key to communicate with the user whose key was compromised. This is a difficult, time-consuming and costly task to perform in a client-centric architecture since copies of the compromised key are distributed widely.

As mentioned in key distribution, a server-centric system holds all the keys and therefore allows the administrator to revoke the keys instantly, an important point for many organizations, particularly those with a high turnover of employees.

Disaster recovery

If a user's private key is lost or rendered unusable through a forgotten password or hardware failure, it is no longer possible to decrypt any documents encrypted for that user. This could have serious consequences for the user's employer.

In a client-centric system, private keys are held on the device, so some mechanism must be put in place to periodically take a back-up copy of keys in case something happens to the copy held on it. This represents a risk for many organizations. For instance, if a user chooses to, or is forced to, regenerate his or her keys, the new keys may not be backed up immediately and any documents encrypted using the new keys will be rendered inaccessible if the key is lost. If a user protects his or her key with a password and then forgets it, it may be impossible to recover access to the key.

In a server-centric system, all keys are on the server, so backing up the server periodically is sufficient. This is obviously much easier and less time-consuming for administrators, allowing organizations to allocate staff to other priorities of their business. Keys are stored encrypted on the server, but they are not encrypted directly using the user's password, so if a user forgets his or her password, the password can be changed to allow access to the keys without any disruption.

Ubiquitous access

Users may wish to protect or verify documents from many different devices in different physical locations. In a client-centric system, each separate device must have its own copy of the user's private keys for this to be possible. These multiple copies introduce management problems, since key regeneration and revocation require every copy to be updated. It also means that the user cannot just use any device with the relevant software to protect or verify documents, since the user's keys are not going to be present on a device. In a server-centric system, as long as users have access to the server, they can access their keys from any device in any location without having had to take any steps to place their keys on that device in advance.

Key escrow

A company has legitimate grounds for allowing certain employees to verify documents protected for other employees. For example, the personal assistant of a law firm might review the incoming e-mail of a partner, or a person might be legally required to access someone else's e-mail. In a client-centric system, users give their private keys to the person they delegate the reading rights to. This is blunt because:

■ *The user does not have technical means to remove access from the reader again* (that is, the person could have copied the private key to some other place).
■ *The user gives full-blown access.* In a server-centric system, the user with this privilege never actually gets direct access to the other user's private key, so there is no way he or she can take a copy of it to use in the future. Instead, access to the key is mediated via the central server.

In a server-centric approach it is possible to limit further the access to the key (for instance, allow reading only of document generated in a certain time span, only generated by a certain group of people, only e-mails but not Word documents, and so on).

Policy enforcement

A company may wish to specify various policies for the use of cryptographic software. For example, restrictions on acceptable passwords may be specified in order to avoid users choosing weak passwords.

In a client-centric system, any such policies can only be enforced if they are done so via the client software. It is certainly possible to do this, but the policies may have to be specified individually on each device, making it difficult to administer them. Also, because users have access to their own private keys, it would be possible for them to copy the keys on to a different machine, perhaps their home computer, with a copy of the client software, which does not enforce the desired policies and presents a difficulty when updating them.

In a server-centric system, the server itself can enforce policies. This provides a convenient single location from which to administer policies. Since users have no choice but to interact with the server in order to use their keys, there is no potential for accidental or deliberate policy breaches by users. In addition, any changes to policy can easily be reflected and administered without incurring the overhead of making changes to individual machines and access devices.

Conclusion

Centralized management is not only more user-friendly for an organization's user population (that is, employees, clients, suppliers and so on) but it allows organizations to have cost-effective and 'always on' security. Users are not forced to worry about whether the device they are using is secure.

Table 4.5.1 Centralized management and device-based management

Centralized management	Device-based management
Keys are stored securely on the server	Keys are stored on user machines, making theft of keys more likely
Keys are generated securely on the server	Keys are generated on the client, so a compromised client may allow an attacker to observe the process
Keys for many users can be generated easily on the server	Users' keys need to be generated on their own client devices
Keys are distributed via the server, so users do not need to be involved, thus security can be as automated as company policy dictates	Users need to exchange public keys amongst themselves or work with an administrator to share them
Key management is performed centrally by administrative staff on the secure server	Users need to manage their own keys, or administrators must visit their machines to do it for them. Client devices must be properly secured for this to be safe.
Compromised keys can be revoked and regenerated immediately	All users with a copy of a compromised key have to be informed when it is revoked and regenerated
Forgotten passwords can be reset by the administrator	Forgotten passwords make a user's keys inaccessible
Keys can be accessed from anywhere there is a network connection to the server	Keys must be copied to a client machine in advance
Keys can be backed up centrally on the server	Keys must be backed up from a distributed collection of client machines
One user can immediately be given access to another user's keys, and this access can be revoked immediately any time in the future	Giving one user access to another user's keys requires giving them physical possession of the keys, which is time-consuming. It is impossible to ensure that the second user has not kept a copy of the keys when he or she no longer has a legitimate reason to use them.
Policies on the use of the system are rigorously enforced by the server	Policies on the use of the system are enforced by client machines, making it more likely that users can subvert them
Policies can be changed and updated on the server and will automatically affect all users	Policy changes must be made on all client machines individually

The function of key management in its entirety is made simpler, resulting in better security and an overall reduction in cost due to the ease of deployment and management of the security infrastructure as a whole. From the perspective of deployment and applications, a server-centric approach not only enables better security but also it saves you time and money.

Indicii Salus, a London-based security services specialist, offers a comprehensive suite of secure services and solutions based on Xenophon, a unique server-centric security solution. Xenophon solutions vary from the protection of e-mail to securing a variety of Web content; its services are delivered via a single user identity, across a wide range of access devices, independent of location.

For further information contact: Zuhamy Colton, Marketing Manager, Indicii Salus, Indicii Salus House, 2 Bessborough Gardens, London, SW1V 2JE, Tel: +44 (0) 20 7836 0123, Fax: +44 (0) 207 836 0567, E-mail: zcolton@indiciisalus.com

Electronic contracting

Contracting online is an attractive development for retailers, who can make their products available to a much wider customer base, but to take advantage of this new opportunity, retailers must take appropriate steps to ensure that the online contract entered into with the customer is valid and made on the right terms, says Peter Brudenall of Simmons & Simmons.

Legal considerations

The core considerations are:

- the ability of parties to contract online;
- formation of online contracts;
- incorporation of an e-tailer's standard terms and conditions.

Can parties contract online?

With the exception of contracts for the sale or transfer of an interest in land, and contracts for the provision of consumer credit, most contracts can be made online and have the same basic requirements as contracting offline. There must be an accepted set of terms, and both parties must intend to enter into a legally binding contract and provide consideration.

An offer or an invitation to treat?

When information, such as a price list, is displayed on a Web site, is this construed as an offer or just an invitation to treat? If the prices displayed amount to an offer, and the customer's selecting and ordering the product amounts to an acceptance, then the e-tailer will be bound to sell the product at the price displayed on the Web site. This is unlikely to be the approach taken by the English courts. To draw an analogy with the treatment of goods displayed in a shop, the price displayed on the Web site is likely to be an invitation to treat and not an offer. The offer would subsequently be made when the customer selects and orders the product. The offer is then accepted by the e-tailer when it confirms the order, or on delivery of the product. This scenario may not always be the case, as the presumption that the prices on a Web site only constitute an invitation to treat may be rebutted by the words or conduct of the e-tailer.

Web sites, therefore, should be designed so that the display of goods does not constitute an offer, and this should be reinforced by including a statement in the Web site's terms and conditions to the effect that the e-tailer is free to accept or reject any offer made by a customer. The significance of this analysis was clearly illustrated when a UK online retailer mistakenly advertised televisions for sale on a Web site at £2.99 rather than £299. The retailer would not have been bound to accept the offers made by customers for the televisions at that stage; however, an automatic e-mail confirmation was sent in response to each offer, which was arguably an acceptance forming a binding contract.

Acceptance of an offer

For acceptance to be effective it must be communicated. How should an e-tailer communicate its acceptance of an offer? The obvious way is by e-mail, although more traditional methods of communication could be used. If e-mail is used, it is unclear exactly when acceptance is communicated – is it when the 'send' button is pressed, when it leaves the e-tailer's ISP mail server, or when the customer receives it? To prevent confusion, it is best to provide details of how acceptance is deemed communicated in the terms and conditions. In commercial contracts, the provision of consideration by each party and their intention to enter into the contract will rarely be an issue.

Incorporation of the e-tailer's standard terms and conditions

An e-tailer will want the contract for sale or supply of goods or services to be governed by its own standard terms and conditions. To be binding, these terms must be incorporated into the electronic contract by bringing them to the attention of the customer before, or at the same time as, the contract is formed. If standard terms are not properly incorporated, in the event of a dispute the court will imply terms to govern the contract based on statute or a past course of dealing, which may be far less advantageous to the e-tailer.

Methods of incorporation

Just including terms and conditions on a Web site is not enough to incorporate them into the contract. The parties must agree to contract on the stated terms. There are three main ways in which terms and conditions may be presented to the users of a Web site and incorporated into the contract:

- hyperlink displayed at base of Web page;
- hyperlink within sentence with wording to the effect of, 'By clicking on the "I accept" button you acknowledge that you have read and accepted the terms and conditions'; or
- click-wrap agreement: where the customer must scroll through the terms before being able to click 'I accept' and proceed with the transaction.

By analogy with earlier case law dealing with incorporation of terms into a contract, it is likely that a court would conclude that incorporation by the second or third option is valid, as the existence and content of the terms is clearly brought to the customer's attention before the contract is formed and so would be binding on the customer. The first option set out above may fail to do this. Although not indicative of the English courts' approach, US courts have confirmed the binding effect of a click-wrap agreement, while confirming that mere reference to terms and conditions as a hyperlink (such as in the first option or by use of a browse-wrap facility) would not be enough to incorporate terms and conditions, as the customer is not required to read the terms before ordering. Therefore a balance must be struck between aesthetics of a Web site and ensuring contractual formalities are complied with.

Reasonable terms

Not only do contractual terms need to be validly incorporated to be binding, they need to be reasonable. In the vast majority of contracts made online there will be no opportunity for the customer to negotiate the e-tailer's standard terms and conditions. As a result, the Unfair Contracts Terms Act 1977 (UCTA) will be applicable and the e-tailer will be unable to exclude or limit liability for breach of contract unless it is reasonable to do so. Whether a term is reasonable will be considered on the facts, and the recent case of *Watford Electronics v Sanderson CFL Limited* (2001) indicates that terms in B2B contracts are likely to be considered reasonable when the parties are commercially experienced and were aware of, or should have known about, the limitation or exclusion of liability.

As a consequence of the Unfair Terms in Consumer Contracts Regulations 1999, e-tailers entering into contracts with consumers will need to take a much more reasonable line on the limitation or exclusion of liability, as reasonableness of a particular term will be judged more harshly against the e-tailer. Plain and intelligible language should be used throughout the Web site.

Other considerations when contracting with consumers

E-tailers contracting with consumers via Web sites must ensure that they comply with the Consumer Protection (Distance Selling) Regulations 2000 (Distance Selling Regulations). Any term in the contract that is inconsistent with the Distance Selling Regulations will be void.

Distance selling checklist

Before the contract is made, the e-tailer must give the consumer certain details, including:

- e-tailer's identity, and address if payment required in advance;
- description of goods or services;
- price of goods or services, including all taxes;
- delivery costs;
- arrangements for payment, delivery and performance;
- existence of right to cancel, where the right exists;
- period for which offer price is valid;
- costs of returning goods on cancellation.

Failure to provide the above information within the required time will affect the length of the consumer's right to cancel, extending the cancellation period beyond three months after conclusion of the contract. Note that certain types of contracts, including those for the supply of food and drink, and for accommodation and transport provided at a particular time, are excluded from the scope of the Distance Selling Regulations.

Evidence of the contract

The e-tailer should ensure that it keeps a record of all online contracts entered into in a durable form to enable later enforcement of the contract, if necessary. Computer systems need to generate an audit trail to prove that the customer accepted the terms and conditions and is bound by them. It is also advisable to keep a record of previous versions of the Web site and past terms and conditions.

Effect of the Electronic Commerce Regulations on online contracting

If a business is trading online, it will almost certainly be affected by the Electronic Commerce (EC Directive) Regulations 2002 (E-commerce Regulations) which came into force in the United Kingdom on 21 August 2002. All e-tailers should ensure that the following minimum information, which must be easily and permanently accessible, is provided to customers, whether businesses or consumers. The easiest way to do this is by including on the Web site:

- The name, geographic address and e-mail address of the service provider. A Post Office box will not be an adequate geographic address, but a registered office address would. The name of the organization with which the customer is contracting must be given, and if this differs from the trading name, the reason for the difference must be explained. It is not sufficient to include a 'contact us' page alone. In addition, an e-mail and geographic address must be provided somewhere easily accessible on the site.
- If a company, the company's registration number must be stated.
- If the business is registered for VAT, the VAT number must be stated.

■ If the business is a member of a trade or a profession, membership details, including any registration number, must be provided.
■ Prices on the Web site must be clear and state whether prices are inclusive of tax and delivery costs.

These requirements are in addition to the information required by the Distance Selling Regulations, if the e-tailer is contracting with consumers.

Additional information to be given before orders are placed online

In addition to the requirements above, the E-Commerce Regulations require the following information to be given when selling online, whether to businesses or consumers:

■ the technical steps that need to be followed to conclude the contract;
■ whether or not the contract will be accessible in future;
■ the methods used to identify and correct errors on the site before orders are placed;
■ languages offered on the Web site;
■ if the contract is not concluded by e-mail (for instance, it is concluded on the Web site), details of any relevant codes of conduct to which the e-tailer subscribes must be provided; and
■ if the contract is not concluded by e-mail, the terms and conditions of the contract must be made available to allow a customer to store and reproduce the terms.

If the transaction is completed by e-mail the acknowledgement need not be immediate, although receipt of the offer should be confirmed as soon as possible. When dealing with other businesses, the terms and conditions can be worded to vary acknowledgement requirements.

When confirming the order, it is better to state that an order has been received and is now being processed, rather than state that the order has been accepted. This helps to avoid the problems set out above of accepting an offer for an incorrectly priced product. It is important for businesses to be aware of the regulation of contracts made online so as to take effective advantage of the commercial opportunities available by selling via the Internet.

Building a relationship of trust online

The perceived risks of online contracting (including the increased risk of fraud, opportunism and the collection and misuse of personal data) lead to greater wariness on the part of potential customers. As such, the e-tailer needs to make every effort to build customer confidence. Customers will want to know that any communication they send will reach the intended recipient unchanged, and without being read by anyone else, and will look to the e-tailer to provide reassurance of this. If it is not provided, custom will be taken elsewhere. Building a relationship of trust will boost customer confidence and will give the business a competitive advantage.

There are several ways in which an e-tailer can build a relationship of trust:

■ Ensure that best practice guidelines are evident and adhered to. As customers grow aware that a business has policies in place to comply with statutory guidelines, they can feel more confident as to the identity of the party they are contracting with, and that their personal data will not be misused.
■ By design and regular review of a business management and organizational structure to provide a secure and trusted management framework.
■ Use of electronic signatures to authenticate the origin of a message, and to confirm whether that message has been altered. Security of e-signatures can be enhanced by the use of encryption to keep messages secret, which can take the form of symmetrical or asymmetrical encryption. The Electronic Communications Act 2000 largely implements the requirements of the Electronic Signatures Directive (1999/93/EC) into UK law and provides that electronic signatures and certificates of electronic signatures are admissible in court as evidence of authenticity of the messages to which they are attached.

E-signatures can come in many forms, including typed names, scanned-in signatures, electronic representations of a handwritten signature, unique sequences of characters, digital representations of a biological aspect (such as the retina) or signatures created by cryptographic means; any of these will increase the security of a transaction.

However, technology can only assist in the creation and maintenance of trust between traders and their customers. Internal adherence to best practice will ensure that customer confidence in the business is built up and maintained, which in turn will reap commercial benefit.

Simmons & Simmons was ranked joint second in the United Kingdom for outsourcing in a recent survey of in-house lawyers by *The Lawyer* magazine.

In 2002, Global Counsel 3000 ranked Simmons & Simmons in the top 10 worldwide for performance in all major practice areas, based on the views of in-house counsel at over 5,000 companies across 74 jurisdictions. Earlier this year the firm won a prestigious Queen's Award for Enterprise in the International Trade category, the only law firm to do so.

For further information contact David Barrett, partner, Tel: +44 (0)20 7825 4032, E-mail: david.barrett@simmons-simmons.com or Peter Brudenall, senior lawyer, Tel: +44 (0)20 7825 4346, E-mail: peter.brudenall@simmons-simmons.com; Web site: www.simmons-simmons.com

Information security training

Alan Calder of IT Governance Ltd looks at the principles involved in ensuring a reliable information security programme through effective IT training.

There are two groups of people in any organization that need information security training: general (non-specialist) users of information and IT equipment (including board members and senior managers), and people with functional specialisms, including the information security specialists themselves. Each group needs a different depth and quality of training.

General information security training

BS 7799, the standard for information security, requires any organization seeking accreditation to train its personnel appropriately. This is to ensure that all users of the organization's information assets are aware of information security threats and are adequately equipped to support the organization's information security policy in their work. Training should include third-party users of the organization's equipment, and all users should also get regular updates on organizational policy.

The key areas of information security that need to be covered for general users are

■ information security awareness, its importance, and the information security management system, including general controls;
■ asset classification and control;
■ responding to security incidents and malfunctions;

- e-mail and Web access awareness and rules (this is particularly important in the context of current legislation and virus threats);
- user access control and responsibilities, mobile computing and teleworking;
- legal compliance awareness and related issues;
- business continuity awareness and procedures.

The organization also needs to have a method for regularly updating users on information security threats and counter measures, as well as on changes to the policies, procedures and IT infrastructure.

Training for staff with functional specialisms

The staff who will require user specific training include the Chief Information Officer, the Information Security Adviser, IT and network managers, IT and help desk support staff, Web masters, premises security staff, HR, recruitment and training staff, general managers, finance staff, company secretary/legal staff, internal quality assurance/system auditors, and business continuity/emergency response teams.

These staff should first be exposed to the all-staff training described above. The additional, user-specific training they require is best identified though an individual training needs analysis (TNA). Any handbook on corporate training, or a training professional, could provide appropriate support on a step that is fundamental to well-designed training delivery. The principle underlying a TNA is that, once the knowledge, skills and competence requirements of a particular role have been established clearly, and documented in the job description, the role-holder's own knowledge, skills and competence can be compared with the requirement and a gap analysis, or TNA, completed. The next step is to map out an individual learning path to meet the requirements of the TNA and close the knowledge, skills and competence gap. This individual learning path will contain a mix of self-learning, instructor-led training and experience. It should identify clearly where the training is to come from, and should set out the dates by when specific steps are to be taken, identified skills or competences acquired, and proof of acquisition generated.

While most organizations will have a TNA process for staff in generic roles, there are individuals who, for information security purposes, must have very specific knowledge, skills and competences that are in addition to those needed by the group of employees of which they may be a part. There needs to be an individual TNA for each of the people in each of the individual or specialist roles identified above. Where this is being put together for a new employee, the offer letter might make permanent employment conditional on achieving certain stages within certain time frames.

It is particularly important that any in-house information security adviser be appropriately qualified, and, if someone who does not have a formal qualification but claims to be qualified through experience is recruited for the role, he or she should be required (as a condition of continuing in employment beyond the initial probationary period) to demonstrate this competence by acquiring an appropriate qualification.

The British Computer Society has a Web site at www.bcs.org. It is based in Swindon and its customer support numbers are:

Tel: +44 (0)1793 417424
Fax: +44 (0) 1793 480270

This site describes a range of training programmes and regimes that are applicable to information professionals, including the Information Systems Examination Board qualifications. The most important of these is the Certificate in Information Security Management Principles. This provides the foundation of knowledge necessary for individuals who have security responsibility as part of their day-to-day role, or who are likely to move into a security or security-related function. BCS claims that the certificate provides an opportunity for those already within such roles to enhance or refresh their knowledge, and in the process to gain a qualification, recognized by industry, which demonstrates the level of knowledge gained.

The qualification is said by BCS to prove that the holder has a good knowledge and basic understanding of the wide range of subject areas that make up information security management. It is possible for someone who has experience in computer support or management to attend this course and to become qualified in information security, but it is not designed for someone who has little or no practical exposure to information technology.

Candidates who have achieved the certificate, which requires a one-week study course followed by a written examination, should be able to understand:

- information security management concepts (confidentiality, integrity, availability, vulnerability, threats, risks and countermeasures and so on);
- current legislation and regulations that impact information security management in the United Kingdom;
- current national and international standards, frameworks and organizations that facilitate the management of information security;
- the current business and technical environments in which information security management takes place (security products, malicious software ('malware'), relevant technology and so on);
- the categorization, operation and effectiveness of a variety of safeguards.

The contact details of those organizations that are accredited to deliver training that leads to the ISEB certificate, as well as current details about examination fees and dates, are all on the BCS Web site. Current training costs and course availability can obviously be ascertained by contacting the training providers identified on the Web site. Those who believe that they are qualified by experience do not need to take any of the training courses offered; it is recommended, though, that their initial employment package require them to refund the cost of a failed examination. This tends to focus the mind of the recruit on the importance of obtaining the certificate. There are about 150 candidates per year for the ISEB certificate examinations and the pass rates are high.

Those IT staff charged with systems administration should be trained appropriately, by either the software supplier or by an approved training vendor (such as those identified on the BCS Web site), as system administrators for the software for which they are the nominated administrator. Evidence of this training should be retained on the individual's personnel file. Those responsible for firewall, anti-virus, encryption and any other security software should have appropriate training certificates from the product vendors and should be required to keep their skills and knowledge current by attending regular refresher and update courses. These should be booked into the individual's training calendar in advance and there should be evidence that they were attended. Certainly, in any Microsoft environment, there should always be a systems administrator who has a Microsoft certificate, such as the MCSE.

Web masters, in particular, need to be thoroughly trained and have their skills regularly updated. Their training needs to cover the security aspects of all the hardware and software for which they are responsible; in particular, they need to be capable of ensuring that the Web servers are fully secured. This is particularly important for organizations that use Microsoft's Internet Information Server (IIS).

Information security staff, company secretarial/legal staff and HR/personnel staff will also need specific legal training. There are a number of specific legal issues to do with information security, and the organization needs to know how to handle them, using standard template documents wherever possible. It does not need to employ an in-house lawyer, as this can be unnecessarily expensive; external expertise can be brought in where and when necessary to deal with specific legal issues.

Staff dealing with telephone systems and network hardware and software will all need specific, supplier-certified, administration and security training that covers these products. The organization will need access to regular updates on information security issues relating to these products.

Conclusion

Effective IT training is an essential component of a secure organization; staff do, after all, make all the difference. Designing and managing an effective information security programme can be done in-house, following the principles identified in this chapter. A specialist vendor, who can ensure that all the necessary steps are taken, can also do it effectively.

Alan Calder is the author of *IT Governance: A manager's guide to information security* and is a founder director of IT Governance Ltd, a company whose mission is to provide best practice IT governance and information security solutions, products and services that are essential for business managers in achieving strategic goals, protecting and securing intellectual capital and the company's whole market value and meeting corporate governance objectives.

For further information: Tel: + 44 (0)1353 659662 or log on to the Web site at www.itgovernance.co.uk

Outsourced solutions

There are a number of benefits to adopting an outsourcing strategy. Martin Saunders, Head of Products at Easynet writes about the options available and what has to be taken into consideration.

In today's corporate environment, it is common practice to allocate a diversity of business functions to external companies. The emergence of outsourcing IT is more of a recent phenomenon, fuelled by awareness of the devastating impact of viruses and their increase in number and virulence.

As a result, businesses are increasingly benefiting from outsourcing communications technology to service providers, offloading their resource-hungry technology requirements to expert organizations, and enjoying improved security coupled with more time and resource to concentrate on core business operations. A host of service providers are jostling for space in a busy market, offering the enticing proposition of management of a full port-folio of communications technology services, from telephone switchboard management, to Web hosting, data back-up and e-mail management, to running an entire corporate network.

For maximum benefit and peace of mind, however, businesses need to adopt an integrated approach to their outsourcing strategy, maintaining an in-house IT function to focus on daily operations and to retain contact with the provider. This chapter will outline the options available to a business adopting an outsourcing strategy, and will identify the considerations that need to be addressed.

Research by IT services provider Synstar identified the importance of outsourcing in terms of risk management. The biggest concerns for IT managers, the survey discovered, are currently security and the economic climate. Within this survey, the most popular method for managing costs was to outsource certain aspects of IT. Selective outsourcing was viewed as the most popular way for IT departments to save money while improving performance, according to half the respondents.

Russell Flower, Director of Managed Services for Synstar, confirmed that outsourced services could help firms manage costs. 'It leaves more time for IT directors to focus strategically,' he said, adding that firms tend to outsource selectively to managed service providers rather than hand over the entire IT function to a traditional outsourcer.

Most respondents said outsourcing was an attractive option. Infrastructure maintenance and user support were the responsibilities IT managers most wanted to hand over to an external specialist. The key attraction was access to skills that were unavailable within their organization.

A diverse range of services is available to businesses looking to outsource their IT requirements but for the purpose of this chapter, these are summarized under the headings of Applications, Physical options and Network options.

Applications   Organizations can benefit from outsourcing applications such as Web hosting, data back-up and e-mail management. Many application service providers, or ASPs, offer the service of managing businesses' e-mail and data. Many providers also offer managed anti-virus and anti-spam services. It is the responsibility of the provider to monitor all traffic entering and leaving a business, removing entirely the burden of traffic control and monitoring from a company's in-house IT department.

Physical options   that can easily be outsourced include colocation and leasing of cage and rack space. With these options, providers offer leased physical space in purpose-built data centre facilities specifically built to provide high-level security including back-up generators, fire suppression equipment, power control and cable management. Companies can hire space to house their own equipment in a fully protected environment without the expense of intensive, complex security systems. The colocation provider is responsible for the maintenance of the physical environment.

An example of such a site is this is 1bricklane®, a colocation and hosting facility owned and operated by Easynet. Providing a resilient and secure environment for organizations' IT equipment and Web servers, the building has been fitted to exacting technical specifications with direct mains power from an adjacent London Electricity primary substation and back-up generators, top-level security and the latest fire detection and suppression systems. The provider offers such managed service options as 24/7 remote hands service, 24/7 device monitoring, professional tape management and managed firewall. Customer servers can also house their operating systems and some applications managed in this facility.

Providers can offer security, access, space, support, cabling, hardware and power. This means that organizations do not have to consider these issues at all.

Network options   involve a service provider taking on the responsibility, to a lesser or greater degree, for the management and maintenance of an organization's network.

Firewalls enable safe connection to and from the Internet. If a company runs a Web site, has a dial-up connection or manages a corporate network, a firewall is critical. While firewalls can be managed in-house, there are clear benefits from outsourcing the service to a specialist who will fully support and maintain the service.

MPLS (Multi Protocol Label Switching) and Internet Protocol Virtual Private Network (IPVPN) are two technologies that enable the transfer of network management from the customer, onto the provider. MPLS connects remote offices for the fast, private exchange of data across a network. Two or more geographically dispersed office locations are linked, creating a managed wide area network (WAN) that connects offices, home-workers, suppliers and field-based staff.

IPVPN is similar in functionality, but offers a higher level of service, and if it is managed by a provider offering Multi Protocol Label Switching technology, can offer users the ability to prioritize data into different classes of service (such as mission-critical account transfer information for a financial corporation, for example). Voice, video and data can be run across the same network. One of the advantages of IPVPNs is that most use IP Sec, a tunnelling protocol that ensures high levels of reliability and security while the data is travelling across a public network.

Many providers offer 24-hour network monitoring to ensure fast discovery (and repair) of outages, high availability and bandwidth at consistent quality. Companies large and small benefit from implementing an IPVPN. According to a survey by InStat/ MDR, 74 per cent of firms that have existing VPNs intend to switch to services managed by providers.

Outsourcing considerations

A diversity of internal and external issues must be addressed before a company adopts a technology outsourcing strategy. Companies may choose to deploy different services to a number of different providers. While this ensures the availability of specialist skills, it can be more of a challenge to maintain communication and can be more costly than adopting a 'one provider fits all' strategy. There is also the argument that security is less of a risk when working with one provider rather than several (eggs in one basket theory and so on).

Internally, a company must have a clear objective in mind of what it is aiming to achieve from outsourcing. Whether this is a cost saving, the adoption of specialist IT skills or the redeployment of in-house IT resource, all will influence the final decision on which provider or providers to work with and indeed what to outsource.

Staff management may need reassessing, as briefings may be required in terms of the division of activity between in-house and external teams. The client's IT management team must establish expectation levels for communication in terms of weekly or monthly contact and ensure the provider has a failsafe contact strategy in place should any outages or urgent security issues arise. The client company may choose to build in checks and procedures to ensure costs are being minimized and the service provider is operating to maximum efficiency.

A range of further issues should be addressed externally, before contracting the service provider. Companies need to assess the levels of security and potential risk if placing hardware on a provider's premises. Does it have all available protection in terms of security and hazard risk? What about back-up in the event of power or network failure? If outsourcing applications, the company need to assess where the data will be held, and look at the reliability and security of the provider's own infrastructure. How financially stable is the operation? It may well be worth assessing financial records to check the provider has a stable financial background. Once all these areas have been considered in-depth, then the decision to outsource or not can be taken.

Outsourcing technology looks set to remain a viable, cost-effective means of streamlining businesses while maintaining specialist skills and implementing secure, robust services.

Outsourcing technology in action

Case study 1

Education recruitment agency Select Education, and sister company Select Appointments, looked to outsource their network management. The companies had a requirement to connect over 30 Select Education branches and 60 Select Appointments offices to their respective head offices over a high-speed connection, enabling fast, efficient shared communication of and access to internal documents, CVs and job specifications, and other client and corporate information.

An IPVPN solution ensured the rapid and reliable exchange of data, greatly enhancing service levels. The client companies were provided with a range of optimized security solutions, a service level agreement and ISDN back-up, ensuring minimum downtime and access to business-critical applications.

The companies are reducing their costs of ownership and are freeing up in-house expertise using their provider's 24/7 monitoring service and remote hosting service, enabling them to redeploy staff at substantial savings.

David Rowe, CEO of Easynet, said: 'Working closely with Select Education, Easynet was able to offer a reliable, cost-effective solution which addressed their concerns about managing the network in-house and offered an alternative disaster recovery solution.'

Case study 2

Bravilor Bonamat specializes in the design and production of filter coffee makers for the professional and the rapidly growing market of instant beverage machines. The company has 250 employees in more than 80 countries. Noticeable growth has taken place in the last decade, placing increasing demands on its network and prompting re-evaluation of the organization's communications technology.

Provider Easynet installed its fully managed EuroVPN solution, a managed pan-European broadband service, giving each of the sales offices permanent fixed lines of communications to each other via an 'always on' Internet connection. As well as safeguarding the network from attack, the managed solution reduces the total cost of ownership and avoids the prohibitive costs of in-house security expertise.

'The fact that my provider offers 24/7 service has revolutionized the way our IT team works. Their time is now free to concentrate on other critical tasks,' observed Jeroen Kok, IT Manager at Bravilor.

Case study 3

Global corporation Tchibo began trading in Germany as a mail order coffee distributor. Now Tchibo is known for much more than just coffee. Through its online store www.tchibo.co.uk, mail order and retail outlets the company provides a large variety of food and non-food products.

In 1997 the company began to develop its e-commerce strategy by opening a German online store. Security and reliability were critical, since the online shop is open 24/7. The company outsourced its server management, and has a high-speed, high-capacity data connection from its provider's data centre to the Internet. Tchibo and its service provider have become close partners and agreed a cost per order model. This means Tchibo does not need to ask for faster connectivity, larger servers or bigger databases because Ision will scale the platform on demand.

The service provider now has responsibility for the availability, performance and uptime of the Tchibo online stores in Germany, Austria, Switzerland and the United Kingdom. Each year the provider adds a number of servers to the platform, in order to meet demand during the busy Christmas period without any drop in service.

Easynet is a leading pan-European business broadband provider and business ISP with operations in eight European countries. Established in 1994, Easynet owns and operates one of Europe's most advanced Internet network and data centre infrastructures. In the United Kingdom, Easynet has a national broadband network spanning 4,450 km. Easynet's experience, infrastructure and vision have resulted in an unrivalled product portfolio. This includes a full suite of scalable broadband access and hosting solutions. In addition, Easynet offers a range of bespoke solutions created exclusively for the education market, delivering Internet access in a safe, appropriate and controlled environment. All services are complemented by quality non-stop technical support.

Further information on Easynet can be obtained at: Web: www.uk.Easynet.net, or contact Anne Perry in the Easynet press office, 1 Brick Lane, London E1 6PU, Tel: 0800 053 4004.

Securing the mobile workforce

A mobile workforce is a positive prospect, but look out for the dangers, warns Andy Baines of Fujitsu Services.

Today's world: new models, new threats

Many organizations are now facing commercial pressures to enable remote access to their sensitive information resources by customers, partners, outsourced service providers and a mobile workforce. Existing perimeter-based security, such as the firewall, cannot cope with these business models. Therefore, a more flexible approach to securing the enterprise is required – balancing risk with a variety of controls, some technical and some soft, including legal and business processes.

Traditional models of security placed sensitive organization assets within defined organizational boundaries and kept everything else on the outside. Known, authenticated users were allowed in, and everyone else was kept out. Today, the Internet has helped to create new business models – commerce is outsourced, distributed, collaborative and interactive. Organizations have to expose internal systems to partners and customers. Concepts of organizational boundaries are blurred.

The wireless infrastructure

The need for security on any network is apparent: the prevention of eavesdropping and the desire for authentication have been the main focuses of many network administrators.

Who's the world's 3rd largest IT company?

However, the problems that already exist are compounded when you add wireless networking to the equation. As wireless networking becomes more popular, the flawed security of most of those networks becomes more apparent.

The security of any network is an important issue. No-one likes the idea that it may be possible that someone could be intercepting their Internet traffic, reading their e-mail, ordering items with their credit cards, or sending inappropriate messages to their boss in their name. Security of wired networks is, therefore, a primary objective of system administrators.

When considering a network that incorporates a Wireless Access Point, or 'WAP', new security concerns come into play. Because wireless is 'broadcast' in nature, anyone within range of a wireless access point or card can intercept the packets being sent out without interrupting the flow of data between card and access point. For this reason, wireless network security must be somewhat more concentrated than that of wired networks.

The two main issues

There are two main issues that wireless security solutions tend to address. First, since all wireless packets are available to anyone who listens, security is needed to prevent eavesdropping. Since it is impossible physically to keep people away from the WAPs, short of erecting a fence around your building, solutions tend to rely on encryption in one form or another.

The second issue is authentication. With a wired network, a system administrator might determine who generated certain traffic based on the physical connection point that the traffic came in on. By assuming that inbound traffic from a particular connection point is always coming from a certain source, there is no need to constantly verify where the traffic is coming from. However, with wireless networking, many users can access the network at the same access point or base station making it more difficult to map who did what. It is often desirable, therefore, to allow users to identify who they are before letting them through the base station onto the rest of the network.

A growing problem

The idea of a no-wires network is becoming more appealing to home and small office users as each day passes, partly because bandwidth becomes less of an issue – wireless networks can theoretically provide speeds of up to 54 Mbps.

In terms of security, it is these ad hoc networks that most often provide the easiest access to outsiders. More often than not, small-network wireless users will utilize only those security features advertised on the outside of the box of the wireless products purchased. Because it is part of the 802.11 specification, a security feature known as Wired Equivalent Privacy (WEP), is available with most base stations sold today. However, WEP is by no means secure. An experienced wireless hacker has a wide variety of attacks with which to circumvent WEP. In most cases, this involves listening in on broadcasted wireless packets and breaking the encryption key. Once enough packets have been gathered the encryption key can quickly be obtained. Once that is accomplished, it is easy to join the network in question.

WEP also falls short in other areas. The use of WEP can have a significant impact on wireless network performance. Most generally available wireless hardware loses significant bandwidth (up to 40 per cent, in some tests) when encrypting traffic in hardware.

Fujitsu,
that's who.

Our name might not be on the tip of your tongue, but you'll certainly have heard of the people we work with. In short, they're the world's biggest businesses and governments. Why do they choose Fujitsu? Because they know that when they have an IT problem, we have the people, the experience and the capability to crack it. And now that's something you know too.

For more information call 0870 234 7800 or visit uk.fujitsu.com/thatswho

THE POSSIBILITIES ARE INFINITE

Source: Fortune 500

uk.fujitsu.com

This means war...

As was mentioned earlier, wireless networking is broadcast in nature, which means that wireless transmissions can be picked up by anyone within range of a base station, whether the owner of that base station knows about them or not. Once this was realized a trend known as 'war driving' started. War driving involves scanning the airwaves for vulnerable wireless networks and attempting to gain unauthorized access.

There is a wide variety of very effective (free) software that helps the would-be attacker detect and compromise vulnerable wireless networks. This software can be run on a laptop or handheld device (a PDA for example) meaning that attacks can take place while attackers are walking around buildings or even driving by. High-gain aerials can be used to increase the range of these scanning devices up to 10 miles.

Is there a solution?

There are a number of solutions that provide additional wireless authentication and encryption controls. In particular the inherent weaknesses in WEP are addressed by using stronger encryption and better management of the keys used to encrypt data. This approach makes the 'sniffing' of wireless packets in order to decrypt keys much more difficult. Additionally, many of these packages require wireless users to authenticate (or identify themselves) before any further wireless communications can take place. These controls can deter all but the most determined attacker.

What is at risk

While attacks and attackers are certainly becoming more inventive, there is more at risk too. In the online world, an organization's virtual assets are at risk. Reputation and brand provide competitive advantage and identity in everything an organization does. Web site defacement, negative publicity surrounding security breaches and carelessness with customers' personal data may not cost money, but will certainly damage reputation and lose customers.

Organizations may not even be a direct target. An attacker may just want to use bandwidth, propagate viruses around the Internet or use systems to launch attacks on other targets. A fraudster may want to steal customers' identities. Organizations may not suffer directly, but they still have an ethical obligation to prevent this exploitation. Many organizations may be unaware that this is happening to them today – but even if they are prepared to take the risk they need to consider the impact of legislation.

Legislation, guidance and regulatory controls may mean that organizations have to put expensive security countermeasures in place. European e-commerce legislation and the UK's Data Protection Act make organizations responsible for the data they use to run their business.

Summary

While a mobile workforce can bring many benefits, to both employer and employee, it is vital that the risks associated with this new model are fully understood. Mobile working and the associated blurring of organizational boundaries mean that the overall level of organizational information security really does come down to weakest link in the chain. Firewalls offer a convenient metaphor for security, and it is not surprising that organizations place such a heavy burden on them to protect their business. But this metaphor is too simplistic – many vulnerabilities occur at the content layer where firewalls can do little to help. The very nature of mobile working means that the human factor plays a major part in determining overall information security levels. It is, therefore, important that users of mobile technology are educated in order that they understand the risks associated with this technology and are aware of their personal responsibilities. The very aspects that make mobile technology so attractive to the end user are also the aspects that introduce many of the security-related risks. So, in summary, the following points should be considered:

- Security policies need to reflect new ways of working.
- Policies should be driven by business requirements and use inputs from risk assessments and industry guidelines.
- Policies must be reflected (by operating procedures and design documentation) within the infrastructure.
- The risks that mobile solutions introduce must be identified and understood.
- Awareness of issues and personal responsibilities is vital.
- Exploit the security facilities available within the technology.
- Use strong authentication and encryption to protect sensitive corporate information.
- Apply the same kind of controls to mobile devices as would be applied to internal systems.
- Assess the use of emerging technologies to assist in increasing levels of security within mobile devices.

This article is an extract from *A White Paper* written by Andy Baines of Fujitsu Services. Andy is a Principal Consultant in the Information Security Practice specializing in the development of security strategies and architectures. He is a regular consultant to government departments and corporate customers.

Andy has a keen interest in the security aspects of mobile technologies, particularly in the area of vulnerability assessment and risk reduction. Andy has spoken at a number of events throughout the United Kingdom and overseas and has made regular appearances on Sky Television's Technology Channel.

Fujitsu is one of the leading IT services companies in Europe. Information Security is one of the areas in which we specialize with a full range of consultancy services and solutions, both stand-alone and managed. Typical consultancy services cover accreditation, architecture, policy development and reviews whilst our managed services group focus on firewalls, anti-virus and intrusion detection services.

For further information contact Ask Fujitsu – Tel: +44 (0) 870 242 7998, Fax: +44 (0) 870 242 4445, E-mail: askfujitsu@services.fujitsu.com

Contingency planning

Business continuity and crisis management

No organization can have complete control over its business environment. It is therefore essential for companies to have a business continuity management (BCM) and crisis management capability, in case of crisis or disaster. This article, written by Dr David Smith, FBCI, Editor of the BCI Good Practice Guidelines, outlines various approaches that can help companies prepare for a business continuity 'event', and explains the BCM lifecycle.

Around the world regulators and governments are putting great emphasis on the need for organizations to have effective business continuity management (BCM) in place. Insurance companies are setting the level of business interruption premiums according to the speed at which an organization is able to resume business. The latest pressures are coming from the credit rating agencies that need evidence of effective BCM at the time of setting ratings, and in the United Kingdom as a result of the Civil Contingencies bill which requires BCM to be established in local authorities and emergency services. It is therefore not in the interest of any organization to ignore BCM.

BCM is defined by the Business Continuity Institute (BCI) as 'an holistic management process that identifies potential impacts that threaten an organization and provides a framework for building resilience and the capability for an effective response that safeguards the interests of its key stakeholders, reputation, brand and value creating activities'.

The BCI's use of the term 'business continuity management' rather than 'business continuity planning' is deliberate because 'planning' implies there is a start and end to the process and can lead to unwanted planning bureaucracy. BCM is, by necessity, a dynamic, proactive and ongoing process. It must be kept up to date and fit for purpose to be effective.

The key objectives of an effective BCM strategy should be to:

- ensure the safety of staff;
- maximize the defence of the organization's reputation and brand image;
- minimize the impact of business continuity events (including crises) on customers/clients;
- limit/prevent impact beyond the organization;
- demonstrate effective and efficient governance to the media, markets and stakeholders;
- protect the organization's assets;
- meet insurance, legal and regulatory requirements.

However, BCM is not only about disaster recovery. It should be a business-owned and driven process that unifies a broad spectrum of management disciplines. In particular, it is not just about IT disaster recovery. Too many organizations tend to focus all their efforts on IT because of its mission-critical nature, leaving them exposed on many other fronts. (See Figure 5.1.1.)

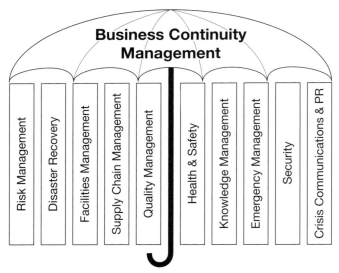

Figure 5.1.1 The unifying process

Because of its all-embracing nature, the way BCM is carried out will inevitably be dependent upon, and must reflect, the nature, scale and complexity of an organization's risk profile, risk appetite and the environment in which it operates. Inevitably, too, BCM has close links to risk management and corporate governance strategies. The importance of a holistic approach across these areas was reinforced in the UK Turnbull Report (1998).

As an organization can never be fully in control of its business environment, it is safe to assume that all organizations will face a business continuity event at some point. Although this simple reality has been etched in high-profile names such as Bhopal, Piper-Alpha, Perrier, Barings Bank, *Challenger*, *Herald of Free Enterprise*, Coca-Cola, *Exxon-Valdez*, Railtrack, the Canary Wharf bombing, Enron, Andersen, Marconi and the World Trade Center, experience also teaches that it is the less dramatic but more frequent business continuity events that can be even more problematic to deal with. Unfortunately, it seems that many public and private organizations still think, 'It will not happen to us'.

Changing the corporate culture

Ignoring business continuity issues can happen for a number of reasons, ranging from denial through disavowal to rationalization. A process of 'group think' can develop whereby an organization genuinely starts to believe its size, or some other feature, makes it immune to disaster. Or executives may firmly believe that insurance will cover them, without realizing that insurance cannot indemnify against lost market share, loss of reputation or tarnished brands.

Research shows that crisis-prone organizations tend to exhibit these tendencies seven times more often than crisis-prepared organizations. While all individuals may make use of such defence mechanisms from time-to-time, the key difference is the degree, extent and frequency with which they are used. Changing such mindsets is not easy, and blindly implementing so-called 'best practice' business continuity techniques is not the best approach. As all organizations are different, techniques that work in one organization will not necessarily work in another. Most executives tasked with addressing business continuity issues are keen to achieve quick wins, and the 'tick box' audit approach, which tries to copy successful strategies used elsewhere, is often adopted without consideration as to suitability.

Underlying the 'tick box' approach is the persuasive belief that a structure, policy, framework and plan are all that is required. While these are critical enablers, relying on structure alone tends to overlook the key issue – that it is people who actually deal with business continuity and crises.

In this context, it is worth remembering (and reminding all senior executives) that 'managerial ignorance' is no longer an acceptable legal or moral defence if a crisis is handled badly. All managers should consider the following key questions that are likely to be asked in a subsequent inquiry:

■ When did you know there was a problem?
■ What did you do about it?
■ If you didn't do anything, why not?
■ If you didn't know there was a problem, why not?
■ What would you have done if you had known such a problem could exist?

Avoiding planning bureaucracy

There is no doubt that some sort of business continuity plan is essential. The plan becomes a source of reference at the time of a business continuity event or crisis, and the blueprint upon which the strategy and tactics of dealing with the event/crisis are designed. In particular, it can provide essential guidance on damage limitation in those short windows of opportunity that often occur at the beginning of a crisis. Unfortunately, reputations and trust that have been built up over decades can be destroyed within minutes unless vigorously defended at a time when the speed and scale of events can overwhelm the normal operational and management systems. A further and critical reason for having a planning process is so that the individuals who are required to implement the plan can rehearse and test what they might do in different situations. Scenario planning exercises are a very helpful technique for destruct-testing different strategies and plans.

Having said this, it is simply not possible to plan for every eventuality, and if you try to, there is a great danger of creating 'emergency' manuals that are simply too heavy to lift. A trade-off needs to be achieved between creating an effective fit-for-purpose capability and relying on untrained and untried individuals and hoping they will cope in an emergency. The spanning of the gap between the plan and those who carry it out can be achieved by either formal tuition and/or simulations. The well-known maxim that a team is only as strong as its weakest link is worth remembering here.

The exercising of plans, rehearsing of team members and testing of solutions, systems and facilities are the elements that provide and prove an effective and fit-for-purpose capability. However, simulations are not easy to devise, and because of this, many organizations do not venture beyond the development of a plan. They are, nevertheless the best way to avoid planning bureaucracy.

Using good practice guidelines: a different approach

Because of the caveats listed earlier, the BCI's *Business Continuity Management Good practice guidelines* (available on the BCI Web site at www.thebci.org) are not intended to be a restrictive, exhaustive or definitive process to cover every eventuality within BCM. Instead, they set out to establish the generic process, principles and terminology; describe the activities and outcomes involved; and provide evaluation techniques and criteria.

These guidelines draw together the collective experience, knowledge and expertise of many leading professional Members and Fellows of the BCI and other authoritative professional organizations. In particular, the guidelines reflect the following BCM principles:

- BCM and crisis management are an integral part of corporate governance.
- BCM activities must match, focus upon and directly support the business strategy and goals of the organization.
- BCM must provide organizational resilience to optimize product and service availability.
- As a value-based management process BCM must optimize cost efficiencies.
- BCM is a business management process that is undertaken because it adds value rather than because of governance or regulatory considerations.
- The component parts of an organization own their business risk; the management of the business risk is based upon their individual and aggregated organizational risk appetite.
- The organization and its component parts must be accountable and responsible for maintaining an effective, up-to-date and fit-for-purpose BCM competence and capability.
- All BCM strategies, plans and solutions must be business-owned and driven.
- All BCM strategies, plans and solutions must be based upon the business mission-critical activities, their dependencies and single points of failure identified by a business impact analysis.
- All business impact analysis must be conducted in respect of business products and services in an end-to-end production context.
- There must be an agreed and published organization policy, strategy, framework and exercising guidelines for BCM and crisis management.

- The organization and its component parts must implement and maintain a robust exercising, rehearsal and testing programme to ensure that the business continuity capability is effective, up to date and fit for purpose.
- The relevant legal and regulatory requirements for BCM must be clearly defined and understood before undertaking a BCM programme.
- The organization and its component parts must recognize and acknowledge that reputation, brand image; market share and shareholder value risk cannot be transferred or removed by internal sourcing and/or outsourcing.
- BCM implications must be considered at all stages of the development of new business operations, products, services and organizational infrastructure projects.
- BCM implications must be considered as an essential part of the business change management process.
- The competency of BCM practitioners should be based and benchmarked against the 10 professional competency standards of the BCI.
- All third parties including joint venture companies and service providers, upon whom an organization is critically dependent for the provision of products, services, support or data, must be required to demonstrate an effective, proven and 'fit for purpose' BCM capability.
- The standard terms and conditions of any outsourced and/or internal sourcing of products, services, support or data should reflect these good practice guidelines.

The structure and format of the guidelines is based upon the most frequently asked questions in relation to BCM, which are listed Table 5.1.1.

Table 5.1.1   The most frequently asked BCM questions

Guideline component heading	Most frequently asked question
Purpose	Why do we need to do it?
Outcomes	What will it achieve?
Components	What do we need to do it? What does it consist of (ingredients)?
Methodologies and techniques	What are the tools we need to do it? How is it done? How do we do it?
Frequency and triggers	When should it be done?
Participants	Who does it? Who should be involved?
Deliverables	What is the output?
'Good practice' evaluation criteria	How do we know if we have got it right?

The BCM lifecycle

The BCI principles and frequently asked questions have been drawn together to create the BCM lifecycle, an interactive process tool to guide the implementation of an effective BCM process. (See Figure 5.1.2.)

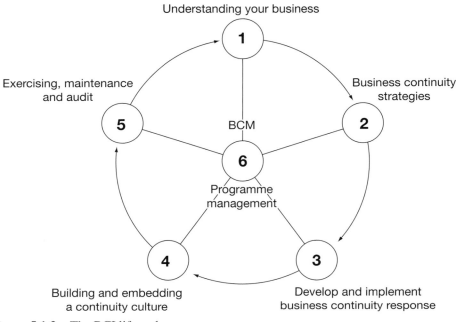

Figure 5.1.2 The BCI lifecycle

The six stages of the life cycle in more detail are set out in Table 5.1.2.

Table 5.1.2 The six stages of the BCM lifecycle

1. Understanding your business	Business impact analysis Risk assessment and control
2. BCM strategies	Organization (corporate) BCM strategy Process-level BCM strategy Resource recovery BCM strategy
3. Developing and implementing a BCM response	Plans and planning External bodies and organizations Crisis/BCM event/incident management
4. Building and embedding a BCM culture	Sourcing (intra-organization and/or outsourcing providers) Emergency response and operations Communications Public relations and the media An ongoing programme of education, awareness and training
5. Exercising, maintenance and audit	Exercising of BCM plans Rehearsal of staff, BCM teams Testing of technology and BCM systems BCM maintenance BCM audit

Table 5.1.2 *Continued*

6. The BCM programme	Board commitment and proactive participation Organization (corporate) BCM strategy BCM policy BCM framework Roles, accountability, responsibility and authority Finance Resources Assurance Audit Management information system (MIS): metrics/scorecard/benchmark Compliance: legal/regulatory issues Change management

The guidelines have been used to generate a tool for evaluating the BCM process, which takes the form of a spreadsheet current state assessment (benchmark) workbook. The workbook enables and facilitates good practice compliance evaluation, current state assessment gap analysis, assurance and benchmarking (process and performance). (See Figure 5.1.3.)

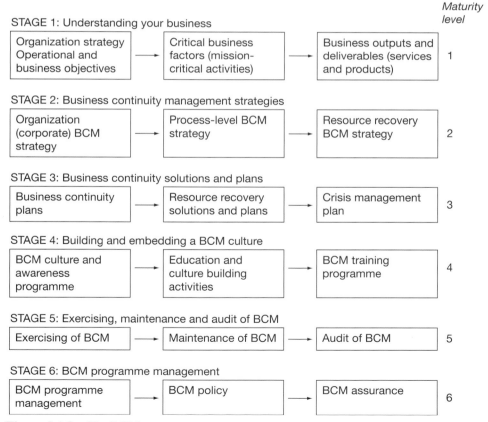

Figure 5.1.3 The BCM process

Each organization needs to assess how to apply the good practice contained within the guidelines. It must ensure that its BCM competence and capability meets the nature, scale and complexity of its business, and reflects its individual culture and operating environment.

Crisis management

The key elements of a crisis management framework are slightly different from the BCM lifecycle, and include those set out in Table 5.1.3, but the list should not be seen as restrictive or exhaustive. There are many advantages to adopting a modular approach to a crisis or business continuity situation, not least that it can be easily and quickly modified to suit local, national as well as global requirements.

Table 5.1.3   Key elements of a crisis management framework

Business risk control Monitoring Prevention Planning and preparation Crisis identification **Assessment** Crisis evaluation (including an evaluation criteria) **Invocation and escalation** **Management and recovery** **Closure and review** Formal closure Ongoing issues, eg investigation and litigation Post crisis review and report **Improvement** Implementation of approved post crisis review report recommendations

However, in managing any event it is critical to recognize that a successful outcome is judged by both the technical response, and the perceived competence and capability of the management in delivering the business response. The stakeholder perception should be seen as the critical success factor, with a priority equal to, if not more urgent than, the technical solution. Consequently, the acid test is convincingly to demonstrate an effective and 'fit for purpose' business continuity and crisis management capability, and to continue business as usual. This is in contrast to the more familiar pattern of a fall and recovery of a business, which is more representative of the outdated disaster recovery and business resumption approaches.

Development of standards

Why is it so important to establish a standard for business continuity management? With BCM we are dealing with a discipline that is designed to protect an organization at the time of crisis or disaster. There must be some commonality of approach in the future, as organizations do not operate within specific sectors or in isolation. Supply chains are extensive and international. The increased use of outsource providers has placed the management of critical operations outside an organization's direct control. Insurance companies, regulators, credit rating agencies and investors require evidence that an organization is able to continue to deliver despite interruption. They are demanding that an effective BCM policy be in place. Governments need to know that their own departments and agencies can deliver their services at the time of crisis. With such pressures on organizations it is essential that a benchmark be established against which they can be measured.

The British Standards Institution (BSI), in conjunction with the Business Continuity Institute and Insight Consulting, has published a guide that clearly establishes the process, principles and terminology of BCM. The *PAS 56 Guide to Business Continuity Management* describes the activities and outcomes involved in establishing a BCM process, and provides recommendations for good practice. It provides a generic BCM framework for incident anticipation and response, and describes evaluation techniques and criteria. The *Guide* is based on the BCI's *Good Practice Guide to BCM*. The BSI Guide is the first step towards the creation of a full standard for BCM. The BSI has indicated that it wishes to proceed with this development in the next 12 months.

PAS 56 has already become an important document in establishing a uniform approach to BCM. Evidence exists of major international businesses adopting the *Guide* for their own approach to the discipline and they are beginning to measure their suppliers against it. In the United Kingdom, central government has stated that all government departments and agencies will be measured against *PAS 56* from next year. The Singapore Standards Authority, SPRING, has developed its own BCM standard which is based on *PAS 56* and the *BCI GPG* and will start to certificate organizations against this standard during 2004. *PAS 56* is being translated into German and Japanese and the *BCI Good Practice Guide* into French.

The move towards a uniform standard for BCM is essential to ensure that there is no confusion at the time of a crisis. *PAS 56* is the foundation on which such a standard can now be built. The first stage is the creation of a British Standard (BS) but as soon as possible there must be a move towards an international (ISO) standard for use in the global village in which organizations operate.

Conclusions

An organization consists of people, and people at the top who give a cultural lead. As a consequence, business continuity and crisis management are not solely a set of tools, techniques and mechanisms to be implemented in an organization. They should reflect a more general mood, attitude and type of action taken by managers and staff.

Individual personalities play a crucial and critical role. It is the human factor that is frequently underestimated in BCM. This is of particular importance because the examination of the cause of business continuity events and crises usually identifies several warning signals that were ignored or not recognized. The key to a successful crisis and BCM capability is to adopt a holistic approach to validate each of the key building blocks of the BCM lifecycle and process.

The first task is always to identify the right people who are not bounded as individuals or within the corporate culture. It is on these criteria that the success or failure of creating an effective and fit-for-purpose BCM capability will be determined. Once the right people have been identified, they should engage in the BCM planning process, using the *BCI Good Practice Guidelines* and *PAS 56*, and training via the exercise simulations of plans, rehearsal of people/teams and testing of systems, processes, technology, structures and communications.

The organization can assist this process by appointing a BCM 'champion' at a senior level whose role is to draw together, under a matrix team approach, representatives from the various organization functions (for instance, human resources) together with key line-of-business heads to ensure a coordinated approach. The key advantage of this approach is that it builds on what already exists and has been done, thereby enabling a 'virtual capability' that provides cost efficiency. A further benefit is that it ensures buy-in throughout the organization.

In adopting this methodology and regularly exercising, rehearsing and testing, the organization maintains an effective, up-to-date and fit-for-purpose BCM and crisis management capability. When a crisis hits the organization, everyone knows what to do and a smooth invocation of the plan takes place, ensuring that the impact on mission-critical activities is minimized and reputation and brand image are not tarnished but enhanced.

References

British Standards Institute (2003) *PAS 56: A Guide to Business Continuity Management,* British Standards Institute, London

Chartered Management Institute (2002) *Business Continuity and Supply Chain Management*, Chartered Management Institute, London

Financial Services Authority (2002) *FSA Working Paper on Business Continuity Management*, Financial Services Authority, London

Pauchant, T C and Mitroff, I I (1992) *Transforming a Crisis-Prone Organization*, Jossey-Bass, San Francisco

Further reading

While the *Guidelines* are predominantly designed for the BCM practitioner, the following publications are strongly recommended as introductory reading by directors and senior managers of all organizations:

Bland, M (1998) *Communicating Out of a Crisis*, Macmillan, London

Business Continuity Institute (BCI) *Good Practice Guide to Business Continuity Management*, BCI, Worcester [Online] www.thebci.org

BCI (2002) *A Strategy for Business Survival*, BCI, Worcester

Central Computer and Telecommunications Agency (1995) *An Introduction to BCM*, HMSO, London

FSA (2001) *A Risk Focused Review of Outsourcing in the UK Retail Banking Sector*, Financial Services Authority, London

Home Office (1996) *How Resilient is Your Business to Disaster?* HMSO, London

Honour, D (2001) Heeding the lessons of 9/11, *International Journal of BCM*, **2**(1), pp 13–17

Institute of Directors (2000) *Business Continuity*, Director Publications, London

Knight, R F and Pretty, D J (2000) The impact of catastrophes on shareholder value, *Oxford Executive Research Briefings,* Templeton College, Oxford

Power, P (1999) *BCM: Preventing chaos in a crisis*, DTI, London

The following video should also be considered as introductory viewing by all managers and staff within an organization:

Business Continuity Institute (2001) *Back to Business: Planning ahead for the unexpected*, Business Continuity Institute, London

The BCI promotes the highest standards of professional competence and commercial ethics in the provision, maintenance and services for business continuity management (BCM). It provides an internationally recognized certification scheme for BCM managers and practitioners. The BCI Professional Recognition Programme creates a benchmark for the assessment of best practice in the field.

There are now over 1,250 members of the Institute working in 40 countries across the world. Members are drawn from all sectors including finance, government, health, transport, retail and manufacturing. The BCI is currently working with the FSA and UK Cabinet Office on good practice guides for BCM.

For further information contact the Institute on Tel: +44 (0)870 603 8783, E-mail: TheBCI@btinternet.com, Web site: www.thebci.org

Dealing with the risks of peer-to-peer

Peer-to-peer networks may incur the wrath of the music industry, but there is danger in them for every Internet-connected business, writes Frank Coggrave, UK Regional Director for Websense.

Pirated music and films are only a small part of the risk, as peer-to-peer (P2P) networks now carry significant amounts of pornography. A recent study analysed over 22 million searches on file-sharing networks, and found that 73 per cent of all movie searches were for pornography, 24 per cent of all image searches were for child pornography, and 6 per cent of all searches were for child pornography of some kind. In fact only 3 per cent of searches were for non-pornographic or non-copyrighted materials. Another study showed that 42 per cent of all searches on one of the most common file-sharing networks were for adult or child pornographic movies or images.

Then there are the viruses. Of the top 50 viruses and worms in the past six months, 19 used P2P and IM applications, quadrupling last year's record. And that is not counting the spyware that gets loaded onto your PCs every time someone downloads and installs one of the main P2P applications.

P2P is a problem that is going to get worse. Free file-sharing systems, like Kazaa, Morpheus and Limewire, will become more and more popular over the next few years, while legitimate music services will struggle to provide what users want. Consumers downloaded more than 5 billion audio files from unlicensed file-sharing services in 2001. Meanwhile, several US universities have reported that P2P applications routinely consume more than half of their network bandwidth. It is not surprising: at any one time, there can be 5 million users on peer-to-peer networks swapping more than 900 million files.

The file-sharing P2P networks are massive, and you have to expect that some of your users will find them attractive. There is a lot of material out there: more than 5 billion music files crossed the P2P networks in 2002, along with 5 million games – and around 500,000 movies a day. It is easy to for a user to think 'I'm just downloading this one song', without realizing the risks his or her employer faces. It is not just seemingly innocuous music tracks that get downloaded, though: studies show that pornography now accounts for more than 38 percent of all online file sharing.

It is not just music and video that is downloaded over P2P networks. You will also find them full of pirated software, and pornographic images and films – many of which depict illegal acts. MP3 and movie files on your servers put you at risk of legal action for copyright violations, while illegal pornographic material can lead to long and complex investigations, and the possibility of criminal prosecution. All it needs is a phone call from a disgruntled employee, and you could be looking at a hefty bill from a copyright enforcement agency, or even a visit from the police. According to IDC, 'As most new computers ship with CD and DVD burners, companies may be crossing new legal boundaries as employees burn down-loaded videos or music onto discs using company owned assets.'

Then there are the additional risks of Trojans and viruses. Downloading files from P2P networks can be risky, especially if they are copies of games or commercial software – quite apart from the fact that you are using unlicensed software that could earn you a visit from FAST, there is no way of trusting your source, and no way of knowing whether it comes with a virus or a Trojan hidden in the installation files. There are even viruses that take advantage of P2P networks, using them to pass from machine to machine. You will also find that many P2P network clients will install spyware on your PCs.

The security risks go well beyond viruses and Trojans using P2P networks as a back-channel into your systems. If they have not been careful, your employees are not just sharing their music and images with the world – they are also exposing confidential documents and files. It is easy enough to accidentally share every single file in a PC's 'My Documents' folder instead of just 'My Music'. While a copy of the latest number one album is coming into your network, your customer list could be on its way out, with no one knowing.

The temptation to use company resources for P2P file sharing is big. Staff will want to take advantage of your network bandwidth, downloading a movie in an hour or so over high-speed connections, rather than taking several hours at home, and that's going to affect network traffic. Not only do file-sharing applications at work have access to more bandwidth than the average home user, but they also have much more in the way of storage space – and with the arrival of low cost terabyte storage appliances there's going to be even more available. Unauthorized P2P downloads can end up using large amounts of disk space, filling your network storage with thousands of music files and movies. While compression technologies like MP3 and DIVX do reduce file sizes, a single song will still take up 4 or 5 MB of space, and a television programme or a movie can fill more than 300 MB.

While you may think you have your networks locked down, using firewalls and port-blocking, P2P applications can be tunnelling through trusted open ports, linking your PCs to a global VPN. What appears to your firewall as a persistent Web connection or an FTP session could actually be someone downloading several episodes of the latest cult American television series. As 64 percent of companies do not monitor or control music and video downloads, you may never know just what is crossing your firewall.

If you are worried about P2P applications running over your network, here are our top five tips for dealing with the problem and keeping the threat to a minimum.

Education

Educate all of your employees and line managers so they should be aware of the dangers of P2P. Ensure an acceptable usage policy is distributed to all so that there is no room for ambiguity.

Report on usage

Employee Internet management software, such as Websense Enterprise, comes with a reporting module that can be used to run historical reports on P2P-related Web access and network usage. This allows management and HR to view employee Internet activity and explore data using a user-friendly reporting tool, Websense Explorer.

Enforce the policy

Websense Enterprise will also allow you to enforce a company policy to block access to P2P-related Web sites. It can also ensure you block P2P network traffic inside the organization, as well as blocking the execution of P2P applications on desktops. This is particularly important for mobile users working on laptops.

Follow up

Make sure that your employee Internet management solution is frequently and automatically updated. The Internet is dynamic and forever changing, so do not choose a static solution. Websense Enterprise enables automatically updated lists of P2P-related Web sites, network protocols and desktop P2P applications to be detected and blocked. Furthermore, Websense has the ability to detect spyware already installed on the PC, as well as block it from sending out any data such as keystroke information.

To find out more how Websense can help you manage P2P and other Internet threats, please visit www.websense.com.

Websense Inc. is the world's leading provider of employee Internet management (EIM) solutions. Websense Enterprise software enables organizations to manage how their employees use their computing resources, including Internet access, desktop applications and network bandwidth. These solutions help improve productivity, security, conserve information technology resources, and mitigate legal liability for organizations. Implemented by more than 19,400 organizations worldwide and preferred by the FTSE 100 and Fortune 500 companies, Websense Enterprise delivers a comprehensive software solution that analyses, manages and reports on employee Internet access, network security and desktop application usage. Websense Enterprise also helps organizations mitigate the problems caused by new emerging Internet threats, such as spyware, malicious mobile code and peer-to-peer file sharing.

To find out more, visit www.websense.com where you can download a fully functional 30-day trial of Websense Enterprise.

Data recovery

Electronic data has become one of the most valued assets any organization or individual possesses. With this increasing dependency on electronic information, there is a growing need for data recovery solutions, writes Adrian Palmer at Ontrack Data Recovery.

When you consider that over 90 per cent of a company's information is created electronically and less than 30 percent is ever transferred to paper, it is astonishing just how few companies actively protect their critical business information and understand the cost to their organization of its loss.

Over 31 billion e-mails are sent every day, yet a virus could destroy all the inboxes of an entire organization at the touch of a button. The corporate data of a whole company could also be erased by simple human error. To lose such valuable information could destroy any company, and for those who manage to survive, downtime would have significant financial ramifications. Yet why are organizations not taking the necessary precautions to protect their primary assets? And why do so many companies not have a comprehensive business continuity plan in place, let alone an effective data recovery programme?

Data loss can strike in many different ways, and companies must be prepared for any eventuality. After all, everyone who works on a computer will eventually experience some form of data loss, ranging from a mechanical failure, software glitch, data corruption, powerspike, virus, fire, flood, disgruntled employee, to even a simple user error.

In recent reports, Gartner analysts have said that the majority of small to medium enterprises (SMEs) have traditionally under invested in business continuity planning, and they estimate that only 35 per cent of SMEs have a comprehensive disaster recovery plan in place. Historically expensive, the cost of business continuity and disaster recovery may have discouraged SMEs from investing; however, today's market offers a broader range of solutions to meet any budget.

So what solutions exist if disaster strikes, and how do you know when it would be cheaper to call in the experts? This chapter explores how to assess the severity of data loss and gives simple advice about how to minimize any damage. It then touches on the most common incidents that require a data recovery specialist and identifies the solutions available. Awareness of the solutions, from do-it-yourself software through to in-lab recovery by engineers, will help any organization build disaster recovery into any business continuity plan.

Assessing the damage

When data is lost, it is easy to panic. However if you evaluate the severity of the damage, and know what solutions are available, a problem need not become a crisis. Data loss can come in the form of physical damage or structural damage, and both require a different approach. However, general advice in the event of either loss is:

■ Never presume that data is lost for good, no matter how damaged the hard drive or magnetic band on a tape appears.
■ Do not shake or remove a damaged hard drive.
■ Do not attempt to dry a wet hard drive or data source by opening it, or exposing it to a heat source, such as a hairdryer.
■ Do not attempt to clean the hard drive; send it immediately to a data recovery laboratory.
■ Do not use utility software or maintenance tools on damaged drives or tapes.
■ Do not attempt to retrieve lost data yourself – you may make a bad situation worse.

In the event of structural damage, caused by accidental file deletion, virus infection and inaccessible or unbootable partitions, free diagnostic tools exist to assess the condition of your computer system and advise whether you can repair the damage yourself. Do not worry if you cannot boot your system to Windows, as the software, which can be downloaded from specialists' Web sites, is self-booting, and runs even when your system cannot.

In many cases of structural damage, do-it-yourself software will be enough to restore data. However, some of the more common incidents that require a data recovery specialist include:

■ **An unreliable back-up system**: without a tested, reliable back-up system, data loss of any size could prove disastrous.
■ **Back-up and restore failure**: unreadable tapes, corrupt data, and improper back-up procedures compromise these processes.
■ **Extensive time required for restoration of back-up process**: in many cases, this could result in significant productivity and financial losses.
■ **Impractical and impossible data recreation**: data recreation or rekeying involves a number of costs including lost time, revenue, and quality that can make it an impractical, if not impossible, option.
■ **Unbootable system**: even minor damage to operating system structures can keep a system from booting.
■ **Mirrored or RAID system failure**: many organizations concurrently copy data into two separate storage locations. However, if that data is corrupt before it is copied, or if

one (or both) of the two systems fails, the data may be destroyed or rendered inaccessible. Additionally, mirrored and RAID systems cannot protect the system from viruses, software corruption or user error.

■ **Intentionally and accidentally altered or destroyed data**: data is susceptible to being deleted or destroyed by malicious viruses, security breaches, or disgruntled employees, as well as accidentally by human error.

■ **Corrupted or deleted database files**: system malfunctions, power failures, and accidental or intentional deletions are some examples that may cause system-critical information to become inaccessible.

The solutions on the market

Data recovery software

Not all types of data loss require the assistance of an engineer. Powerful do-it-yourself software solutions exist that are capable of recovering and repairing lost or inaccessible data safely. Data loss caused by accidental file deletion, virus infection or software corruption can be recovered from downloaded software. This solution can restore data from most hard drives, diskettes and digital media, and works on systems that cannot boot to Windows.

There is software that is specific to e-mail recovery, inbox restoration or file system repair to name but three, and many are tailored for different sized organizations and the scale of the damage. Advanced disk diagnostics are also available to assess the health of your hard drive and identify problems that could lead to data loss, before it happens.

Remote data recovery (RDR®)

Ontrack Data Recovery is the only data recovery company in the world that offers a remote data recovery (RDR) solution. Engineers can recover certain data loss situations directly on your desktop, laptop or server (including RAID systems), via a modem or Internet connection. Returning an organization to productivity in minutes/hours instead of days, this solution ends unnecessary downtime and consequently saves the inconvenience and expense involved in the removal and shipping of equipment.

For many users, the key benefit of RDR is time. A typical in-lab recovery can take about two to five days to complete. Restoring data from back-up tapes, which will never be as current as the data that was just lost, can take just as long. RDR, which is available 24 hours a day, can be completed in as little as an hour and can be performed anywhere in the world. If a drive is physically healthy, RDR can usually recover lost data. This secure solution offers the same client confidentially and security procedures implemented in labs.

In-labs, clean rooms or on-site data recovery

In more serious cases of physical damage, such as fire, flood or earthquake, recovery may take place in a lab or 'Class100 clean room'. This solution is particularly suitable for internal or mechanical failure, and can be carried out under different time scales, depending on the priority placed by the organization.

Whether it stems from security concerns or critical deadlines for the recovery of your lost data, on-site data recovery solutions also exist. Highly trained engineers will come to your location to diagnose and recover your data so that you do not need to send your systems to the labs.

What to look for in a data recovery specialist

- Do they have the expertise? Data recovery is technologically complex and requires in-depth knowledge. Look for companies that make a substantial investment in research and development, have created a significant number of proprietary tools and tech-niques, and have performed data recovery for a large number of clients.
- Look for a company that is a certified developer or solutions partner for MicrosoftÅ, Novell, Apple, Sun, SCO, and other major hardware and software companies. Your data recovery provider should also be able to retrieve data from every type of system (including portable and desktop PCs, Apple Mac, Unix, HP, DEC, and IBM platform servers), media (hard disks, optical disks, removable disks, flash media, multi-drive volumes and RAID systems) and tape. Also, major hard drive manufacturers should recommend a data recovery specialist.
- To protect sensitive business data, a data recovery company must have strong data security procedures in place, including proprietary protocols, data encryption, and secure facilities.

Conclusion

Until recently, data loss due to hardware and software failure, unbootable computers, viruses and human error was considered lost forever. Today however, most lost data is recoverable. Data loss can happen in the most strange circumstances and when least expected, but knowing what steps to take ensures that all is not lost. Below is a taste of some of the more bizarre situations in which Ontrack Data Recovery recovered lost data:

- An American user became so frustrated with his laptop, he shot it with a gun, before realizing there was important data saved on the computer.
- A man threw his computer out of the window, in an attempt to destroy evidence, when he found out the police were coming to seize his PC and arrest him.
- One man's laptop dropped out of his bag while he was riding his moped. The computer was then run over by a lorry before he even noticed he had lost it and needed access to the data.

However, too many companies rely on an untested back-up system as their safety net, and this too often proves to be inadequate when it really matters. Over the course of performing more than 150,000 data recoveries, Ontrack Data Recovery has identified some of the top tips to help an organization minimize data loss:

- Back up all data as often as possible, especially before 'going mobile'.
- Protect against power surges by buying an uninterruptible power supply. This avoids the risk of electrical failure leading to incorrect data being written to the disk surface, making some data inaccessible.
- Do not install software without a firm understanding of the system set-up. This is a major cause of accidental file deletion.

∎ Regularly test data back-up and restore capabilities. Just because you have a back-up system does not mean it will be able to restore successfully when you need it. There is also the danger that the wrong data is being backed up.

∎ Scan all new programmes for viruses. Awareness can be the best form of protection in data loss avoidance. Virus software should also be updated with regular virus signatures.

∎ Set up a thorough business continuity plan. Data disasters can happen at any time. Spending a little time thinking about the services you would need in the event of a fire, flood or simple server failure could mean valuable time and money is saved in the long run.

∎ Do not panic at any apparent damage and attempt to operate or repair a visibly damaged hard drive yourself. This may cause further data loss and cause more damage to the computer hardware.

Ontrack Data Recovery, a wholly-owned subsidiary of Kroll Inc, is a leading provider of data recovery and electronic evidence services. It enables customers to protect, manage, back up and recover their valuable data.

Using its hundreds of proprietary tools and techniques, Ontrack Data Recovery is able to recover lost or corrupted data from all operating systems and types of storage devices through its do-it-yourself, remote and in-lab capabilities. Ontrack's award-winning utility software tools help prevent critical data loss through problem-solving and file-management utilities.

Ontrack Data Recovery, The Pavilions, 1 Weston Road, Kiln Lane, Epsom, Surrey KT17 1JG; Freephone: 0800 389 4216, Tel: +44 (0)1372 741 999, Fax: +44 (0)1372 741 441, Web site: www.ontrack.co.uk

Crisis or disaster management

It is vital for companies to prepare contingency plans in case of crisis, says Simon Langdon of Insight Consulting.

The threat of disasters

During the last three years, there have been many examples of natural or man-made disasters. There have been widespread floods and droughts in Europe, the Sars virus, a petrol strike, the foot-and-mouth epidemic, major power cuts in London, the United States and Italy, and terrorist attacks around the world. Many of us have anecdotal evidence of crisis caused by extraordinary events. Recently, I have heard of the evacuation of a London mainline station because of toxic fumes coming from batteries on charge which boiled over, and an office block being evacuated because a drunken driver crashed into it and the back-up generators failing when a company suffered a power cut.

Currently, there is nervousness about the threat of terrorism – particularly in major cities. There is nothing new in this, unfortunately. The bombs on the railway in Madrid on 11 March 2004 just being the latest. In 1996, suicide bombers drove a lorry into the central bank in Colombo, Sri Lanka, which exploded and set eight buildings alight, killed over 60 people and injured 1,200 more. London has suffered at the hands of the IRA. The events of 11 September 2001 were an awful escalation of terror and have done much to focus minds. As a result, many companies have been reassessing their crisis management procedures. To think the unthinkable is not so difficult now. Who would have envisaged the closure of air traffic in the United States following 9/11 or the closure of Congress as a result of the threat of anthrax contamination? Global terrorism has led to a global tension kept alive by the media. The modern media, with its worldwide reach, meant that it did not take long for us all to hear of the bombs in Madrid or the bombing of the British Consulate and the HSBC bank in Istanbul in November 2003. Is it surprising that we are all increasingly aware of the threat from disasters?

Definition of crisis management

In the light of these threats, how should companies deal with crisis or disasters? A definition of a crisis provides a foundation from which to work. A crisis is an abnormal situation or perception, which threatens the operation, staff, customers or reputation of an organization. Crisis management is the process by which the organization manages the wider impact of a crisis such as the business issues and media coverage.

Characteristics of disasters

To study how to respond to a disaster or crisis it is useful to consider the characteristics. Disasters are no respecters of people, buildings, companies or governments. Disasters such as a fire, flood, earthquake, airline crash or terrorist bomb are often unexpected and sudden. The timing and location may be unpredictable and the impact cannot normally be contained within boundaries. Disasters cause chaos. They have a very human impact. There may be casualties, people may be frightened, it may be difficult to think and there is a thirst for knowledge.

Making order out of chaos

Disaster or crisis management must therefore be aimed at making order out of chaos, providing a timely and effective response to ensure the safety of people, and returning the business to normal as quickly as possible. We must be prepared before the disaster – that is, now – and therefore we need a well-rehearsed plan based on good communications.

Public scrutiny following a disaster or crisis can be intense, and there are many examples of companies that have suffered a crisis or disaster without an apparent crisis management plan that have subsequently not survived. A good crisis management plan, properly implemented, will not only focus a practical response but will also do much to provide confidence to management, staff and customers that the company is able to cope.

After the Hatfield rail crash in 2002, the disruption to the railway caused by the search for hairline cracks on the line was immense. The rail industry lost almost £1 billion in three months as a result of a loss of confidence by the public, business, the media, the government and the rail industry itself. All parties felt the railway was unsafe and unreliable. The result was that eventually Railtrack went into administration and the chief executive left to seek employment elsewhere.

Risks in today's business environment

In addition to the almost traditional disasters already mentioned, there are many other types of risks in today's business environment – industrial action, fraud, espionage, human error, viruses, technical failure and the failure of suppliers, to name a few. While some of these risks can be quantified, it is difficult to predict exactly what might happen, when or where. It therefore makes good sense to develop a generic plan to ensure that there can be a focused response to any major incident, of whatever magnitude, whenever and wherever it might occur. In simple terms, if the right people are around a table, working together with a well-rehearsed and straightforward crisis management process, they will be able to cope with whatever might happen.

Geographic nature of disasters

Major incidents or disasters are often geographic in nature. In other words, they happen where they happen and the immediate effect is local from where the impact might spread rapidly. The effect is similar to a pebble being thrown into a still pond. If you imagine that where the pebble enters the water is where the incident happens, then the ripples that spread out represent the impact. September 11 was like a boulder being thrown into the pond, with the ripples being waves of impact that are still going round and round the world. It follows also that the response to a major incident must counter the impact, and that a major crisis or disaster will require a major response.

Once the geographic nature of major incidents is understood, it is easy to see why a key principle of crisis management is that responsibility must remain at the local level, where the immediate response to an incident will start. At the same time, support for the local level must be coordinated throughout the organization. As with a football team, individual skill is important but is largely ineffective if not supported by all members of the team. Communication, of course, remains the bedrock on which crisis management is built. Crisis management is all about managing the information flow, and without communication it is impossible.

Media handling

When a major incident happens there are two stories – one is how the company responds and the other is how the media reports how the company responds. The public tend to believe what they read and hear in the media. They believe the media's interpretation or perception of what has happened and so 'perception becomes reality'.

As a result of the growth of 24-hour news channels, it has become necessary to plan carefully how the media will be handled. The media's requirement is to inform the public of the facts. They will ask the simple questions following a disaster – 'What happened, how did it happen and what are you doing about it?' They will soon add 'And who is responsible?' These are all understandable questions and should be answered with facts and honesty.

The media are useful. If asked, they will include on their news bulletins contact numbers for friends and relatives to call, and they may even relay important messages. Remember that reporters are human too, they have a job to do and they like to help. Use them.

All communications with the media should be coordinated from company head-quarters. Responsibility for the media at the scene, however, should be delegated to the front line. Local managers should be enlisted and trained as spokespeople in an emergency. Such a strategy positions the company to release information rapidly and effectively, anywhere and at any time, and will satisfy the demands of the media. Importantly, it will also reflect the company's ability to cope with the crisis.

The two phases of crisis management

There are two clearly defined phases in crisis management – the immediate response and the recovery. Part of the first phase, the immediate response, is identifying and confirming that there is, in fact, a crisis. This is not always as easy as it seems, as some crises appear to creep up almost unnoticed. To counter this, it is good practice to use a Crisis Impact Criteria Table that quantifies the impact of an incident against pre-determined criteria under different headings such as Operations, Staff, Reputation, Legal and Finance. The table acts simply as a tool to aid the decision on when to invoke the crisis management plan. A common adage is 'If in doubt call it out!' That is, if undecided invoke the plan and call out the crisis management team. Not to do so may mean that you are always trying to catch up rather than taking control in a timely way with positive, proactive action.

The recovery, or second phase of the response, should start almost at the same time as the immediate response and run parallel with it. It is a project in its own right that requires planning and coordination. An early start will speed the return to business as usual. As the immediate response tails off, so the recovery will become the priority.

Content of a crisis management plan

A crisis management plan should first of all identify and define the responsibilities of those managers involved in a response. Although this sounds obvious, it is often overlooked. It is important for members of the Crisis Management Team (CMT) to know not only their own responsibilities but also those of others. A list of tasks that members of the CMT should complete in order to fulfil their responsibilities should be included.

The crisis management plan should also contain the invocation procedure and list the external groups and organizations with which the company may wish to communicate at the time of a crisis. Examples include business partners, customers, suppliers, regulators and other major stakeholders. It should contain the system by which business continuity plans are invoked and coordinated, as well as the procedure for the resolution of conflicts of interest, the decision-making process and some detail about how the incident is managed 'on the ground'. An understanding of the latter assists the CMT in knowing how best to support the actions at the local level.

The plan should contain a section on communication, outlining the lines of communication within the company and responsibilities for communicating to external organizations. Contact details and a list of communication equipment to be used should be contained in an appendix.

Immediate actions on being notified of a major incident

There are many ways that one may be informed of a crisis. You could be told by a colleague, the duty manager, a neighbouring business, a passing stranger or even hear about it on the news. However the notification is made, it is important first to verify the facts. The next action is to start a log of events, to note down the time and the detail of the incident and who informed you. Then keep a note of all actions.

Once a decision to invoke has been made, it is necessary to activate the call-out system and to confirm who should attend the CMT meeting, and where and when it is to be held. It may be necessary to arrange a conference call to allow managers who are unable to attend to take part. Typically the CMT will consist of representatives of all the main departments within the company such as operations, human resources, customer services, IT, finance, marketing, facilities management and corporate communications.

It is a good practice, at this stage, to consider standing by contingency sites such as a Recovery Centre if one is available. Finally, you should consider briefing a deputy and establishing the latest status of the incident before moving to the CMT meeting.

The crisis management meeting

The first action to be taken at the CMT meeting is to appoint a scribe to take the minutes and to confirm attendance to ensure all are present. The next task is then to establish the detail of the incident and access the impact. The chairperson should obtain reports from all the members of the CMT in turn and ask them to outline their priorities. He or she should then summarize the company or corporate key issues and priorities for action. It is at this point that any conflicts of interest should be discussed between members of the CMT. The meeting should be conducted in an autocratic style – there is not time for too much democracy in a crisis. Once the priorities are agreed, decisive action is necessary in order to gain control of the situation.

It is a good idea for the CMT to have an agenda for their first meeting – not only to ensure that nothing is overlooked but also as members may be 'off balance' because of what has happened. A good way to develop the CMT meeting agenda is to hold a crisis management (table top) exercise, where a scenario is 'played' and the CMT discuss their response and raise issues as the response progresses.

Reporting

As crisis management is all about managing the information flow, there are a number of reports that can be standardized to assist in the process such as the initial Incident Report and the follow on Status Report. The Incident Report is a simple form which should describe the detail of the incident, its location and time, whether it is confirmed or uncon-firmed, the impact, whether there are any injuries, what action has been taken, who has been notified and an estimate of the time to recover. The report should also include any other relevant information and list the actions that are needed. Finally, the report should indicate when the next update will be made.

A Status Report might typically contain the latest information of the response and outline other important issues such as HR, operations, the status of buildings and equipment, business impacts and details of the security of the incident site. It should contain the prior-ities of all the departments involved and may, when appropriate, include comment on the long-term strategic impacts, the legal and insurance implications and priorities for action. Consideration should be given to the requirement for holding a press conference.

Summary

The risk of disaster is ever present. Organizations that do not prepare contingency plans to deal effectively with them may not survive the impact that disasters bring. The aim of crisis management is to make order out of chaos, to maximize the safety of people and to return the business to normal as quickly as possible. An understanding of the characteristics of disasters will help in developing effective response procedures. The crisis management process is about managing information, and therefore the ability to communicate effectively is vital. Handling the media, by providing them with the facts of what has happened in a timely manner, must form an important part of the overall process.

A crisis management plan must be practical and simple. It is all too easy to over-plan and include ever more detail, so that the process becomes overcomplicated and the plan so thick that no one ever reads it. Even worse is to think that the plan is finished and to put in on the shelf where it will only gather dust. The plan must be a 'living document', and should be generic and sufficiently flexible to be used to respond to any crisis of whatever size, whenever or wherever it might occur.

Finally, the members of the CMT must be trained in the crisis management process and the plan must be exercised and maintained – there is little value in investing in a plan if no one knows how to implement it and it has become out of date.

Insight Consulting is a specialist provider of information security, risk management and business continuity solutions. Simon Langdon is a Principal Consultant with Insight Consulting Ltd and the Chair of the International Disaster and Emergency Readiness Conference (IDER). Simon has undertaken crisis management assignments for the SRA, IATA, NATS, BA and a number of major banks and media organizations.

For information about crisis management, visit www.insight.co.uk.

Forensics

There is more to e-security than meets the eye. Robert Brown, Technical Director and Forensic Analyst at DataSec, reports on effective forensic process and underlines the importance of following certain precautionary measures in order to reach the right conclusions.

To catch a thief?

When we turn our minds to matters of e-security, our first thoughts tend to be about defences such as firewalls and intrusion detection – and rightly so. After all, there is much wisdom in the pursuit of prevention before cure. But what happens when our defences are breached? How should we respond to such an incident?

Those investigating crime have long understood the value of evidence. In its most literal sense, evidence is '*that which demonstrates that a fact is so*'.[1] By acquiring evidence we build a picture of what happened, how it came to be and, hopefully, *who* did it. The digital world is no different to the physical world in that every event leaves a trace. This *digital evidence* can be gathered and pieced together to help develop our understanding of the what, how and who of an incident. Over time, this process has come to be referred to as *computer forensics*.

The term 'forensic' is associated, by definition, with legal process. That is, the methods used to gather evidence during an investigation allow it to be deemed admissible in a court of law. Therefore, the most influential factor in the court's decision whether or not to accept evidence is the way in which it was obtained, and in particular, consideration as to whether such methods may have affected the original data or its subsequent interpretation.

---

[1] Patterson, R F, *The University English Dictionary*, University Books

Every good incident response plan will have some form of investigative foundation. An effective response relies on an understanding of what has taken place and how it occurred in order to identify the appropriate course of remedial action. But, without the appropriate precautions, the way in which such action is taken may modify or even destroy the data on which the evidence is based and, in doing so, may significantly affect the possibility of attributing accountability for the cause of the incident. By adopting some simple and logical practices when conducting an investigation it is possible to avoid compromising such evidence. The core of computer forensic best practice can be defined by three generally accepted principles :[2]

- No action taken should change the data held on a computer or other storage media that may be relied upon subsequently.
- Where original data must be accessed, the person doing so should be suitably qualified and able to explain the relevance and implications of his or her actions.
- An audit trail or other record of all processes should be created and preserved such that a third party might examine such processes and achieve the same result.

The forensic process could therefore be summarized as *preservation*, *documentation* and *justification*.

Understanding the problem

When responding to an incident, it is important to identify the circumstances in which it has occurred and the objectives of any subsequent investigation. This puts us in a position both to assess the risks that the situation may present to our business, and to form a strategy for conducting the investigation itself. In this way the type of incident will begin to define the required course of action. But what if an investigation is not expected to end in tribunal or litigation? Can we relax the standards that would normally be applied? Quite simply, what initially appears to be a simple, straightforward incident can quickly escalate into something far more serious and dangerous. For example, an investigation into a simple denial-of-service attack on an e-commerce server suddenly and unexpectedly turns out to be a platform for extortion by organized criminals. Nothing should be taken purely on face value. If we apply best practice from the outset, we avoid any possibility of compromising the investigation at a later stage, or the integrity of the evidence we may come to rely on.

We can begin to define the scope of the investigation by forming an idea of what we think has happened. This, in turn, will help to identify where we should be looking for evidence and what needs to be done in order to acquire it. Throughout the investigation it is necessary to constantly assess our understanding of what has happened and consider adapting the chosen strategy if necessary.

The methods employed in the investigation should be proportional to the seriousness of the incident. For example, it would be reasonable to consider examining the e-mail of employees suspected of sending threatening or abusive messages to colleagues or

---

[2] Association of Chief Police Officers, *Good Practice Guide for Computer Based Electronic Evidence* [Online] http://www.nhtcu.org

customers, but it would probably be considered unreasonable to place 24-hour surveillance on them and install a keystroke logger in their home computers!

It is vital that an investigator possesses a clear understanding of the legislation that affects the way in which an investigation is conducted. Such legislation includes, but is by no means limited to, the Human Rights Act 1998, the Regulation of Investigatory Powers Act 2000, the Business Interception Regulations 2000, the Data Protection Act 1998 and the Computer Misuse Act 1990. Familiarity with the relevant legislation allows an investigation to be conducted in such a way that it will stand up to any subsequent scrutiny. The quantity and complexity of such legislation means that it may often be appropriate to seek advice from a lawyer in order to form a legal strategy for the investigation that is to take place.

Ultimately, any investigative process will consist of both operational and strategic elements typically involving the following:

- preserving data for forensic analysis;
- forensic recovery of data;
- presentation of evidence (reports and orally);
- acting lawfully;
- working within a business (or disciplined) environment.

Preserving the evidence

The first principle of digital evidence defines the need to preserve the original data on which the investigation is based. Typically, a forensic investigator will take a low-level, or bitstream image of the media containing the data. Provided the method used complies with the first principle, the image produced can be treated as 'best evidence', which means a court of law would accept it as an accurate and true copy of the original data. An obvious benefit of this is that, now a legally acceptable copy of the data exists, it is easier to justify returning the original equipment to service, thereby minimizing business interruption.

However, it may not always be possible or practical to take a system out of service in order to capture the data it holds. In these cases we may revert to the second principle of digital evidence, which makes provision for such access and defines the restrictions and obligations with which the investigator must comply. Key to this compliance is ensuring that the way in which access may affect the data is clearly understood. The mere act of starting a computer can cause numerous modifications to be made to the data it holds. If such modifications affect the evidence that we wish to produce, we must be able to identify what changes have occurred and the effect they might have on its interpretation.

It is at this point that the importance becomes evident of maintaining an accurate and detailed record of the actions that are taken and the reasons for taking them. Such a record acts as an audit trail for the investigation. It allows an assessment of the methods used and the decisions made in order to establish the admissibility of the evidence, and brings with it compliance with the third principle of gathering digital evidence.

After the data has been acquired, it is important to maintain its evidential integrity. This can be achieved by strict control of access and by maintaining a record of its movements and the identity of those in whose custody it has been. By doing this we are creating a 'chain of custody' for the evidence with which we can demonstrate its provenance.

Building the picture

Once the data has been identified and acquired, the next phase of the investigation involves its examination and analysis. The objective is to identify evidence of what has happened with a view to establishing how the incident occurred and, if possible, who was involved. The quantity of material that can be produced by apparently trivial actions on a computer can be quite staggering. This information can present a vivid picture of the various events that have taken place in relation to an incident. The downside to such rich potential sources of evidence is that a detailed and proper analysis can be both complicated and time-consuming. There is a risk that a vital piece of evidence may be overlooked or misinterpreted. Consequently it is necessary to ensure that investigators are properly trained in forensic methodology and techniques, and possess an appropriate degree of knowledge about the systems and software they are examining.

The analysis will result in a report describing the investigation and its findings. In the main such findings will be restricted to statements of fact such as the presence of specific items of data. At times it may be appropriate for the investigator to offer an opinion on the meaning of these facts. However, such an opinion must be based on significant knowledge and experience for it to be considered reliable. An opinion should be an appropriately educated interpretation of the facts at hand and not a best guess.

If an investigation ends in legal proceedings, the investigator may be required to present his or her findings orally in court and face cross-examination as to content and reliability. This is not something to be undertaken lightly, and can be a daunting experience. Accordingly investigators should seek to gain experience of court proceedings, and preferably undertake training to act in the capacity of a professional or expert witness.

The end result of this entire process should be a clear understanding of the events associated with the incident under investigation: in other words, answers to the original questions of what, how and, perhaps most importantly, who.

By adopting a 'best practice' approach to the acquisition and examination of digital evidence we can ensure that our investigation remains forensically sound and will stand up to the most rigorous scrutiny. It is certain that as e-business becomes increasingly prevalent, so too will the attempted abuse of the systems and infrastructure that make it possible. While we do our best to prevent such abuse it is vital that we have the ability to act effectively and lawfully when it eventually happens, and ultimately bring accountability to those responsible.

DataSec are one of the United Kingdom's leading providers of computer forensic services and as such are registered with the Law Society as expert witnesses. The DataSec range of services includes awareness training for IT and HR managers and consultancy services for organizations considering setting up an incident response team or who already have one in place. DataSec also provides independent investigations and analysis for internal incidents, criminal cases and civil litigation and legal services including expert witness testimony.

For further information contact DataSec Ltd at Allen House, Station Road, Sawbridgeworth, Herts CM21 9JX, Tel: 01279 313007, Fax: 01279 313130, E-mail: office@datasec.co.uk, Web: www.datasec.co.uk

Index of advertisers